CLIMBERS' CLUB GUID
Edited by Geoff Milbur

CW00552137

7

Gogarth

Andy Newton (Updated the entire script, adding the Historical and other sections)
Andy Pollitt (Gogarth Bay)
Steve Haston (South Stack)
Paul Williams (Rhoscolyn)
Mike Gresham (The Range and Holyhead Mountain)
Geoff Milburn (Worked on the whole script, particularly the First Ascents)
Greg Griffith (Maps and crag diagrams)
Ian Smith (Proof read the script and obtained the photographs)

Cover photographs by Bernard Newman and from the Paul Pritchard collection.

 Published by the CLIMBERS' CLUB

1966 Craig Gogarth - First Edition Peter Crew.

1967 Craig Gogarth - First Edition Revised by Peter Crew.

1967 Holyhead Mountain by Dave Durkan.

1969 Anglesey - Gogarth by Peter Crew.
Published by West Col.

1969 Mona by Dave Durkan.

1977 Gogarth - First Edition by Alec Sharp.
Published by the Climbers' Club.

1978 Gogarth - 1978 Supplement by Geoff Milburn and Al Evans.
Published by the Climbers' Club.

1981 Gogarth - 1981 Supplement by Geoff Milburn.
Published by the Climbers' Club.

1990 Gogarth - Second Edition by Andy Newton, Andy Pollit, Steve Haston, Paul Wiliams and Mike Gresham.
Published by the Climbers' Club. Reprinted (without the colour photographs) - 2000

© The Climbers' Club 1990

Newton, Andy
    Gogarth. – (Climbers' Club guides)
    1. Rock climbing – North Wales
    I. Title   II. Climbers' Club
    III. Pollitt, Andy   IV. Series

    ISBN 0-901-601-48-9

front cover: *Andy Pollitt on the 2nd ascent of The Bells! The Bells! (E7), North Stack.*
Photo: Bernard Newman

back cover: *Paul Pritchard and Andy Popp on Schittlegruber (E6), Left-Hand Red Wall.*
Photo: Pritchard collection

Prepared for printing by: Synergy, Royal Oak Barn, Cartmel, Cumbria, LA11 6QB.
Produced by: The Ernest Press, Glasgow.
Distributed by Cordee, 3a De Montfort Street, Leicester, LE1 7HD.

Contents (Diagrams in *italics*)

Editorial Introduction

After the 1981 Gogarth Supplement plans were made to produce a new definitive guidebook to the Anglesey cliffs. Consequently in 1982 Jim Perrin 'signed up' Steve Haston to start work on the guidebook. Operating from the laid back atmosphere of the Llanberis climbing community Steve added several new routes to Gogarth in 1982 and 1983 and then time slipped away until the urgent need for a new guidebook spurred Steve on to further action. In addition to completing the South Stack section of the script Steve also claimed some hard new routes in 1986 and 1987 to show that actions sometimes speak louder than the written word.

Time however was going by and Andy Pollitt took over the script writing to produce a first draft manuscript. Later Paul Williams and Mike Gresham joined the guidebook team for the Rhoscolyn and Holyhead Mountain sections. The initial script was word-processed by Jean and Les Ainsworth. Long before the script had been checked Greg Griffith had taken on the challenge to draw a full set of crag diagrams, despite the fact that it has often been said that such a project would prove to be impossible. Greg completed his daunting task in no time at all – compared to many past projects.

Guidebook work then came to a full stop as the guide writers ran out of both steam and enthusiasm. Time passed by ... and a new injection of enthusiasm was urgently needed. Andy Newton was originally approached to write the historical section, but instead he got involved with the script as a whole. Eventually he single-handedly word-processed the whole script and finally completed the historical section – the whole job being a mammoth task which only those who have word-processed a complete guidebook will appreciate. Without Andy's persistence this guidebook would have been delayed a few more years.

A further recent development has been the opening of a second-hand bookshop by Jack Baines at 1 Thomas Street, Holyhead, farther down the street from the Brittania Inn. As a specialist in mountaineering books Jack has a wide range of second-hand guidebooks as well as copies of this latest Gogarth guidebook. If the weather is bad then this may be a good refuge for literate climbers.

A further suggestion for a group of jaded climbers is to sail round the cliffs on Girl Kilda. The owner Mr Biddlecombe can be contacted on 0407 710 812 and his boat could take a dozen climbers without any problem. In addition to the superb view of the cliffs the echo sounder on the boat shows all the local wrecks and the shoals of fish that surround them.

It is now 25 years since climbing started at Gogarth and within this guidebook there are over 500 routes to satisfy and test even the most ambitious climber. Much of the early ironmongery has now gone – undoubtedly for the good as the routes are mainly all free. In addition the use of bolts is frowned upon as these cliffs are the preserve of climbers who aspire to a more pure approach. Gogarth can now match the best of inland crags but in addition it has a unique character of its own. On tranquil days when the sea is calm one can sit amongst a rich carpet of flowers and idly contemplate the wonders of a vast ocean. At the other extreme there are the wild days when the howling wind sings in the wires and pounds the mountainous waves against the rocky ramparts which guard the coastline. Whatever your experience long after you are back in the warmth and safety of your home part of Gogarth will remain with you and in the years to come far away from the west you will feel its compelling call which will speak to your inner soul. Then one day you will return.

Acknowledgements

Any guidebook relies, for its accuracy and authority, on a great many people, and the authors would like to thank everyone who has helped in the production of this guidebook, and especially: Paul Trower, Leigh McGinley and Mike Owen, with Mike Howerd and Ian Wilson, for their checking, advice and criticism, and Kath Griffiths for a great deal of intricate word processing.

Geoff Milburn's 'eagle eye' spotted myriad tiny errors in the text, thus ensuring a fine finished product.

The fine drawings and diagrams were produced by Greg Griffith, after Geoff and Alan Milburn raced down to Wales one afternoon to shoot an extensive series of photographs of the cliffs from a boat (moored near the Holyhead coastguard station). Girl Kilda, is owned by J R Biddlecombe, who, for a reasonable fee (about £40) will take a party of climbers round the Gogarth cliffs -- a unique experience. This trip was organized by Jack Baines who put the feelers out for locals.

Thank you all those who responded to the call for photographs.

Previous works by Pete Crew and Dave Durkan provided a great deal of, otherwise overlooked, information. Bangor University Mountaineering Club's production of a Rhoscolyn supplement greatly aided the identification of particular routes.

John Ratcliffe and Alistair Moralee, of the Nature Conservancy Council and the Royal Society for the Protection of Birds respectively, generously provided information and assistance in environmental and access matters.

The authors would also like to extend particular thanks to the following: Steve Andrews, Martin Barnicott, Tony Brindle, Joe Brown, Celia Bull, Malc Campbell, Martin Crook, Dave Durkan, Grant Farquhar, Alan Hinkes, Trevor Hodgson, Tim Jadwat, Dave Jones, Ray Kay, Dai Lampard, Mark Leach, Jim Moran, Martin Murray, Bernard Newman, Elaine Owen, Chris Parkin, G Peters, Dave Pearce, Paul Pritchard, Mike Raine, John Redhead, Mike Thomas, John Tombs, Simon Tong, Dave Towse, Mike Turner, Crispin Waddy, John Whittle, and the Staff of Glenmore Lodge.

Introduction

The green quilted island of Anglesey, or more properly Ynys Mon, meets its watery surround on a coastline dotted with steep ragged heights and gentle sandy swathes. One such rocky bastion is Gogarth, the name given to an intermittent stretch of sea cliffs, over five km long, encompassing the north-west corner of Holy Island. Only explored once technical and psychological frontiers permitted, this area now provides hundreds of fine atmospheric climbs. This guide also encompasses climbing areas on other parts of Holy Island, and those dotted around the whole of Anglesey.

The nature of the climbing here is, almost without exception, steep and demanding, both physically and mentally. The rock is often good, but should never be treated with disregard, and is generally covered in a profusion of possibilities, if one is strong enough to take advantage of them. A relatively modern crag, the development covering a mere 25 years, it has occasionally been subject to grievous attack, but in general has developed in a dignified and respectful way, never more so than at the present time.

A number of the routes have been climbed very infrequently, but perhaps with the publication of this guide, many more routes will see ascents each year. Those less popular routes may well be vegetated, but any that are hugely unpleasant have generally been noted in the text. It has proved possible to climb here all year round, the weather out on the island being substantially better than in the mountains of Snowdonia. The crags dry relatively quickly, especially in a breeze, although cracks may hold lingering dampness for some days. After a rough sea, or in sea mist, the crag appears dry, yet at close quarters harbours an annoying dampness that is a little off-putting. Some routes finish onto steep grass slopes which, when wet, are especially terrifying.

It has been 12 years since the last comprehensive guide-book to these crags, and a considerable number of new climbs have been added in that time. As with all crags, Gogarth has dropped in and out of fashion, and exploration has often occurred in waves, each corresponding to the attention of a new generation of climbers. Each one has been more ethically aware than the climbers of previous eras, and the present vogue for on-sight adventures can only be applauded as a standard bearer for the vanguard of a very British school of climbing. A number of the more recent routes have had few, if any, repeat ascents, and it would be fair to say that they should be treated with a little caution, although every effort has been made to ensure that they are not dangerously undergraded.

The standard adjectival grading system has been employed, and it assumes that the climbers will be carrying a modern rack of gear, and wearing 'sticky' rock boots of some description. The grades are as follows:

Moderate	Hard Severe
Difficult	Very Severe
Very Difficult	Hard Very Severe
Severe	Extremely Severe

The Extremely Severe grade is now an open-ended system of increasing difficulty, represented by the symbols E1, E2, E3, E4, E5, E6, E7, and currently E8. These, like the other adjective grades, represent the overall impression of a climb's difficulty, taking into account the technical difficulty, strenuousness, seriousness and position of the route.

Numerical Pitch Grades are included in the text, and will be familiar to most climbers. They are: 3c, 4a, 4b, 4c, 5a, 5b, 5c, 6a, 6b, 6c, and 7a. It will be noted that these grades have not been included for some of the more esoteric gems, and the symbol XS (unspecified Extremely Severe) is used, where the exact grading is uncertain, or unknown. The few artificial climbs have been graded for difficulty on a scale of A1, A2, A3, A4.

The given grades are a consensus opinion from a large number of local activists, but are of course subject to individual anomalies, even the will to live being vital for success on some of the more committing horrors contained within!

The familiar 'star' system has been used to indicate the quality of routes, irrespective of grades. A route must be excellent in all respects to qualify for ★★★, and even a ★ route must be out of the ordinary. Absence of a star does not mean that a route is unsatisfactory, as poor climbs are specifically described as such in the text.

As a relatively modern area, and in line with guidebooks nationally, the entire text has been standardized into metric units. As a rough guide a metre is 3.25 feet, and pitch lengths have been calculated accordingly. These are a rough guide only, usually estimated by first ascensionists in the cafe afterwards, although a large number in this guide have been adjusted from experience to more accurate estimations. It should be noted that the measurements are for the amount of rope run out, and pitches of more than 45m will obviously require 50m ropes to be used. The increased protection and escape possibilities of double ropes make their use here universal.

Many pegs (pitons) are mentioned in the text, and they vary greatly in condition and age (up to 20 years old!). Some have been made redundant by subsequent improvements in protection devices, but many are still considered vital protection or are used as belay points. They should, without exception, be considered as suspect, the action of salt-laden sea air seriously affecting their strength. Indeed, they often appear good, but have their buried part completely rotted away, and hardly hold the weight of a quick-draw, never mind a plummeting climber. They are included in the text as waymarks, but vanish at regular intervals, and should not be taken as truly permanent. Back-up runners should be used, if at all possible. Replacement, with the stainless steel variety, by any charitable party, would be very much appreciated.

Bolts have occasionally appeared on these cliffs, but these have been reduced to a few rusty relics, and the infamous Cad bolt. It should be well noted by all visiting parties that any bolt appearing on any sea cliff in this guide will be removed, and the perpetrators discouraged from repeating their unwanted actions. A few aid points still exist on routes, and these have been specifically mentioned in the text.

Visitors to Gogarth may find the situation and climbing to be rather gripping, and should consider competence at Very Severe a fair minimum. It would be wise to pick a route well within the team's usual ability on a first visit.

It would be handy for parties to carry 'Friends' both as runners, and to back up many belays. A number of slings should also be carried, 12mm tape proving particularly good for tying off pegs, and wrapping around rock protrusions. If particular gear is thought vital for any route, it is mentioned in the text. Equipment should be rinsed in fresh water after each visit: salt water and sea air rapidly corrode aluminium alloys, and rot many fabrics.

Many of the climbs are affected by the tide, and some knowledge of tidal movements would be helpful. Spring Tides, which coincide with a full moon, rise and fall the most (and have a faster rate of movement), Neap Tides do not rise and fall over so great a range. They interchange on a two week period, and the lowest and highest tides occur when low water is around 6 pm. The black, paint-like, lichen marks extreme high water level; however the swell, particularly after high winds, may cause the waves to break tens of metres up the cliff. The time of high and low water moves on by a little over half an hour each cycle, so for example, high water today will be just over an hour later tomorrow. Tide tables are available in Holyhead, for those who can understand them!

Crags around the island have been located by means of a standard Map Reference, and all those mentioned are to be found on the Ordnance Survey sheet 114-Anglesey, in the 1:50 000 Landranger Series.

All the amenities one would expect in a town are available in Holyhead, which is also well served by public transport, both rail and bus. There are a few reasonable cafes and take-aways, and a couple of chippies may also be found at the Valley crossroads, on the A5. The two pubs here are also better than most, but the pub at Rhoscolyn should be avoided until the ownership changes.

Campsites abound on the island, and a visit to any Tourist Information office will provide phone numbers and addresses. Near the crags, however, The Anglesey School of Sea Canoeing (0407 860201), at Porth Dafarch (just down the road to Holyhead from the bay), provides a handy camping base (with its own bar), as does Carreg yr Adar (0407 860469), on the approach to Rhoscolyn Bay.

The inclusion of any climb or crag in this guide does not imply a right of way exists to that point. Rock-climbing is a potentially dangerous activity, and any directions or information contained herein is acted upon at the reader's own risk.

Access

All the crags mentioned in this guidebook either lie on, or are approached over, private land, and their inclusion in this guide does not necessarily imply any right of way. However, providing that the described approaches and parking areas are used, there should be few problems. A number of the cliffs are nesting sites for sea birds, and should be treated with great sympathy by climbers, not to mention the consideration of serious injury inflicted by irate parent birds.

At South Stack, the colonisation of the cliffs by sea birds, and Peregrine Falcons, is so important that there is a voluntary agreement by climbers not to climb within the areas of Mousetrap Zawn, Left Hand Red Wall, Red Wall, Penlas Rock, Smurf Zawn, Blacksmith Zawn and part of South Stack Island between 1st February and the 31st of July inclusive. It is absolutely imperative, for both the birds, and everyone wishing to climb here that all parties visiting these cliffs co-operate with this ban. Information concerning the ban is also posted on signs around the crags, and all the concerned routes in this guide are marked with an (R) symbol to remind users. The plea not to break this ban could not be stronger.

Other cliffs also have resident nesting birds during the spring, and these should be left undisturbed if at all possible. Any deliberate harm caused to these birds is totally unacceptable to all reasonable climbers.

Many of the cliffs mentioned in this guide are Sites of Special Scientific Interest (SSSI), under the control of the Nature Conservancy Council, due to their important geological, botanical or biological interest. It is important to the continuation of access to these sites, and all others, that no environmental damage is inflicted by climbers.

The recent practice of driving along the private road to the top of the Gogarth Main Crag approach should not be continued; the track will shortly be blocked anyway. Extra car parking can be found in the disused quarry 800m before the South Stack road junction, on the way from Holyhead.

An extra hazard facing climbers in the Smurf Zawn area is an unpredictable, and sometimes violent, landowner. As little time as possible should be spent on the private ground at the top of the crag. Any violent incident should be reported as below, and to the Holyhead police.

Any incident concerning access should be reported to the Access Officer of The British Mountaineering Council (BMC), (phone 061 273 5835), as quickly as possible to prevent any deterioration of the situation.

The Crag Environment

Many climbers must have sat on belay ledges and wondered what sort of birds were buzzing around, and diving into the water beneath the cliffs. The Gogarth region, and many of the other areas mentioned herein, are particularly interesting in terms of flora, fauna and geology, and perhaps the best way in which to promote harmony between climbers and their environment is to educate and inform.

The cliffs at South Stack display some of the most magnificent exposures of folded rock strata in Great Britain. They consisted originally of sandstone beds, separated by thin shale layers, and they are part of the South Stack Group of the Mona Complex, very ancient rocks (600 million years old) which underlie most of Anglesey. Metamorphosis has taken place to produce quartzite, which makes up most of the cliffs. The friable red rock of South Stack is due to a higher iron concentration in that area. The strata are now so convoluted that older rocks overlie younger rocks in some places. Rhoscolyn consists of similar, superbly contorted, rocks. Carboniferous limestone is found on the eastern side of the island, at Red Wharf Bay and Penmon for instance.

The rocks are home to colonies of sea birds, some of which are briefly described here: The first three birds belong to the Auk family, and dive underwater to feed on small fish and crustacea. The Guillemot, a white chested and black-backed bird, is very similar to the Razorbill, a tall-beaked bird, with a white stripe across the eye area. Both birds nest around the South Stack cliffs in large numbers. Puffins are slightly smaller than the previous two, and are usually identified by their brightly coloured stubby bill. They nest in burrows on the grassy slopes above the cliffs. A rare bird anywhere in Wales, the Chough, a red-legged and red-beaked member of the crow family, is occasionally seen here. Ravens also appear in the area from time to time.

The Herring Gull, a grey-backed, white-chested and yellow-beaked bird, is the most common species of gull here. They will eat eggs, fledglings and even household rubbish. Kittwakes have recently colonised the area, being essentially a maritime bird, and they resemble the Herring Gulls, but are much less noisy! Cormorants and Shags are often seen, the former having a wing span of a metre and a half, and a white patch on the throat and cheeks. Shags are

Gogarth Bay showing the crags from North Stack to the Upper Tier.
Photo: Geoff Milburn

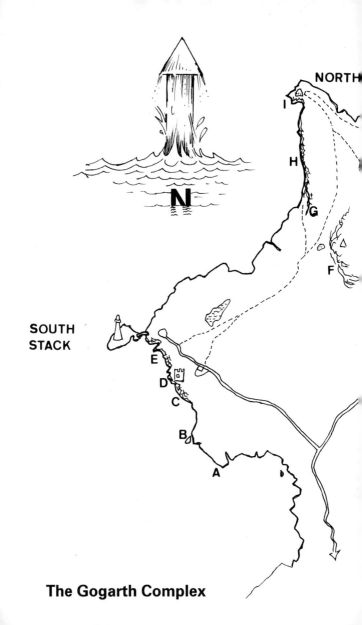

NORTH

SOUTH
STACK

N

The Gogarth Complex

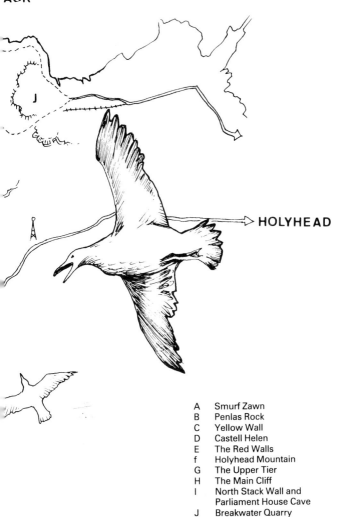

'ACK

J

HOLYHEAD

A   Smurf Zawn
B   Penlas Rock
C   Yellow Wall
D   Castell Helen
E   The Red Walls
f   Holyhead Mountain
G   The Upper Tier
H   The Main Cliff
I   North Stack Wall and
    Parliament House Cave
J   Breakwater Quarry

slightly smaller, and darker, with a yellow patch at the throat. They both swim underwater to catch fish.

On the heathland above the crags other birds often appear: Stonechats, Linnets, Whitethroated Warblers, Wrens and Meadow Pipits. Butterflies are well seen on warm sunny days, amongst the flowers of the coastal heathland. Many of these are particular to this type of habitat, and during the summer months form a superb display of colour.

Other animals of interest are: the Grey Seals, which often appear to inspect the performance of waterside climbing teams; and Adders, found dozing in the sunshine in the grass at the top of the cliffs. The latter can inflict a serious, though not usually fatal, bite.

Historical

Long before the potential of the Gogarth sea cliffs was realised, local climbers and members of the RAF Valley Mountain Rescue Team climbed on the small sunny crags of Holyhead Mountain. Cliff Fishwick, K C Jones and Dave Durkan were the main pioneers, and Durkan even published a guidebook to the area.

The mainstream climbers in Snowdonia were, during the early Sixties, starting to run out of possibilities, and the pursuit of 'Crag X' had become a favourite game. One of the most active groups around that time was the Alpha Club, and it was two of their members, Bas Ingle and Martin Boysen, who 'discovered' Gogarth, and climbed the first two lines: *Gogarth* and *Shag Rock*. They returned with Pete Crew, and beavered away to produce nine routes, after which, astoundingly in retrospect, they felt that the cliff was worked out. The Alpha Club later drifted apart, and nothing further happened for some time. South Stack got a look in when Stan Wroe, Dave Crilly and Paul Braithwaite failed on what was to become Mousetrap, and climbed *The Green Slab* instead. That was the only route added all year.

1966 saw two events that were to spark off the first great wave of exploration at Gogarth. The first was when Claude Davies and Alli Cowburn climbed *The Rift*. Not the greatest climb ever, but it made Crew and others sit up and take notice of the potential again. The second event was the rape of Red Wall by a team of All Stars to provide a live television outside broadcast. Joe Brown was called in to replace an unavailable Bonington, and after initial suprise, put his mind into gear and considered the possibilities of the place. Shortly after this, Crew and Jancis Baldock broke a psychological barrier when they completed *The Ramp*, a line that had puzzled Crew for some time. Crew and Dave Alcock also uncovered *Central Park* after a marathon gardening session.

Brown started his explorations at Gogarth with not just a new route, but by discovering one of the most latterly popular areas of all the cliffs here. Out with friends on a sea-level traverse, Brown spotted the top of Wen Slab, and borrowing gear from the others, went into the zawn to climb *Wen* with Boysen. He returned the next weekend to claim *Dde*, whilst Boysen added *Scavenger* and *Fifth Avenue*. Rowland Edwards added a few routes to the Upper Tier, and Brown climbed *Winking Crack*. Crew had a secret weapon at this time in the form of a set of aerial photographs of the cliffs, and was able to climb the hidden *Big Groove,* followed by *Cordon Bleu* and a girdle on the Main Cliff, with Geoff Birtles.

Crew and Brown then teamed up to attack the steep central area of the Main Cliff. *Dinosaur* was the result, on a day when Crew climbed like a a demon and Brown was forced to take a back seat. It would be easy in retrospect to say that this period was characterised by the use of too much aid, but this was on-sight climbing at the psychological limit of its day. It should also be remembered that many points of aid were used because of the loose and dirty nature of the rock. *The Rat Race* illustrates well the desire not to use aid, if possible, but that the importance of the line eventually overwhelmed the ethical stances. Several leaders had tried the line; Malcolm Howells reached a high point, but was loathe to use a peg. Brown used a peg, and gained the stance, but his second could not follow. Twice this happened before Howells and Barry Whybrow took advantage of the in-place gear to complete the meat of the climb. Brown and Crew repeated the route the next day, adding a final pitch in the process.

That summer Crew published an interim guide with 39 routes. Mountain magazine published photographs and articles about Gogarth, which ensured a growing popularity.

Brown returned to examine the lines he had spotted on Red Wall, and bagged both *Red Wall* and *Wendigo.* Attention turned to Castell Helen and within a few weeks Brown, Crew and Alcock had accounted for most of the classic lines, with *Doppelgangen* being slotted in for good measure. Mousetrap Zawn was next on the list, the magnificent *Mousetrap,* climbed with Crew, being the major find. Geoff Cram and Mike Yates added the serious *Pterodactyl* to the lost world of Yellow Wall before Brown and Crew trekked up *The Sind. Resolution* was a good find by Crew at the close of the year.

Easter Island Gully was discovered early in 1967 and again Brown, Crew and Alcock dominated the proceedings. Alcock and Rogan also found *Britomartis* at this time, while *Concrete Chimney* fell to Crew and Brown; another puzzling piece of rock. Activity continued although nothing major was climbed until Crew teamed up with Ed Drummond to climb *Mammoth,* felt at the time to be a better line than Dinosaur. This spurred Brown, with Ian MacNaught-Davis into a spate of activity in the Easter Island area.

Attention now moved to those blanker areas as yet unexplored. *Left Hand Red Wall* was climbed by Brown and Crew but only after the use of a peg in a drilled hole. The cliffs became the focus of attention of an emerging generation of climbers and Ed Drummond was the first to make his mark. *The Strand* was a superb addition followed a few weeks later by *Transatlantic Crossing*. Drummond's ability and eye for a line were however a little shrouded by his blaze of self publicity.

Doug Scott, by contrast, beavered away in obscurity for several weekends to produce *The Big Overhang*, which followed the big roof of Parliament House Cave. The Holliwell brothers, Lawrie and Les, attacked the cliffs with great zeal, although their first addition fell down and was re-climbed as *Yellow Scar*. *Park Lane*, *Black Spot* and *U.F.O.* were better lines. Exploration slowed a little and the next route of note was *Deygo*, forced up the blank right-hand side of Left Hand Red Wall by Tom Proctor and Geoff Birtles. Dave Durkan had also been busy with a number of minor additions to the Upper Tier and The Holyhead Mountain crags. *Hypodermic* was another fine addition from the Holliwells. Brown and Crew ventured into the huge arch opposite Wen Slab to climb *Spider's Web*; Brown had nearly drowned on this, on a previous attempt, with Brian Fuller. Drummond and Dave Pearce traversed Wen Slab to produce one of the most popular climbs in Wales with *A Dream of White Horses*. With Ben Campbell-Kelly, Drummond also added *The Quartz Icicle* and *The Horizon*, the latter an incredibly long girdle traverse. *Citadel* was also ascended during this period, although an unfortunate lapse by Jack Street meant that the main pitch was hammered into submission and the crack left littered with ironmongery (until it was removed many years later by a falling American visitor).

Climbing has always relied on the honesty of first ascensionists, and it had become clear that a certain climber had claimed a number of lines that had simply not been climbed. *Afreet Street* was climbed by Drummond to provide fairly conclusive evidence of the fabrication, and the discredited climber vanished from the scene; if only contemporary liars had the same remorse. It was also during this period that there were without doubt a number of first ascents that were never recorded, sometimes because the climbers were not in the mainstream, but also because the concept of what constitutes a climb and makes it worth reporting has also changed. Remnants of these early explorations have often turned up on latter-day lines, sometimes in extraordinary locations.

The first proper guidebook, written by Crew was published in 1969 and it contained around 130 routes. Crew commented that he felt Gogarth to be fully developed, and he expressed some doubt as to the future popularity of the area; in retrospect he could not have been more wrong.

Crew himself rendered the guide out of date when he and Brown climbed *Perygl*, the first route on Yellow Wall to approach the ominous mass of overhangs. Lawrie Holliwell found *Wonderwall* and the serious *Mantrap*; the former was not repeated for several years. He also climbed *Supercrack* around this time but did not record it as a couple of points of aid were used. The most important ascent of this period, however, was the ascent of *T.Rex* by Drummond, Pearce and Holliwell, with Janet Rogers. Powerful climbing and intricate route finding reflected the composition of this 'super team'. *Red Haze* marked the close of the Brown and Crew era, although Brown was to put in several re-appearances in later years. The Holliwells continued to find good routes such as *Spider Wall* and *The Savage*. John Gosling ascended *Falls Road* to produce a serious problem, and he also added a number of fragile routes in the Breakwater Quarries.

Dave Durkan added a number of routes to The Upper Tier, but more importantly began, with Len Costello and others, to develop the sea cliffs at Rhoscolyn. Worthwhile climbs of all grades were added although the area was not felt at the time to rival the much more extensive cliffs of Gogarth, and it had to wait over a decade for belated recognition.

The Maze was another fine addition from Drummond, again in a serious position. The Holliwells added their own serious line, *Zeus*, to Wen Slab, whilst Cliff Phillips and Nigel Horne provided the first route on North Stack Wall with *Wall of Horrors*. Wen Slab also received an intricate new line, from Drummond and Pearce, called *Games Climbers Play*; so named for the variety of techniques used on the ascent.

1971 opened with a route that advanced the grades a full step, when Alan Rouse and Pete Minks forced *Positron* up the steep walls between The Rat Race and Dinosaur. Although the new routing continued it was more a consolidation in terms of existing difficulty rather than Positron being used as a spring-board for greater things. This would have to wait another few years.

The evergreen Martin Boysen climbed a line of pockets left of Winking Crack to give the hugely named *Fifteen Men on a dead man's chest, Yo ho ho and a bottle of rum. Drink and the devil have done for the rest, Yo ho ho ...etc*; in fact the climb was probably shorter than the name. Ray Evans, whose contributions to Welsh climbing have always commanded respect, added *Bubbly Situation Blues* to The Main Cliff; a line that would still halt a few E6 leaders. *The Needle* was another fine Evans creation. Drummond re-appeared to find *The Moon* – many a Gogarth devotee's favourite climb; pushing its way through the central overhangs of Yellow Wall. Lawrie Holliwell's last major contribution before his untimely death on Craig Yr Isfa was *Hysteresis*, on the left-hand side of Mousetrap Zawn. Marred on the first ascent by a drilled peg, Holliwell re-climbed the route free shortly afterwards.

Another lull in activity was followed in 1973 by probings of yet another wave of activists. Pat Littlejohn, with Andy Houghton, visited South Stack and added the impressive *Pagan* to Left Hand Red Wall. Deygo was climbed free by Ron Fawcett, and the aid on Mammoth reduced, before Pete Livesey dispensed with the aid on Falls Road. *Puzzle Me Quick* was another contribution from Evans and Brian Wyvill, taking the groove left of The Big Groove.

Alec Sharp, at College in Bangor, was to be the major contributor of the next two years. With John Zangwill he forced the difficult eliminate line of *The Camel*, freed the aid on The Moon, Wonderwall, and Supercrack before adding *Creeping Lemma* with Steve Humphries and *The Eternal Optimist*; the last of the bogus routes to fall. Probably Sharp's major contribution to The Main Cliff was *Ordinary Route*, a rising traverse of The Main Cliff's central wall. Climbed with John Whittle and Chris Dale (part each) it included the crux section of Positron.

In 1976, ten years after his first new route at Gogarth, Malcolm Howells, with Paul Trower, climbed the difficult and serious *Dogs of War*. Trower then partnered Pearce on *The Cow*, a very fine prize in this steep area. Littlejohn returned to Red Wall and added *Redshift* with Hugh Clarke, while Sharp and Ray Toomer followed a line left of Citadel to give *Graduation Ceremony*. Fawcett and Livesey spent a day frightening themselves whilst each added a route to Wen Zawn. Mick Fowler and John Stevenson found a new girdle of the central wall of The Main Cliff; *Trunk Line*. Littlejohn and Nipper Harrison returned to free Games Climbers' Play, providing a new start in the process.

Around this time climbing entered an era where the freeing of points of aid on existing routes was considered very important. There was also a change of attitude to the manner of first ascents. Previously the majority of routes had been climbed more or less on sight with minimal preparation; this now became the exception, with the majority of lines being well cleaned and examined before the first ascent. Other less savoury tactics were also suspected. This surprisingly did not stop the odd point of aid being utilized, and there were some instances of routes being top-roped before a conventional ascent. Again, in retrospect, this was probably greatly preferable to the use of excessive ironmongery, or worse, the chipping of extra holds (as happened on the odd occasion).

1977 saw the appearance of the first Climbers' Club guide to Gogarth (although not without some legal wrangling) written by Sharp. He rightly surmised that the boulder problems of the day would tomorrow be taken to the crags in the shape of hard new routes; Gogarth was poised for its second major wave of exploration.

Ben and Marion Wintringham set the ball rolling in 1978 with *Bitter Days*. While Al Evans gardened extensively to produce the fine *Freebird*, Dave Knighton set a dubious precedent when he top-roped *Street Survivor* prior to a clean lead. Pete Whillance and Dave Armstrong disdaining such tactics added the serious *Staying Alive*. Brown re-appeared yet again finding *The Flytrap*, a gem nestling in a neglected area. *Wandering Wall*, another Brown creation, required novel tactics to complete. Jim Moran and Evans began to examine Easter Island Gully with fresh eyes, and produced a string of interesting routes. May Day saw four major teams completing new routes; Whillance and Armstrong producing the route of the day with *Energy Crisis*. Andy Hyslop and Knighton in addition to the Moran/Evans party produced classic middle-grade lines, while Mick Fowler battled with poor rock on Yellow Wall to produce *Paddington*. Fowler had previously added the serious *Ludwig* to this area.

The next major line, involving a whole sequence of boulder problem moves, was *Barbarossa*, Moran's fine but slightly flawed line right of Bloody Chimney. Pat Littlejohn also contributed a major line with *Hunger*, forcing a way through the steep band of rock right of Citadel. *The Horrorshow* was another fine lead by Moran, a sustained and strenuous pitch. The routes kept flowing from Moran, with Evans and Geoff Milburn, many being very worthwhile additions such as *This Years Model* and *The Assassin*, but most impressive was the big line of *The Wastelands*. Brown returned to Smurf Zawn, an earlier find, with Wintringham and produced a number of steep and interesting routes. Milburn was determined to explore North Stack Wall, and with

Moran, Evans and Simon Horrox, the team added a number of fine amenable climbs such as *South Sea Bubble*.

The Red Wall area quickly came under scrutiny as the bird ban lifted; Evans and Moran adding two man-eating routes *Alligator* and *Cannibal*. Moran continued, with Paul Williams to firstly free Television Route and then add his own line of *Khmer Rouge*. Wintringham and Brown produced their own line *Rapture of the Deep*, and also found *Anarchist* and *Infidel* on Left Hand Red Wall. The big line here however was Fowler's *Heart of Gold*, which involved some hair-raising situations before it was eventually climbed. Fowler also added a fine girdle; *The Missionary*. Knighton returned to grab the obvious line of *Communication Breakdown*, free Blind Pew and produce the well-positioned line of *The Emotionary*.

The most controversial event of this dynamic period was the ascent of *The Cad* by Fawcett. In order to claim probably the finest line on this wall, Fawcett placed two bolts on this otherwise very poorly protected pitch. Although Whillance dispensed with the lower bolt on the second ascent, it was some time before the route was led without either. The controversy over the bolt still in situ drags on, and in an effort to make progress the route is recorded in its purest form. Whillance and Armstrong picked up consolation prizes in the form of the bold *Blue Peter*, and a free ascent of Wall of Horrors. Fawcett again pushed back the frontiers when he produced the technical and serious *Blackleg*, one of the hardest leads in Wales at the time.

In response to the 75 routes climbed that year, Milburn and Evans produced a 1978 Supplement to Sharp's guide book. Many of the routes found in this period became instant classics, and a number of the harder routes gained reputations in the way that some lines had ten years previously.

1979 saw Wintringham produce a string of new climbs, but it was Moran who returned with Paul Williams to claim several big lines that had been inspected the previous year. *The Tet Offensive* and *Sebastopol* both took steep and impressive lines, whilst *Mein Kampf* took a blank section of Left Hand Red Wall. Whillance returned to North Stack and produced yet another serious line with *The Long Run*. The Original Start to Games Climbers Play was freed by Fawcett, who went on to free The Horrorshow, Afreet Street and the much tried Dinosaur. 1980 also saw a concerted attack on the remaining gaps on the steep central section of The Main Cliff. *Alien*, an obvious but very difficult line, fell to Littlejohn and Steve Lewis, before Fawcett and Moran teamed up to produce the daunting *Wall of Fossils* and *The Big Sleep*.

At South Stack, Gordon Tinnings and Trower added another two serious routes with *Another Roadside Attraction* and *Blue Remembered Hills*. Overshadowing the other contributions of this year was the outstanding ascent of *The Bells! The Bells!* by John Redhead, which brought a new grade of difficulty and seriousness to Gogarth. In addition to this Redhead also showed his great technical ability by freeing Barbarossa.

At this point the previous supplement was up-dated to 1981 by Milburn, with the consolidation of comprehensive E grades, and the inclusion of the notorious graded list.

On Holyhead Mountain Jim Donnely had whittled away at old aid routes, and Keith Robertson also added a number of hard climbs. This was to be continued by Dave Hazelaar, Julian Dalton and latterly Mike Gresham to result in a fine modern, but largely ignored, outcrop. Attention also started to be shown in other areas of rock around Anglesey including The Range and the Bull Bay area.

Fowler returned to Mousetrap Zawn and added the terminal *Death Trap*, but little else of consequence was climbed for a couple of years.

The next major development really occured in 1983/4 with the rediscovery of Rhoscolyn, initially by Steve Haston, Bangor University students and then to great effect by Williams and Moran. Contributions such as *The Sun*, *The Savage Sunbird* and *Godzilla* from Williams, and *Magellan's Wall*, *Warpath* and *The Jub Jub Bird* from Moran, dragged the crag into the modern era. Joe Healey also got a look in here with his route *The Trail of Tears*.

Back on Gogarth Redhead had started to blitz North Stack Wall with serious and committing lines. *The Clown*, *Birth Trauma* and *The Demons of Bosch* all of which commanded great respect, although the latter unfortunately saw the placement of another bolt on this wall. Andy Pollitt joined in with *Art Groupie*, being obviously influenced by this style of climbing. He also added his own very difficult climb to the steep section of The Main Cliff with *Skinhead Moonstomp*, an unusually obvious remaining possibility. Pollitt also claimed the obvious prize of *Mammoth Direct*, and freed the difficult Ludwig, a pitch that had defeated some very strong leaders. Haston soloed Positron; Johnny Dawes' impromptu solo of the main crack of Citadel, and Jim

Jewell's solo of The Cad are other outstanding events of this ilk. Just as impressive was one climber's jump from Castell Helen's half-way ledge into the sea, although apparently swim-inspected beforehand! Fowler and Tony Saunders returned to South Stack to add *Helmet Boiler* whilst Moran free-climbed the old aid route of The Nod to give a popular pitch, *The Cruise*.

After a two year lay-off Redhead returned to North Stack Wall and produced more serious climbs with *The Stroke of the Fiend* and *Flower of Evil*, but now a new generation was snapping at his heels; activists that were to produce routes of even greater seriousness and commitment. With the sterilization of hard climbing in some areas of the country, old traditions re-surfaced at Gogarth, and it became again a matter of pride to be able to comment 'on sight' after writing up one's latest creation.

Martin Crook continued his far flung explorations, producing a series of minor classics all around the cliffs; the best of which is probably *20,000 Leagues Under The Sea*, a painfully obvious line opposite North Stack Wall. Crispin Waddy began, with *Agrophobia*, to explore the Cryptic Rift beneath Wen Zawn's promontory, but it was Steve Haston, with Ray Kay and John Tombs, who made the major contribution with a series of difficult and serious climbs around South Stack. *Me*, *The Drunk*, *Rosebud*, *The Electrification of the Soviet Union*, *Free Stone Henge* and *Isis is Angry* were all major lines through very imposing and sometimes outrageous territory. Craig Smith added the difficult *Psychocandy* to The Upper Tier, but the serious side of Gogarth climbing again emerged when Smith and Johnny Dawes investigated the huge archway in Wen Zawn to produce the bold and muscular *Conan The Librarian*.

Dawes continued in a serious vein with Paul Pritchard when they teamed up to climb the appalling *Come To Mother*, a portion of which later fell down. Pollitt, after repeating The Bells! The Bells!, went on to add his own line *The Hollow Man*, another totally committing lead. Pritchard returned to Left Hand Red Wall adding *Schittlergruber*, *The Enchanted Broccoli Garden*, *Outside The Asylum*, *Salem* and the most serious route in this guidebook with *The Super Calabrese*. Bob Drury, Piggy Johnstone, Nick Harmes and Mike Thomas were his horrified partners during these escapades. Pritchard also visited Wen Zawn with Nick Dixon to produce *The Unridable Donkey*, another climb to lose a portion into the sea shortly afterwards.

Rhoscolyn received attention from a number of teams and many obvious gaps were plugged, while Malcolm

Campbell, Ed Stone et al investigated The Equestrian Walls. The Range also received another session of exploration at this time. Haston, Kay, Dave Jones, Trower and Leigh McGinley continued to investigate the more esoteric areas around South Stack, but it was at Breakwater Quarry that a potentially disturbing development took place with two bolt-protected lines being produced by Pritchard and George Smith. The only reason these bolts survived is that they were not placed on waterside crags, but no one could doubt that both creators were fine climbers without this ironmongery; Smith producing routes such as the excellent *Arachnid* and *The Cruel Seam*. The area beneath Left Hand Red Wall also received investigation from Crook, Waddy, Andy Popp and Tombs.

The real world returned soon enough when Dawes, with Drury made the first totally on-sight ascent of an E7 climb with *Hardback Thesaurus*, a very fine effort indeed. Pollitt, with Adrian Hughes, added yet another line to the crowded North Stack Wall with *A Wreath of Deadly Nightshade*, and eliminated the bolt from The Demons of Bosch. This prompted Redhead and Dave Towse to keep abreast of the game with *The Angle Man* and variations on The Cad and The Long Run. Pritchard began to fill some of the obvious gaps with *Hang Ten (in the Green Room)*, a serious boulder problem style route. The last notable find was *Eraserhead* by Grant Farquhar and Waddy, an instant classic on a crowded section of The Main Cliff.

At a time when climbing is bogged down in a sea of commercialism and controversy; when bolts, red-points, pink- points, and French style is the vogue; when egotistical and paranoic prima-donas spend more time putting down their fellows than actually climbing; when chipping and cheating are used more than ever to bring routes down to the level of the worst performer – Gogarth has remained relatively unaffected by this irrelevant nonsense. The climbs here still overwhelmingly embody a sense of adventure and escapism. There are still new lines to be sought out, but to use Geoff Milburn's words of 1978 'they will be hard...very hard.' It has certainly become obvious that a number of the crags can be climbed anywhere at a given grade; here restraint might be nobler than gluttony. There is great scope on a number of the smaller crags; there may well even be some worthwhile routes! Most important is the timeless atmosphere of the area, the restless pounding seas and the cries of the sea-birds, and often peace and solitude – an antidote to our scurried modern existence.

Gogarth

Approaches

SOUTH STACK

The area is usually approached by the A5, which crosses Anglesey to Holyhead. Enter the town on this road until, crossing over a bridge, a large wall bounds the road (Victoria Road) on the right (the ferry port lies on the other side). Continue down this until some 900 metres after the bridge a junction to the left is met. Here the wall gives way to a fence; turn left into Prince of Wales Road. This passes the Coastguard post, and emerges by the waterfront of Holyhead harbour. 200 metres past the Coastguard post, a left turn, signposted South Stack, is taken. This leads, via another signposted right turn, to open fields, and eventually a right turn, up the small road to South Stack. The road ends beyond the cafe, and at the top of the Lighthouse steps. The cafe car park is for customers only, so buy your Mars bars before cragging! The cliffs all lie in the area below the road. Ellin's Castle, easily seen over the wall, is a good landmark, as are the Lighthouse steps.

It is also possible to reach the same point via Trearddur Bay. When approaching via the A5, turn left at the Valley crossroads (the only permanent traffic lights met on the way across the island), and follow the road, and signs, to Trearddur Bay. Just across Four Mile Bridge is the Rhoscolyn turn-off. Carry on to Trearddur Bay, and turn left at the garage, to meet the waterfront in the bay itself. This road is followed, past Porth Dafarch, and The Range, to reach the turn-off up to South Stack.

THE UPPER TIER, MAIN CLIFF and HOLYHEAD MOUNTAIN

Follow the South Stack route to the car parks. From the highest one, a path leads away from South Stack, to join a track leading to the intrusive microwave relay stations. The path carries on to the right of these, and 300 metres after the second station, the path splits at a vague col. The left fork leads downhill, with an impressive view of the Main Cliff, to a couple of large boulders, at the top of the gripping approach gully, where sacks are usually stashed. This area is being undercut by the head of the gully, and the nearest boulders may soon become part of it! The right fork leads up onto Holyhead Mountain, and can be used to gain the Wen Slab and North Stack areas. The Holyhead Mountain

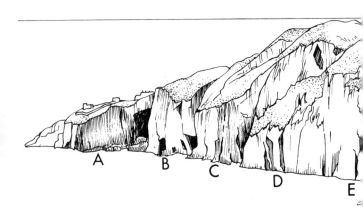

Gogarth Bay

A North Stack Wall
B Flytrap Area
C Wen Zawn
D Easter Island Gully Area
E The Main Cliff
F The Upper Tier

Crags are obvious on the right, just along this path, and a path runs down along the bottom of these.

An alternative approach is to park in the disused quarry, 800 metres before the South Stack road junction, and follow the footpath up, beneath the Holyhead Mountain Crags, to reach the path divide at the vague col.

EASTER ISLAND GULLY, WEN SLAB AREA, NORTH STACK AREA, TSUNAMI ZAWN and BREAKWATER QUARRY.

Take the South Stack approach as far as the Coastguard post, and the Holyhead Harbour. Carry on along the waterfront until, near the far end, a small road forks off left and goes over a bridge. This ramped road leads to a pot-holed track, under a bridge, and into the Breakwater Quarry. Cars can be parked at the track end on the right (Map Ref 225834). Take the path, up an incline, to where it flattens at 400 m. At the path junction, the right fork leads downwards, alongside the telegraph poles, and passes above Tsunami Zawn, to reach the North Stack Promontory. The left fork carries on rising, alongside the electricity poles, and is exited leftwards where it turns down right. Ahead is a small col, beyond which lies Wen Zawn, and a path leading down to the promontory. Easter Island Gully lies up left from the Wen Zawn col, and from a second small col, just beyond the top of a heathery hill, a path runs down into the fearsome approach gully, and so to the abseil point.

Gogarth Bay

The northern side of Gogarth Bay is formed by a continuous line of cliffs extending for nearly a kilometre, and reaching over 100 metres in height. They are divided into sections, both by the structure of the cliffs, and by the access to the climbs. The most southerly of the cliffs is the Upper Tier, the base of which is around 70 metres above the sea, and extends from the descent gully (described in the Approaches) to where the walls merge into The Main Cliff. The Main Cliff rises directly from the sea, and provides the highest area of the crags, running north until it becomes The Easter Island Gully Area, an access, rather than physical, division. This area terminates where Wen Zawn slices into the cliffs, the huge arch of the Promontory forming one side of the zawn. Beyond this, the cliffs become lower and more broken, and are collectively known as North Stack. The massive sea-cave of Parliament House and the connected North Stack Wall are the best known sections of this area. Also included in this area are routes on the very broken Holyhead side of the North Stack peninsula.

The Upper Tier

The Upper Tier is perhaps the most frequently visited area of all the Gogarth crags, due to the relative ease of access and a lesser degree of commitment than the waterside crags. Although bristling with test-pieces, there exist here a number of the more amenably graded climbs in the area.

The crag is made up of an alternating series of bays and walls which start immediately left of the foot of the short approach gully and open out into the large amphitheatre bounded on the right by the Central Park wall, and on the left by the vegetated area beyond Bezel, where the rocks merge into the upper section of The Main Cliff. Above the routes, steep heathery slopes lead upwards to a narrow and very obvious path which contours above the cliff line. To regain the top of the approach gully, this path is followed rightwards (facing in) to a heather and rock step. Just beyond this the path splits, and the right fork leads down to a short rocky gully, which runs out into the area at the top of the approach gully.

From the base of the·approach gully a path runs along the foot of the crags, complete with several collapses that constantly cause the path to be re-routed. Several branches lead up to the starts of the various climbs. Just past the obvious pinnacle of Shag Rock, a short rock traverse leads, with care, to a better path continuing around and rising to gain the Gauntlet area. Beyond Bezel the path heads downhill to gain the start of Cordon Bleu etc. and the grassy ramp ends abruptly just beyond.

Nomad   52m   Very Severe   (1968)
A vegetated and rather obscure route, starting beneath a six-metre slab at the foot of the descent gully.
1   30m. Take the slåb then the groove on the right to a wall. Traverse right and go up a short arête moving left onto a ramp, which is followed to a crack leading to a block belay on the left.
2   22m. Move across to the crack behind the belay, go up this, and go over blocks to a wide crack on the right which gains the top.

The Upper Tier – Right-Hand Section

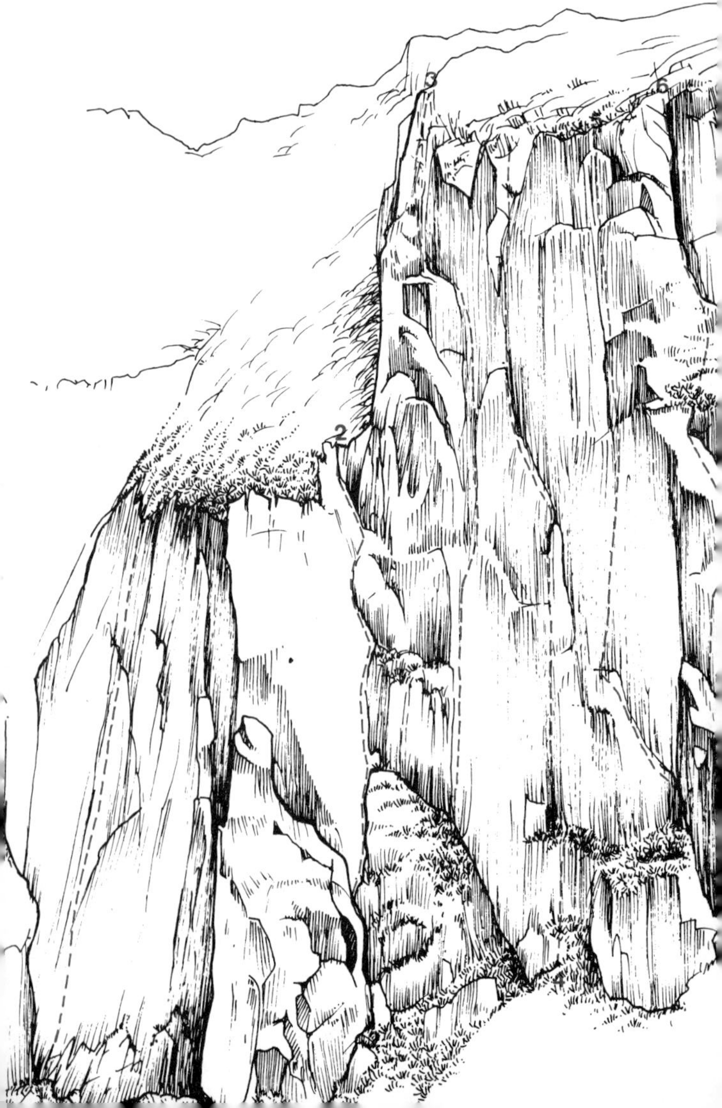

1	The Strand	E2	10	Bloody Chimney	VS
2	Black Spot	HVS	11	Barbarossa	E6
3	Crowbar	E1	12	Blackleg	E6
4	Blind Pew	E2	13	Strike Direct	E6
5	Winking Crack	E3	14	Strike	E3
6	Campion	HVS	15	The Rift	VS
7	Puffin	S	16	Dropout	E2
8	Pantin	VS	17	Dirtigo	VS
9	U.F.O.	E2	18	Psychocandy	E6
			19	Trogg's Way	HVS

Trogg's Way 40m Hard Very Severe 5a (1970)
A chossy route and not recommended. Start by scrambling up to a peg belay at the foot of the obvious slabby corner left of the descent gully. The tricky crack on the right leads to a grassy ledge. Climb a slab on the left wall followed by a slight groove. From the top of this gain the flake on the left then take the crack above to finish.

Psychocandy 18m E6 6c (1986)
A thin and bold pitch taking the obvious thin crack trending rightwards up the cleaned wall. Start as for Trogg's Way. Climb the corner for a few metres then move right to the crack. Follow this with great difficulty, past two pegs, to finish on the arête.

Dirtigo 49m Very Severe (1966)
Not as bad as the name suggests. Start as for Trogg's Way.
1 34m. 4c. Climb the corner skirting slightly leftwards around the bulge. Continue up to grassy ledge with peg belays.
2 15m. 4a. From the belay traverse right and follow a chimney to the top.

Variation
2a 15m. 4c. Climb the slab up and leftwards to finish, more in keeping with pitch 1.

Acid 52m Hard Very Severe (1970)
This takes the crack-line in the centre of the slab to the left of Dirtigo, starting at the foot of the corner, as for Trogg's Way.
1 34m. Go up and left to gain the crack and follow it over the bulge above, where a slight groove leads to a second bulge. Take this on the left before moving right to belay on the grassy ledge, as for Dirtigo.
2 18m. Traverse right and climb the chimney, as for Dirtigo, for 5 metres. Follow the ramp leftwards to the top.

Dropout 49m E2 (1978)
A serious and poorly protected pitch which takes the arête left of Acid, starting at the foot of the corner, as for Trogg's Way.
1 37m. 5b. Follow Acid over the first bulge, then traverse left to the arête and climb this, with difficulty, to a small ledge. Move up right and climb the slab just right of the arête to a belay.
2 12m. 4a. Ascend easily in the line of the arête to finish.

To the left of the above routes, the next portion of the cliff is formed by a huge flake, The Rift taking the right-hand side and Bloody Chimney the more impressive left-hand side.

The Rift   57m   Very Severe   (1966)
A good outing for the chimney addict. Start at a chockstone
belay beneath the right-hand side of the gigantic flake.
1   37m. 4c. Enter the chimney and 'ascend' until it is
possible to escape to a small ledge on the left. Shuffle to
the edge of the flake then climb up and left to a spike belay
on top of the flake itself.
2   5m. A short scramble up behind the stance leads to a
second spike belay in a small recess.
3   15m. 4c. The crack behind the belay provides a sharp
finish.

★★ **Strike**   57m   E3   (1966)
A very strenuous, but well protected and popular main
pitch, taking the obvious twin diagonal cracks up the
right-hand side of the front face of the gigantic flake. Start
beneath the cracks.
1   37m. 6a. Move up a little and make a hard move left to
get established on the line. A good rest after six metres is
followed by a baffling sequence to enter the slabby groove
above. Follow this, and then the wide crack on the right to
belay on top of the flake.
2   20m. 4c. Gain the crack above and follow this to finish,
as for The Rift.

Variation
Strike Direct   30m   E6   6c   (1982)
A vicious and scary direct start up the faint arête, protected
by small wires, and starting down to the left of the original
start. Boulder out the arête to join Strike at the good resting
place, just below the slabby groove. Continue as for Strike.

Between Strike and the next slabby corner is an impressive
steep wall, containing two difficult, but contrasting, routes.

★ **Blackleg**   48m   E6   (1978)
A vague right-trending depression provides the line of this
serious pitch. A good selection of wires and a large sling
can be placed en-route, but few of the runners are really
inspiring. Nevertheless, a most worthwhile route.
1   22m. 6b. A strenuous start leads up and rightwards to a
spike runner. Pull straight up to a small flake on the left
which accepts further protection. Move up right to a good
hold where the wall steepens, and a very long reach leads
to an excellent hold and so to easier ground on the ramp of
Strike. Belay.
2   11m. 6a. Gain the flake on the right and move up
strenuously to its top. Follow a lichenous ramp leftwards,
then go up to belay on top of the flake.
3   15m. 4c. Finish as for The Rift.

★★★ **Barbarossa**   52m   E6   (1978/1980)
An excellent, strenuous and sustained route taking a direct line up the front face of the huge flake. Start left of Blackleg, directly below a line of pockets in the middle of the wall, from which a peg protrudes at eight metres.
1   37m. 6b. Strenuously work up to the peg, after which technical moves lead slightly leftwards to regain the line of pockets. Follow these to a small overlap and continue in the same line to an old peg. Step right, then go easily up to belay on top of the flake.
2   15m. 4c. Finish as for The Rift.

★ **Bloody Chimney**   55m   Very Severe   (1966)
A good route with a bold start, taking the chimney up the left-hand side of the huge pinnacle. Start below a crack at the foot of the slabby corner to the left of the pinnacle.
1   22m. 4c. Climb the crack and continue up the chimney to a sloping ledge, and belay.
2   18m. 4b. Regain the chimney and follow it, passing the large chockstone on the right, to exit on top of the huge flake.
3   15m. 4c. Finish as for The Rift.

Immediately left of Bloody Chimney is a large slab taken by Pantin and Puffin. This is bounded on the right by a steep wall which provides a number of harder routes.

★ **U.F.O.**   64m   E2   (1967)
A pleasant and interesting route, starting at the bottom of the slabby corner, as for Bloody Chimney.
1   30m. 5b. Climb the slabby corner, until a thin crack in the right wall can be reached at eight metres. Follow this, a little fragile, moving firstly right then back left, and continue to a pinnacle, where a short descent can be made rightwards to belay in Bloody Chimney.
2   34m. 5b. Return to the pinnacle and follow grooves and cracks to a ledge. Another crack, up to the left, leads to a niche. Continue to the top.

Pantin   67m   Very Severe   (1964)
A straightforward approach leads to a steep and impressive finish, providing a worthwhile route. Start as for Bloody Chimney, at the foot of the slabby corner.
1   37m. 4b. Follow the corner for nine metres then go diagonally leftwards across the slab to reach short cracks in the left wall. Climb these to a ledge and spike belay.
2   30m. 4c. Step down and traverse across the steep wall on the right to reach a big spike in the corner. Finish up the main groove above.

Get The Stroll   43m   E3   (1978)
Bold climbing, but not as strenuous as Run Fast, Run Free.
Start from a belay below the short cracks on Pantin.
1   31m. 5c. Cross the slab on the right, and gain the foot of
the crack, which is followed to below the obvious pod.
Traverse delicately right on quartz holds to gain rattly flakes
and follow these up rightwards to reach a crack, which
leads to a good stance.
2   12m. 5c. From the left-hand end of the ledge, follow the
obvious leftward slanting crack to the top.

★★ **Run Fast, Run Free**   43m   E5   6a   (1978)
An excellent example of sustained crack climbing, starting
from a belay below the short cracks on Pantin. Cross the
slab to gain the foot of the crack on the right, as for Get The
Stroll. Climb this leftwards, past a pod, and continue, pegs,
stepping right to a continuation crack which leads to the
top.

Canned Laughter   45m   E2 (1 pt. aid)   (1970/1978)
The original aid route of this wall has been superseded,
although it can be followed to give a disjointed route. Start
from a belay below the short cracks on Pantin.
1   33m. 5c. Cross the slab rightwards to gain the crack, as
for Run Fast, Run Free. Follow this, and from the top climb
leftwards to a second, thin crack. Go up a couple of metres,
then go left to a corner and peg. Climb this, moving left into
the corner of Pantin and ascend this to the stance. One rest
sling was used on this pitch.
2   12m. Move right into a broken chimney and climb this to
finish.

Dangerous Rhythm   62m   E3   (1978)
The meat of this route is provided by the golden corner left
of Run Fast, Run Free. Start at the foot of the slab a couple
of metres left of Pantin.
1   28m. 4b. Follow a crack in the slab to belay below the
short cracks of Pantin.
2   34m. 5c. Cross the slab on the right to a shallow
depression just left of the initial crack of Run Fast, Run Free.
Climb the depression and the wall above to reach a large
hollow spike, with a peg on the wall out left. Ascend the
shallow corner above to the overlap, which is passed on the
right, and continue for five metres before moving left into a
chimney. Finish up this.

Force 8   68m   Hard Very Severe   (1970)
A good route taking the left-hand edge of the Pantin slab,
and the arête above. Start at the edge of the slab, left of
Dangerous Rhythm.

1   43m. 4c. Climb up and right for five metres, then head back left to gain the arête at a small bulge. Follow the crack up the edge of the slab then take a slight groove leading to the back wall. Go up the break in the wall to gain a ledge on the skyline. Step right and go up the crack to belay at the top block.
2   25m. 5a. Move down into a chimney and climb the crack in the back wall, which is actually the right-hand side of a flake. From the top of the crack, step right across a steep wall and climb the groove by its left branch. Step right again to ledges and go up easy cracks to the top.

Puffin   64m   Severe   (1966)
A meandering climb although pleasant, and overall offering a reasonable introduction to The Upper Tier. One of the few easy routes at Gogarth. Left of the Pantin slab is a subsidiary slab, the corner between the two being filled by a bulging flake of rock.
1   15m. 4a. The groove, on the left of the flake, is climbed to a belay on top of the flake.
2   24m. 4b. Cross rightwards for three metres and climb a short crack up onto the edge of the Pantin Slab. Climb up rightwards to reach short cracks in the wall above, junction with Pantin. Take the cracks to gain a ledge and spike belay.
3   25m. 3b. On the left is an obvious broken corner. This is followed to finish.

Variation
Direct Start   18m   Hard Very Severe   5b   (1967)
The crack two metres right of the normal start leads past a bulge to the stance on top of the flake.

Campion   81m   Hard Very Severe   (1967)
A varied climb, loose in places, with some frightening grass climbing on pitch 3. It would seem better to climb across and join Force 8 after the first two pitches to give better climbing. Start below and left of the slab of Puffin at some large blocks, below a groove.
1   25m. 4b. Climb the groove and crack above the belay to the top of the pinnacle.
2   9m. 4c. Go up the crack behind the belay to a small stance on the edge of the upper slab.
3   22m. 5a. Move right to a short crack and take this until it is possible to move onto the wall on the left. Climb this, peg, then step left onto a short brown slab. Move left again then go up over vegetated ledges to reach a large spike belay.
4   25m. 4c. The crack in the wall above leads to a flake. From this transfer to another crack on the left and finish up this.

★ **Hang Ten (in the Green Room)**   28m   E6   6c   (1988)
A serious and very difficult pitch up the blunt arête left of
Campion. Start by the pinnacle, up and left of Campion.
Gain the top of the pinnacle, and step onto the arête. Climb
this on the right-hand side, past a peg to reach a second
peg. Swing round left and climb the blunt arête direct to a
desperate slap for a good hold in a serious situation.
Continue easily up the rib to a belay. Finish as for The
Cruise, pitch 2.

To the left of Hang Ten is an impressive orange-tinged wall
which contains the next route. Left again is the towering
continuation of this wall, cleft by the striking fissure of
Winking Crack.

★ **The Cruise**   65m   E5   (1970/1984)
A good crack climb, with excellent protection ensuring
popularity. Start with an easy scramble up rightwards from
the path to a nut belay in a corner.
1   37m. 6b. Move left and climb the arête to a small ledge
beneath the crack. Gain the crack and follow it, two pegs, to
a shake-out just short of the chimney above. The ensuing
thrutch, which leads awkwardly to the ledge above, can be
protected by medium Friends.
2   28m. 4c. Climb more easily up slabs and vegetated
ledges to the top.

Noddy   60m   E2 (1 pt. aid)   (1978)
A somewhat contrived beginning leads to a well positioned
climax on the wall between The Cruise and Winking Crack.
Start as for Winking Crack.
1   15m. 5a. Follow pitch 1 of Winking Crack as far as the
base of the corner and belay.
2   9m. 5a. Climb the corner for a little way until the shallow
groove in the left arête can be gained. Follow this to the
stance and block belay on Winking Crack.
3   18m. 5b. Gain the prominent crack directly behind the
belay and follow it to a horizontal break. Cross this using an
aid peg to reach a flake slanting away up right. This leads to
easier ground and belays.
4   18m. 4c. Finish up broken rocks to the top.

★★ **Winking Crack**   67m   E3   (1966)
A fine route taking the striking crackline in the towering
wall. The crux, an off-width finish, has a gripping reputation,
most leaders finding just enough adrenalin to glue them in
place. Start by scrambling up for about ten metres to a
good ledge and belays below a short wall.
1   30m. 5a. Move right and go up a short easy groove
before moving left around the arête (start of The Cruise) to

The Upper Tier – Central Park Area

13	Fifteen Men	E4	20	Barbarossa	E6
14	Blind Pew	E2	21	Blackleg	E6
15	Winking Crack	E3	22	Strike	E3
16	The Cruise	E5	23	Strike Direct	E6
17	Hang Ten	E6	24	The Rift	VS
18	U.F.O.	E2	25	Trogg's Way	HVS
19	Bloody Chimney	VS			

gain a corner up on the left. Climb this until a stance and block belay can be reached on the left.

2   37m. 5c. Climb the crack, peg, to where it divides and follow the left-hand branch, a little friable, to a small overhang. Move left then step back right and go up the cracks to the final off-width. This leads, with some effort, to the top. Yosemite enthusiasts will eat this up, others may find it particularly trying. An unsporting lunge for ledges on the right can be made, from below the crux crack, but this negates all those guidebook ticks!

Variation
Blue Oyster Cult   55m   E3   (1978)
A spiralling line weaving in and out of Winking Crack, on which it is based. Start beneath the overhanging corner left of the start of Winking Crack.

1   10m. 5b. Climb the corner to a nut belay halfway up pitch 1 of Winking Crack.

2   15m. 5a. Move left around the corner and gain a ramp/groove, which is followed to an awkward exit rightwards to the block belay at the end of pitch 1 of Winking Crack.

3   30m. 5c. Move up into the corner then boldly gain the arête, rounding it by blind moves before climbing up into the crackline of Winking Crack. This is followed to the swing right onto ledges, and so to the top.

Blind Pew   74m   E2   (1966/1978)
Not a bad route, but one which is likely to be rather vegetated, taking the area of rock between Winking Crack and the back of the bay. Start by a short scramble up to a short wall split by a crack, three metres right of the corner.

1   10m. 4c. Climb the crack to the good ledge and belay below the left-hand groove.

2   15m. 5b. Follow the groove past two old pegs to an easier groove which leads to a good stance.

3   15m. 5b. The overhanging crack leads to the next belay.

4   12m. 5b. Continue up the crack to the final stance.

5   22m. 4c. Climb the detached flake above on its left side and continue in a similar line to the top.

The Emotionary   25m   E5   (1978)
This takes the, once brushed, wall high up between Blind Pew and Winking Crack, starting from the belay at the end of pitch 3 of Blind Pew.

1   15m. 6a. Step right to a peg then climb straight up to a second poor peg at the overlap. Continue rightwards with difficulty to a handhold before following a leftward-slanting crackline, peg, to a good stance.

2   10m. 5a. Climb the slab on the left to finish up the headwall via a short, thin crack.

★ Fifteen Men on a Dead Man's Chest   62m   E4
(1971/1981)
Good and technically interesting climbing up a line of
pockets on the first pitch, but with a rather friable and
serious second pitch. Start by scrambling up to a ledge just
left of Blind Pew.
1   25m. 6a. Move boldly left around the arête and go up to
the first of a line of pockets. Continue in the same line with
increasing difficulty until it is possible to move right to a
ledge and pinnacle belay.
2   25m. 5c. From the top of the pinnacle follow a flaky
crack until scary moves up and slightly right lead to a good
ledge and belay.
3   12m. 4c. Ascend a short groove on the right to a ledge,
trend right up a short slab into a corner and finish up the
easy crack.

★ The Horrorshow   62m   E5   (1978/1980)
The excellent main pitch offers sustained climbing
with good protection. Start by scrambling (4a) 12 metres up the
groove corner of Crowbar and taking a belay beneath its
initial corner.
1   25m. 6b. Climb the short crack in the right wall, then
work up right to a peg before trending back leftwards to a
second peg in the depths of a pocket. Follow the faint
crackline to a peg high on the right, before a tricky move
left gains a good hold above. Traverse right along the
obvious line until moves up and right lead to a junction with
Fifteen Men etc. in a corner on the sloping ledge.
2   25m. 5c. As for Fifteen Men etc. From the top of the
pinnacle follow a flaky crack until scary moves up and
slightly right lead to a good ledge and belay.
3   12m. 4c. As for Fifteen Men etc. Ascend a short groove
on the right to a ledge, trend right up a short slab into a
corner and finish up the easy crack.

Crowbar   55m   E1   (1966)
A quite bold route which follows the overhanging corner
system up the back of the bay, unfortunately often damp.
Start by a 12 metre scramble up the groove below The
Horrorshow to the foot of the first corner.
1   15m. 4b. Take the corner direct to a stance and peg
belay.
2   12m. 5a. The overhanging corner crack is followed to a
poor stance.
3   28m. 5b. The continuing overhanging groove leads past
some old pegs to an overhang. Surmount this on the left
and continue to block belays on the top ledge. Scramble
off.

The Grim Reaper 53m   E3   (1978)
This eliminate fills the gap between Crow Bar and Black
Spot with difficult climbing in a good position. Start as for
Crowbar, below the corner.
1 25m. 5a. Climb steep slabs to a ledge and peg, as for
Crowbar. Move left then climb the steep ledged wall to a
large ledge. Take the groove, rising from the middle of the
back wall, moving right to belay as for Crowbar.
2 28m. 6a. Go left along the ledge then climb steep rock
diagonally rightwards and go up rightwards to good
footholds. Move steeply up right until forced left to a small
pillar. Go up rightwards to a ledge where an easy escape is
possible up to the left.

The left edge of the bay is bounded by a huge detached
rock pinnacle, that has fallen away from the slab above.
This is Shag Rock.

Black Spot 55m   Hard Very Severe   (1967)
A fairly serious route which takes the shallow grooves up
the left-side of the bay, starting just right of Shag Rock.
1 25m. 5a. Climb the short steep wall then move
rightwards onto a ledge. Follow a crack to a second ledge
and peg belay.
2 30m. 4c. Go up the ramp on the left to gain a scoop,
which leads in turn to the top.

Bitter Days 62m   E1   (1978)
A reasonable line in a good position, although a little
lichenous, taking the arête overlooking Shag Rock. Start as
for Black Spot.
1 25m. 5a. Follow Black Spot up the short steep wall, or
go up behind Shag Rock, to gain the arête. The wall above
leads to a sloping ledge which is traversed to the belay on
Black Spot.
2 37m. 5b. Traverse back left to the ledge and climb up
leftwards to a crack near the arête, peg. Climb the crack,
peg, to easier ground. Traverse left onto the arête and finish
up this.

Shag Rock 25m   Hard Very Severe   5a   (1964)
The original of two routes that reach the top of the huge
pinnacle at the right-hand side of the Central Park wall. A
careful descent can be made from the summit by abseil.
Start inside the chimney behind the pinnacle, and near its
right-hand side. Chimney up behind the pinnacle and pull
up onto a ledge on the arête. Climb the arête and take the
last few metres on the inside face, peg, with interesting
moves to reach the summit. Quite good fun.

Shag Rock area.
Photo: Ken Wilson

The Main Cliff and Upper Tier.
Photo: Ken Wilson

Shagorado   37m   E3   5c   (1978)
An unusual route which spirals its way up Shag Rock, with
some friable rock at the start. Start beneath a right-trending
crack in the front face of the pinnacle. The crack leads to a
ledge, where a step right gains holds leading up and left to
reach a small ledge. Climb steeply up the sensuous (!) crack
above, to reach the slab above. Trend left up this, peg, to
reach the arête and move around this to the start of a
narrow ledge crossing the face. Follow this across to the
other arête and climb this to the summit.

To the left of Shag Rock is the very popular Central Park
Wall. Central Park itself makes for the wide crack in the
upper right-hand reaches of the wall whilst The Strand
takes the stunning thin crack up the clean strip of rock just
left of centre.

★ **Fifth Avenue**   46m   E1   (1966)
An interesting and varied route taking the groove up the
right edge of the Central Park Wall, starting in the chimney
formed by the left edge of Shag Rock, just up from the path.
1   40m. 5b. Chimney up until it is possible to pull boldly
into the groove running up leftwards. Follow the groove
over two bulges and go up to a stance and peg belay.
2   6m. 5a. Climb the short wall above to the top. Scramble
to belay at the back wall of the slope above.

Tequila Sunrise   50m   E2   (1978)
A reasonable route, the crack of which is obvious from
below. Start at the chimney, as for Fifth Avenue.
1   25m. 5b. Go up the dirty flake on the left to its top, then
ascend the wall above to a peg. Gain the thin crack above
and follow it to the belay of Fifth Avenue.
2   25m. 5c. The obvious crack is quite tricky and leads to
the arête, up which an easy finish is made.

★ **Times Square**   50m   Hard Very Severe   (1978)
A sustained route following a direct line up the wall left of
Fifth Avenue. A little dirty at present, but the quality should
return with traffic. Find a belay just above the short rocky
traverse on the path and beneath a shallow groove.
1   40m. 5a. Keeping left, climb to the top of the grassy
groove and move right to boldly climb some thin cracks.
These lead to a right-trending groove and so to a peg belay
at the top of the groove on Fifth Avenue.
2   10m. 5a. Go out left from the belay and climb a series of
flakes heading to a finish near the top of Central Park. Quite
scary. A belay can be constructed here, or better go well up
the slope above.

Street Survivor   53m   E2   (1978)
A fairly good route, starting directly below the final crack of
Central Park.
1   25m. 5a. Climb the wall and crack which leads directly
up to the stance on Central Park, to belay as for that route.
2   28m. 5c. Move up the top crack of Central Park for two
metres then make awkward moves left to gain flakes out on
the wall, which are followed to a peg. The steep shallow
groove above leads with difficulty to the top. Belay way
back.

★★ **Central Park**   60m   Hard Very Severe   (1966)
A very enjoyable and popular route which gains and follows
the obvious wide crack in the upper right-hand side of the
wall. Start in the small niche on the left of the short rock
traverse on the path.
1   30m. 4c. Climb the slabby wall on the left to reach a
shallow groove which in turn leads to a ledge on the left.
Move up right then take the obvious left-trending line and
steep groove to a wall. Go up this to an old peg below an
overhung niche, and make an interesting traverse right to
belay in a fine position beneath the wide crack.
2   30m. 5a. Climb the crack past a couple of tricky moves
near the top to reach a ledge in a niche. A belay can be
constructed here. Scramble up steps in the steep grass
above to reach easy ground.

★ **Manor Park**   58m   E4   (1978)
An interesting route with an intimidating start and an
enjoyable, but difficult, finish. Start as for Central Park.
1   30m. 5c. Follow Central Park for 15 metres until it is
possible to move right and climb a thin crack directly to the
belay of Central Park.
2   28m. 6a. Follow the obvious thin crack out and up
leftwards past a peg at nine metres, to another at 25
metres, and climb to the top with some difficulty.

Hyde Park   67m   E4   (1977)
This has been rendered somewhat more difficult than
before by some absconded holds. Start midway between
Central Park and The Strand.
1   22m. 5b. Follow a series of flakes before traversing right
into Central Park, and belay at the start of the Central Park
traverse, below a groove.
2   45m. 6b. Step left then climb rattly flakes to reach the
top of the groove, on Transatlantic Crossing. A thin crack
above leads with difficulty past three old pegs to easier
ground and the top. Belay higher up the slope.

★★★ The Strand   49m   E2   (1967)

A classic pitch, with well protected and sustained climbing in a fine position. One of the outstanding climbs of North Wales. Start below, and a couple of metres left, of the compelling crack running up in a wide cleaned swathe through the lichen.

1   43m. 5b. Climb up rightwards to reach the crack and follow it, steepening gently, over a tiny overlap, finishing on good holds to a peg belay below a short slab. Back-up runners for the pegs are advisable.

2   6m. 4b. Climb the broken slab above then follow steps up the steep grass to belay at the far back wall.

★ Park Lane   70m   E1   (1967)

A once pleasant route taking a curving line to the left of The Strand, the last two pitches now being very grassy. The first pitch is still very good. Start as for The Strand.

1   30m. 5b. Climb up rightwards to the crack, but follow holds leading up left to below the bulge. Move up left, then step back right into the crack, and climb up to a stance and peg belay on top of the large flake.

2   28m. 5b. Go up left to a crack and gain the groove above. Follow this to exit left onto a stance with peg belays in a corner.

3   12m. 4b. Take the slab above then scramble up the slope to belay high up the slope.

★★ Park Lane/Doomsville Connection   55m   E1   (1967)

An excellent and varied climb combining pitch 1 of Park Lane (5b) with pitches 3 and 4 of Doomsville (5b,4b) that has become the *'voie normal'* up this area of the crag.

Mayfair   48m   E3   (1978)

Although an eliminate, the climbing is worthwhile. Start a couple of metres left and up from The Strand.

1   30m. 5c. Go up to a peg then break out rightwards and climb the right-hand side of the flake to the stance on Park Lane.

2   18m. 5c. Follow Park Lane a little way until it is possible to climb flakes to a peg. Climb the slab to the top and belay well back up the slope.

Doomsville   67m   E1   (1967)

A good top pitch but with a chossy and vegetated start below a groove up left from The Strand.

1   18m. 5a. The groove leads to grassy ledges and a peg belay.

2   18m. 5b. Go rightwards, past a peg, to the belay on top of the flake as for Park Lane. Well overgrown.

3   25m. 5b. Move up and climb rightwards up the ramp, past a peg, with interest, to finish up a short crack to a peg belay below a slab, as for The Strand.
4   6m. 4b. Climb the broken slab above then follow steps up the steep grass to belay at the far back wall, as for The Strand.

Broadway   64m   Hard Very Severe   (1969)
An uninspiring climb taking the cracks up the left-hand side of the wall, starting as for Doomsville.
1   18m. 5a. The groove leads to grassy ledges and a peg belay.
2   34m. 5a. Climb the thin crack then the wider crack above to belay on slabs as for Park Lane.
3   12m. 4b. Take the slab above then scramble up the slope to belay higher up.

Transatlantic Crossing   123m   E2   (1967)
An interesting girdle of the Central Park wall, starting as for Fifth Avenue. The route is described as finishing as for Park Lane, but it would seem better to finish up Doomsville, the latter being much cleaner.
1   40m. 5a. Chimney up and gain the groove, as for Fifth Avenue. At the first bulge, move down left and around the corner to gain holds leading leftwards past a large spike on Times Square. Continue across to belay below the wide crack, as for Central Park.
2   43m. 5c. Traverse left to climb a groove, peg, then move left to The Strand and climb down this for six metres until it is possible to climb across to the flake, on Mayfair, and go up to the stance on top of the flake.
3   28m. 5b. As for Park Lane, pitch 2.
4   12m. 4b. Finish as for Park Lane, pitch 3.

The next few routes start in the steep, grassy-floored amphitheatre, up and left of the Central Park Wall. It is gained by a rather frightening pitch up a vague gully in the centre of the broken rocky band, which leads onto the steep vegetated slope. It is also possible to abseil into this area from the crag top, an approach that requires a detailed knowledge of the cliff topography, and is probably even more gripping than the normal way.

Gladiator   50m   Hard Very Severe   (1967)
Reasonable climbing, but with worrying sections of loose rock on both pitches, taking the obvious break slanting up right. Start at the foot of the break, by a pinnacle in the centre of the bay.
1   22m. 5a. Climb the broken groove to a ledge, and carry on up the diagonal break to reach a small stance and peg belay.

The Upper Tier – Left-Hand Section

2   28m. 5a. Go up the groove and ramp on the left, then traverse left into a light-coloured groove and follow it to the top.

Kira His   48m   E4   (1989)
This fairly serious route takes the wall right of Amphitheatre Wall, starting at a block belay right of the corner of that route.
1   18m. 6a. Climb the crack in the red wall, just right of the corner, to a block belay.
2   30m. 5c. Go straight up the groove behind the belay to a loose finish.

Amphitheatre Wall   52m   Hard Very Severe   (1964)
A serious route, finishing on very poor rock, taking the broken corner on the left-hand side of the amphitheatre. Start by scrambling up to the foot of the corner.
1   18m. 4b. Climb the corner crack, past a sloping ledge, to a small niche on the right. Peg belay.
2   34m. 4c. Take the groove behind the stance then go right around the arête and onto a slab. Go right again to a wide crack which leads, through very loose rock, to the top.

Mill Street Junction   50m   E1   (1980)
This follows the obvious dog-leg crack system right of The Cracks, with pitches of 4c and 5b.

The Cracks   50m   Hard Very Severe   (1967)
Pleasant climbing up the obvious crackline left of Amphitheatre Wall, the only drawback being the terrible approach. Start by scrambling up to the base of a thin crack in the slab.
1   25m. 4c. The crack leads to a large ledge.
2   25m. 5a. Move right and climb the wide crack, just right of the arête, moving left where it narrows to finish up the arête.

Staying Alive   53m   E4   (1978)
A serious and aptly named route, with a poorly protected first pitch. Start six metres down and left of The Cracks.
1   28m. 6a. Climb the slab, keeping right of the arête and passing a peg at 18 metres to land on the belay ledge of The Cracks.
2   25m. 5a. Finish by taking the obvious crack system 3 metres right of the top pitch of Ceilidh.

Moving left from where the amphitheatre ends, the crag steepens and becomes more continuous. The broken grassy ramp running along the base gradually rises until it eventually sweeps up to divide the Upper Tier from The Main Cliff just beyond the corner of Bezel. The right-hand side of this area is marked by a huge yellow scar, the scene of a large rockfall in 1969. Left of this is the hanging groove of The Gauntlet, and left again, the slabby grey corner of The Ramp.

Ceilidh 80m E2   (1966)
This takes variable rock in a good, exposed situation to the right of the yellow scar. Start at the base of a groove at the bottom right-hand corner of the wall.
1 18m. 4a. Climb the groove, keeping to the left, to belay on top of a block.
2 9m. 4c. Move right and climb a deep crack a little way before moving right again, over a bulge, and going up to a small stance on the edge of the wall.
3 28m. 5c. Take the steep ramp up left, past a peg, then go left and climb onto a loose flake. Take the shallow groove up to and over a small overhang, peg, and continue leftwards to a large ledge.
4 25m. 5a. Climb up left to beneath a large pinnacle, traverse right for six metres and take a crack to a narrow ramp leading up left. This is followed to a good spike, before moving left to a small spike and finishing direct.

Mondo Hard 81m E4   (1987)
An adventurous route with some bold climbing. Start left of Ceilidh, below an overhanging wall.
1 18m. 6a. Layback up on fins to reach a crack and enter a yellow niche, peg. Exit right at its top, peg, to easier climbing and a block stance.
2 In10m. 5b. Climb a short wall and a fine crack direct to a poor belay.
3 28m. 5c. Take the steep ramp up left, past a peg, then go left and climb onto a loose flake. Take the shallow groove up to and over a small overhang, peg, and continue leftwards to a large ledge (Ceilidh, pitch 3).
4 25m. 5c. Go straight up the corner groove to the top, exiting right to easier ground.

Yellow Scar 78m E1   (1967)
An intricate route up the area of rock right of the rockfall, taking in some poor rock. Not really recommended. Start at a small pinnacle below the scar.
1 18m. 5a. Climb to the top of the pinnacle and boldly surmount the overlap on the right. Move up left then step right across an overhang into a broken groove. Climb this exiting right to the stance on Ceilidh.
2 30m. 5b. Go up the short wall on the left, then follow this obvious line left to a pinnacle on the edge of the yellow scar. Move up onto the scar and traverse left then back up right to gain big holds leading leftwards to a small pinnacle stance.

3   30m. 5a. Take the corner crack on the right to the top of a large pillar, then descend (junction with Celidh) and traverse six metres right to a crack. Climb this to a narrow ramp leading up left. This is followed to a good spike, before moving left to a small spike and finishing direct.

Hurricane   30m   E2   5c   (1980)
Start as for Yellow Scar. From the pinnacle, climb straight up cracks in the steep wall to an awkward mantelshelf at the top. Continue up a short groove and swing right to belay on Ceilidh. Finish up this route.

★★ **The Gauntlet**   50m   Hard Very Severe   (1964)
A fine route offering interesting and well-positioned climbing, to provide one of the better routes on the Upper Tier. Start in a shallow groove directly below the crackline left of Yellow Scar.
1   40m. 5a. Climb the groove, peg, and go over the bulge to reach better holds above. Continue up the groove, using a steep wall on the right to gain a small ledge, pegs. Move left and follow the groove, then move right into another groove and go up to a stance and peg belay.
2   10m. 4b. Return to the groove-line on the left and finish up the steep corner crack onto a broken ledge. Construct a belay here, or higher up the slope.

Ziggurat   61m   E3   (1971/1981)
A poor route, giving scrappy climbing with a lichenous top pitch. Start five metres left of The Gauntlet.
1   28m. 5b. Follow a depression up slightly left for 22 metres then traverse right to the good belay on The Gauntlet.
2   18m. 6a. Go left onto the arête and climb it via a short and technical sequence, peg, before going leftwards across two shallow grooves to an exposed belay above a very steep wall.
3   15m. 5b. From the right-hand end of the ledge go straight up to finish up vegetated slabs.

★★ **The Ramp**   55m   Hard Very Severe   (1966)
A fine route, taking a reasonable line through a very steep area of rock. Start left of The Gauntlet, at the foot of a pinnacle beneath the line of the ramp.
1   30m. 5a. Climb to the top of the pinnacle then step right on to a ledge. Follow the corner, peg, and carry on up the slab to reach spikes on the left. Go over the bulge and up to a large spike at the top of the ramp. Traverse left to belay beneath a steep corner.
2   25m. 5a. Climb the crack in the corner, peg, and grope rightwards to the base of a bottomless chimney. This leads more easily to the top.

Dave Alcock on the 1st ascent of Fail Safe.
Photo: Ken Wilson

To the left of The Ramp is a very steep wall, split by a number of impressive cracklines.

★ **Energy Crisis** 58m E5   (1978)
Very strenuous and sustained climbing, with reasonable protection for the strong. Start beneath the right-hand of two wide cracks a little left of The Ramp.
1 28m. 6a. Climb the crack direct using a variety of techniques to the welcome haven of the belay on The Ramp.
2 30m. 5c. From the right-hand end of the belay cross to a bottomless groove. Climb up, then step left to a thin crack, which leads to a slabby groove on the left. This provides an easy finish.

Afreet Street 53m E4   (1969/1980)
A strenuous and technical route, but not as worthwhile as Energy Crisis. Start beneath the left-hand of two wide cracks a little left of The Ramp.
1 28m. 6a. Climb narrow slabs until it is possible to enter the crack on the right. Take this direct, passing the odd ancient peg to the stance on The Ramp.
2 25m. 4c. Climb shallow cracks above, finishing up a chimney.

★ **Fail Safe** 53m E2   (1966)
Powerful climbing, with some long reaches, taking the wall left of Afreet Street, with a difficult exit from the top of the first pitch. Protection is adequate, but not generous. Start as for Afreet Street.
1 28m. 5b. Climb narrow slabs, past a quartz spike, to reach the overhang. Move right with difficulty and climb small ledges to gain the belay on The Ramp.
2 25m. 5a. Finish up The Ramp, pitch 2.
(The poor original finish went left around the arête from this point).

★ **The Eternal Optimist** 46m E2   (1975)
Good climbing taking the corner/crack running up to an overhang, above the foot of the slab that forms the left-hand end of The Upper Tier. Start at the foot of the crack.
1 37m. 5b. Steeply gain the start of the crack and climb it, using good holds on the left, to a tricky move over the overhang. Easier rock and a wide crack lead to a ledge and belay on the left.
2 9m. 4c. To the left of the belay a wide loose crack leads to the top.

Cartwheel 52m E2   (1978)
A reasonable but poorly protected route featuring the
right-hand of two cracks left of Bezel. Start a little to the
right of Bezel.
1 15m. 4c. Climb the slab, just right of Bezel, via the
prominent quartz vein, to cross Bezel and follow a right-
trending crack which leads to the stance on Bezel.
2 37m. 5b. Step left and take the crack until a prominent
V-niche on the left can be gained. Continue more easily to a
ledge, possible belay, and finish up easy rocks on the left.

★★ **Bezel** 49m Very Severe   (1964)
A pleasant and interesting route taking the curving groove
to the left of The Eternal Optimist. Start at the foot of the
groove.
1 15m. 4b. Gain the top of the small pinnacle on the left
and take a diagonal crack slanting up rightwards. Move left
then go up to a small ledge and peg belay at the foot of the
groove.
2 25m. 5a. Pull through the bulge and follow the groove
until it is possible to move right to ledges and belays.
3 9m. 4b. The short crack on the left leads to the top.

Slow Dancer 49m E1 5a   (1978)
A serious pitch up the left-hand flake crack between
Cartwheel and Sulcus. Start from the pinnacle just left of
Bezel. Follow Sulcus to a ledge at nine metres then climb
the discontinuous flake crack to reach the V-niche on
Cartwheel. Continue more easily to a ledge, and belay.
Finish up easy rocks on the left.

Sulcus 43m Very Severe 5a   (1969)
This follows the obvious crack in the arête left of Bezel, and
is quite worthwhile. Start from the pinnacle, as for Slow
Dancer. Follow the crack as far as the overhang and move
left around it into a niche. Step left then go up to spike
belays. Finish up broken ground.

GIRDLE TRAVERSES

Rolla Costa 257m Very Severe   (1968)
A poor route, which avoids the issue of a true girdle line,
taking the right-hand area of The Upper Tier. Start at the
foot of the approach gully.
1 30m. As for Nomad, pitch 1.
2 28m. Follow cracks right of Nomad, pitch 2, then a
chimney leads to a crack on the left. Take this to a stance.
3 21m. Go left to a break on the skyline, then descend a
chimney to belay on Dirtigo.

4 12m. Traverse left again, around the arête before descending slightly and crossing a chimney to gain a belay.
5 18m. Descend the chimney and belay as for Bloody Chimney at the far end.
6 22m. Abseil down Bloody Chimney, pitch 1.
7 37m. As for Pantin, pitch 1.
8 28m. Go left along the ledge, below the final pitch of Puffin, and continue across to near the top of Winking Crack.
9 40m. Abseil down Winking Crack to the large ledge.
10 21m. Abseil down the groove and wall to the path.

The Underground 209m Extremely Severe (7 pts. aid)
(1970)
Certainly not the most popular route on the crag, but it is potentially entertaining nevertheless with some hard and sustained climbing. Much of the aid might well be dispensed with by a strong team. Start as for Strike.
1 37m. 6a. As for Strike, pitch 1.
2 37m. 5c. Pendulum from a pinnacle, on the upper edge of the huge flake, across the wall on the left to a peg. Descend the slight groove to another peg before moving left, with difficulty, past a yellow flake and into Bloody Chimney.
3 21m. 5b. As for U.F.O. up the grooves and cracks to a ledge, block belay.
4 30m. 5b. Go to the left-hand end of the ledge. At foot-level a peg can be used to gain a small pinnacle, on reddish rock. Tension left from this to a hidden peg at waist level, in the middle of the wall, and using this and a nut, gain the corner on the left. Follow this (Canned Laughter) to the corner of Pantin. Descend and cross to a spike belay on the left.
5 15m. 4c. Go diagonally left to belay at a quartz ledge on the skyline.
6 18m. 5b. A peg on the left is used to gain Winking Crack. A crack leads left to a steep crack, parallel to the top of Winking Crack. Climb this to the top.
7 30m. 4c. Descend the broken crack on the left to a ledge, then take the ramp on the left to a corner. Go down the slab to the arête. Go round this to a groove then on to a quartz ledge. Belay on the grass below. A dirty pitch.
8 21m. 5a. Climb the centre of the wall behind the stance, trending left to a small bulge near the top. Surmount this and scramble to a belay higher up.

Suspender 129m E1 (2 pts. aid) (1968)
A steep and sustained girdle of the left-hand area of The Upper Tier, starting below The Cracks. Rope manoeuvres are used to pass the steep ground right of The Ramp.

1 21m. 4c. Drop down a little and move around the corner to a ledge. Carry on left, past a flake, to a shallow groove which is climbed for three metres to a stance.
2 15m. 5a. Continue up the groove to a pinnacle on the edge of the yellow scar. Move up onto the scar, peg, and go left then back right to gain big holds leading up left to a stance on a pinnacle, as for Yellow Scar.
3 22m. 4b. Descend part of The Gauntlet.
4 25m. 5a. Go left to the arête, peg. Lower six metres on the rope, and swing left to a ledge, peg. Climb up and leftwards across the wall to a peg, and again use the rope to descend and swing across to the slabby corner of The Ramp, peg. Climb down to a ledge and belay.
5 21m. 5a. Go back up continuing as for pitch 1 of The Ramp.
6 25m. 5a. As for The Ramp, pitch 2.
(Originally the poor finish of Fail Safe was used.)

The Main Cliff

This area epitomizes all the facets of sea-cliff climbing at its best, with a tidal traverse to gain most of the routes, uncompromising climbing, and interesting route finding. Here the cliffs reach their maximum height, well over 100m, and are virtually unbroken until the heathery slopes above are reached. The central area, as crossed by Ordinary Route, is one of the showpieces of Gogarth.

The crag is reached by taking the path along the foot of The Upper Tier until just beyond the short rock traverse, below the Central Park Wall. Here the left-hand fork of the path should be followed downward towards the foot of a steep slabby wall, taken by Aardvark. Scramble easily left beneath this wall, and climb down a 10 metre section of rock steps to gain ledges at sea level. Immediately above and left is the obvious 20 metre pinnacle of Gogarth, which marks the beginning of the Main Cliff proper. At low tide an exciting 6-metre traverse can be made around the foot of the pinnacle to reach higher platforms beneath The Rat Race. Alternatively, if the water is too high, climb up and over the pinnacle, and make a short abseil down the far side. Left again from these platforms is the central overhanging section of the crag, Gogarth's pièce de resistance. The obvious groove/chimney lines of Dinosaur and Mammoth are blatant landmarks, and some way along the traverse a prominent square block marks the start of Pentathol. This higher section can be traversed at most states of a calm sea, but beyond the block the traverse gets a little trickier, not to mention tidal, and leads to the overhung corner of Heroin, some 20 metres left of the block. A further 20 metres left again lies the corner of Hustler, after which the traverse peters out and the crag merges with the Easter Island area.

From the top of the routes in the Aardvark area scramble up the steep grassy rake to the foot of Bezel, and either climb one of the routes to the top or, follow the approach path back rightwards beneath The Upper Tier to the descent gully. Scramble up this to the starting point.

For the rest of the routes scramble up the grassy slopes above the crag to the obvious narrow path which leads back rightwards, above The Upper Tier, to the rock and heather step.   Just beyond this the path splits, the right-hand fork leading down right to a short rocky gully, which runs out by the starting point.   When returning at dusk, care should be taken to ensure the party is high enough to cross the top of the Upper Tier. For routes left of Scavenger, it is possible to scramble off leftwards to join the upper parts of Easter Island Gully.

The first routes are situated above the grassy rake, just left of the Upper Tier. The best approach is by following the path along beneath Bezel, then descending steep stepped grass to the foot of the routes. These climbs can also be combined with the routes, right of Resolution, arriving on the grassy rake from below, to finish at the top of the cliffs.

Interrogator   60m   Hard Very Severe   (1968)
A rather scrappy route, starting ten metres up right from Interpolator and below a large depression with a shallow left- trending groove.
1   25m. 5b. Climb the back of the depression then follow the groove leftwards for six metres. Traverse leftwards across the slab to gain and climb vertical cracks to reach a belay ledge.
2   35m. 4c. Step right off a block to climb a short wall then a shallow groove. Climb the broken rake to reach steep broken rocks on the right, which lead to the top.

Interpolator   75m   Hard Very Severe   (1966)
Not a particularly worthwhile route. Start from a large embedded flake directly below a groove.
1   30m. 5a. Follow the groove to a niche, pull out left, then head up right to a belay.
2   45m. 4a. Climb up the shallow corner then move left across the slab to a crack, which leads to the top.

★ **Sunstroke** 55m E1   (1970)
A good stiff route with interesting climbing. Start as for
Interpolator.
1 30m. 5b. Gain the steep corner, over a bulge, and follow
it to where it becomes a flake. Take the wide crack leftwards
to the arête and move around it to a slab, with belays in a
corner above.
2 25m. 5a. Climb the corner for five metres until better
holds lead to a small ledge on the left arête. Follow the flake
crack left, as for Diogenes, to a belay around the corner.

★ **Diogenes** 53m Hard Very Severe   (1966)
A fine route, with good positions, which breaches the
overhangs above the grassy rake with a couple of difficult
sections. Start as for Interpolator.
1 10m. Descend the rake a little then cross the slab to a
stance on the arête, with a belay on the left.
2 25m. 5a. Climb up above the belay to gain the shallow
square chimney on the right. This is turned, with difficulty,
via the flake on the left, stepping back right to the top of the
chimney, or by climbing the chimney direct. The slab above
leads to a steep corner, then a step left onto the arête
allows the belay niche, peg, to be gained by a steep pull.
3 18m. 4c. Step right and climb the short arête to gain a
good flake crack, which is followed, in a brilliant position,
leftwards to belay around the corner.

Revelation 56m E1   (1979)
A rather eliminate line, starting as for Diogenes.
1 10m. As for Diogenes.
2 21m. 5a. Follow Diogenes to its first bulge then bear
diagonally leftwards to a loose spike. Traverse leftwards
across the slab to reach a hanging belay, as for Resolution.
3 25m. 5b. Climb onto the spike on the left, and step right
to a crackline which is followed to the top.

★★ **Cordon Bleu** 145m Hard Very Severe   (1966)
An excellent girdle crossing the top of The Main Cliff,
passing through intimidating surroundings, with fine views
and situations. Most of the climbing is reasonable, with one
mean section. Careful ropework will pay dividends. Start as
for Interpolator, on the grassy rake.
1 38m. 4a. Go down the rake for a few feet (with a metric
calculator) then traverse out across the slab on the left to
reach the arête. Go around this and descend a short
chimney to reach a good ledge and belay on the left. (The
steep groove above is on Gogarth.)
2 37m. 4b. The left wall of the groove above is formed by
a huge flake, and by descending a little the base of it can be
traversed leftwards to reach a corner on its left. Climb this,

then traverse left along the top of the massive flakes to belay just past the apex.

3 45m. 5b. The short steep wall on the left is climbed, with difficulty, into a corner. Protection for the second should be arranged somewhere here. Follow the obvious slabby ramp leftwards, possible poor belay, to climb a short chimney before crossing a slab to reach a groove and belay at the top, on the arête.

4 25m. 4b. Go easily round the corner, behind a large flake and ascend a short groove to the top.

The remaining routes on The Main Cliff start at, or just above, sea level. The first routes are on the clean wall at the base of the previously described approach path, below and right of the last few routes.

Seeyerlater 46m Hard Very Severe (1981)
An unpleasant proposition, being loose, dirty and serious. Start six metres right of Imitator, at a short corner.

1 10m. Climb the corner to a large ledge and belay on the right beneath a crack.

2 15m. Climb the crack to the bulge and surmount this to gain the stance on Imitator.

3 21m. Go straight up above the stance onto a slab, then slightly right, following a gap in the bulge above, onto slabs. Trend slightly leftwards up these to bay, and climb the left wall of this to a flake belay.

★★ Aardvark 45m E2 (1978)
A fine popular route, alternately bold and difficult, up the clean wall right of Emulator. Start five metres right of Imitator and beneath the centre of the wall.

1 30m. 6a. Climb diagonally left on good holds then move up to a thin crackline. Go up this awkwardly to gain the traverse of Imitator. Move up to gain the left-hand of two thin cracks, and follow it round two small overlaps until it is possible to move right to good holds in the right-hand crack. This leads to a small ledge and nut belay.

2 15m. 4a. Climb easier ground to join the steep path, and belay well up the slope.

Imitator 60m Very Severe (1966)
A pleasant route which winds its way up the slabby wall right of Emulator, which can be combined with Bezel to produce an excellent long climb of fairly consistent standard. Start about 15 metres above the sea and beneath the obvious large corner.

1 30m. 4c. Go steeply up right to gain and climb a groove in the blunt arête. From some way up this, tricky moves gain the slab on the right and good narrow ledges above.

Follow these easily rightwards to a good crack and climb this to a belay.
2 30m. 4b. On the left is a shallow groove, which leads to a small bay. Move right onto the arête and go up to easy ground.

★★★ **Emulator** 45m E1 5b (1964)
An excellent climb which takes the large corner/groove up the slabby wall which forms the lower right-hand side of The Main Cliff. Start as for Imitator, 15 metres above the sea and beneath the obvious corner. Climb up easily for five metres to where the groove steepens, surmount the bulge, and continue to the top on good holds and jams. A fine sustained pitch.

Stimulator 50m E2 (1978)
A good steep climb, starting just left of the arête between Emulator and Simulator.
1 10m. 5c. Climb the overhanging groove just left of the arête to a good ledge and belay.
2 40m. 5b. From the belay go diagonally rightwards around the arête, passing a loose hold, to gain cracks in the wall which lead to another obvious crack. Follow this to the top.

Simulator 38m Very Severe 4c (1964)
A short route, with an even shorter amount of good climbing, up the groove left of Emulator. Start below the groove and climb it to the top, taking the best line through poor rock at the top.

Direct Start to Diogenes 45m Hard Very Severe (1969)
An interesting way of extending the parent route. Start as for Resolution.
1 12m. Climb the overhanging crack to reach a good stance with peg belays.
2 33m. Step left, climb the steep crack onto the slab and continue up to belay at a spike below the parent route.

★★ **Resolution** 93m E1 (1966)
A fine direct way up this part of the cliff, with good climbing in exposed positions, on the arête right of Gogarth. Start in a bay of overhanging friable rock, to the left of Simulator.
1 45m. 5a. Climb the obvious, aptly named, overhanging crack (The Razor Blade Crack) until it widens into a chimney. Traverse left along the diagonal break to the arête, then climb up into a clean-cut groove and follow it to a good belay ledge, on the left.
2 28m. 5b. Climb the overhanging wall just left of the arête, stepping right after ten metres to a crack in the arête

The Main Cliff – Right-Hand Section

GREG 87

itself. Follow this directly to a good flake and a hanging belay.

3 20m. 5b. Climb the crack on the left to the top of the block. Move left into a groove and climb this, tricky, to finish up an easier crack.

Variation

★★ **Resolution Direct** 71m E2   (1982)
An eliminate version of Resolution, as good as the original, but more sustained, starting as for the parent route.

1a 43m. 5b. Move left and climb the crack in the arête (as for Trunk Line) to join Resolution after the traverse, and follow the groove to the good belay ledge.

2a 28m. 5b. Climb the crack in the main arête direct, joining Resolution at 12m, and follow it to the hanging stance. Finish as for Resolution.

★★★ **Gogarth** 109m E1   (1964)
A marvellous route with varied, and interesting, climbing in fine positions throughout. It has become the most popular introduction to The Main Cliff. Start from the right-hand side of the huge pinnacle rising from the sea at the right-hand side of The Main Cliff proper.

1 18m. 4b. Climb the wide crack up the right-hand side of the pinnacle to a stance on the top.

2 18m. 5a. Step down and traverse four metres right across the black wall, around the arête and into a shallow hidden groove. Climb this, keeping left of a small overhang, before traversing back left to a peg belay on a sloping ledge, directly above the previous stance.

3 18m. 4c. From the left-hand side of the ledge climb the short crack before easier ground leads up rightwards to a good ledge, and belay, at the foot of a steep groove on the left, formed by a huge grey flake.

4 15m. 4b. Go delightfully up the groove to a stance at its top.

5 40m. 5b. Traverse right across the steep wall to a ledge below a thin crack. Difficult moves up the crack lead to good holds, and so to the top, in the same line.

Variation

Devotee 110m E2   (1978)
A direct line on Gogarth, contrived in places, starting as for that route.

1 18m. 5a. Climb diagonally left to the arête, and follow this to belay on top of the pinnacle.

2 37m. 5b. Climb directly up the short steep wall above to reach the sloping stance on Gogarth. Step right and follow a groove until a move left gains the large ledge stance, on Gogarth.

3 25m. 5b. Traverse left and climb directly up the front of the big pinnacle to the stance, on Gogarth.
4 30m. 5c. Traverse right, as for Gogarth, for about three metres to a small groove. Follow this, and the bulge above, continuing with some difficulty in the same line to the top.

Falls Road   102m   E4   (1969)
Not an especially worthwhile route, with a loose and serious top pitch. The second pitch, however, is quite good and could perhaps be combined with Resolution to give a better outing. Start beneath the obvious groove in the front face of Gogarth pinnacle.
1 15m. 4b. Climb the groove to belay on the large platform.
2 25m. 5c. Behind the stance is a steep reddish wall, containing a thin crack. Climb this then transfer to the slightly wider crack on the left, which leads to a sloping belay above.
3 37m. 5a. An obvious line trends left and leads to a large block at the foot of a corner. Climb this for a few moves, then transfer into another corner on the right. Go up this and the slab above to belay on Cordon Bleu.
4 25m. 5c. This takes the obvious wide crack splitting the wall above. Move up to the overhang from the left, then move right and go up, peg, to the wide crack. Follow this to the top. A worrying pitch.

★ **Bubbly Situation Blues**   55m   E4   (1971)
A good route with two contrasting pitches, very strenuous then technical, the main feature of the route being the obvious groove just left of the Gogarth pinnacle. Start on the lower left-hand platform of the Gogarth pinnacle, at the end of pitch 1 of Rat Race.
1 30m. 6a. Step off the left-hand side of the platform and climb the groove immediately above to reach some ledges. The groove above is somewhat easier, and leads to another ledge containing a large block, peg belay on the right.
2 25m. 5c. Move left, and climb the corner above the block until it is possible to traverse left across a steep slab to the top of the chimney of The Rat Race. Go up to a stance on Cordon Bleu, and finish up this, or Dinosaur.

★★ **The Rat Race**   116m   E3   (1966)
A continuously steep and exciting route through some impressive rock scenery. Pitch 2 is outstanding. Start on a large ledge to the left of the Gogarth pinnacle. At high tide, the start of pitch 2 can be reached over the top of the pinnacle, via Gogarth pitch 1.
1 12m. 5a. Climb slightly left up the steep wall, then go diagonally up right to gain the large belay platform, on the pinnacle.

Alec Sharp on the 1st ascent of Ordinary Route.
Photo: Chris Dale

2   30m. 5c. Step left and climb diagonally left, past a tricky move up, peg, to a rest. Carry on left into a chimney groove and climb up to the overhangs. Climb up left to follow the curving overlap, often damp, around to a steep slab, all very strenuous, and pull up right to gain a good stance below a nasty-looking chimney. A fine exposed pitch, with one very hard section.
3   25m. 5b. Climb the chimney, steep, strenuous and bold to reach the slab above by exiting right. Belay at the top of the slab, on Cordon Bleu. A gripping little pitch.
4   8m. Shuffle right, down the flake, to belay at the base of the obvious corner.
5   13m. 4c. Climb the steep corner to belay on top of the pinnacle, on Gogarth.
6   28m. 5a. Step down left and go across the wall to the foot of a crack. Follow this, and the right-hand branch at the divide, before moving left across a rib to an easier finishing crack. Belay well up the slope above. Odd climbing on even odder rock.

Variation
3a   30m. To avoid the chimney, follow the ramp right of the belay around the corner, and across a groove, to reach easier ground which can be taken to gain the large slab. Go up right to belay at the foot of the corner, below pitch 5. Easier, but not really in the spirit of things.

★★★ **Positron**   60m   E5   (1971)
A phenomenal outing, continuously sustained, crossing the stunning central headwall of the Main Cliff. Interesting climbing with considerable exposure, on a route that has a really big feel about it. Start just left of The Rat Race.
1   18m. 5c. Move up right into a scoop then go back left to an obvious flake. Go up left to a small ramp on the arête and pull over the small overhang above to belay at the foot of a chimney groove, below the crux of The Rat Race.
2   12m. 6a. Pull up left and go over another small overhang. Move left around the arête, below the next overhang, into the corner of Alien and climb more easily up this, stepping right to an excellent stance, on The Rat Race.
3   30m. 6a. Go left to a spike on the arête, then move up to gain an obvious diagonal line across the headwall. Follow this until a short traverse left leads to a small overhang. Surmount this on its left then move up more easily, until it is possible to step left into the groove of Dinosaur, which leads to a belay on blocks above. A brilliant pitch. Finish up Dinosaur, or Cordon Bleu.

Pete Crew and Joe Brown on the 1st ascent of Dinosaur.
Photo: Ken Wilson

★★★ **Ordinary Route**   136m   E5   (1975)

A magnificent route, strenuous and sustained, and in fine positions. The classic of its grade. Start as for The Rat Race at the foot of the pinnacle.

1 37m. 6a. Climb steeply up, left of the pinnacle (as for The Rat Race), bearing slightly right, then go back up left to enter a groove (which is eight metres along the traverse of The Rat Race). Climb this exiting left at its top, then go up the short leaning wall on the left, with a hard move to enter the groove above. This leads to a good stance, below the chimney, as for The Rat Race.

2 25m. 6a. As for Positron, go left to the spike on the arête then, diagonally across the headwall, to reach the small overhang by a short traverse. Climb this on the left, and go up until it is possible to step into the groove of Dinosaur. Climb down this to a hanging belay, in a great position, on a ledge, level with the small overhang on the right.

3 40m. 5c. Go left along the ledge into a groove, on Mammoth, and climb this to a small ledge, peg. Possible belay. Traverse left on the overhanging wall to join Citadel, which is followed to the first small ledges on the left. Go across these to a short corner, and go up this until moves left, around the arête, lead to a large sloping ledge below a small hollow.

4 34m. 5b. Step left, and climb the steep groove just before the arête to a small cave below twin cracks. Climb the right-hand crack to finish.

★★ **Eraserhead**   87m   E6   (1988)

A finely positioned and sustained route following the arête between the two facets, as directly as possible. Start left of The Rat Race, just right of the arête.

1 35m. 6a. Climb just right of the arête to gain and follow Positron, up the arête and into the groove, to belay on the good ledge, as for The Rat Race.

2 40m. 6a. As for Positron, step left and go around the arête, to arrange runners in the base of the diagonal line. Step right to climb a vague flake, just left of the arête, to a poor spike. Continue to a large niche, with good spikes, right of the 'bucket seat' belay on The Big Sleep. A strenuous and exciting pitch.

3 12m.   Ascend easily to a belay above the slab, on Cordon Bleu. Finish up Alien or Dinosaur.

★★★ **Skinhead Moonstomp**   80m   E6   (1984)

A great route taking a direct line up this part of the cliff. At first it follows the big corner left of Positron, before taking a mind blowing run out up a hanging flake in the middle of the Positron headwall. Start beneath the big corner.

1 25m. 6a. Climb the corner, mainly by its left wall, to a bulge and surmount this on the left to reach a sloping shelf.

Pull onto this, and move up into the overhanging corner above. Cross the right wall to an obvious jug near the arête, then swing right on to the arête, junction with Positron, and pull over the small overhang to belay in the chimney groove, as for Positron.

2 43m. 6b. Step up left, and go round the arête into the corner of Alien. Ascend this for a few metres, then cross left along the obvious line, and move up to a resting place beneath a steep wall. Pull up and reach right to the base of a blind flake, which is followed for eight metres to its top. Three obvious flat jugs lead straight up to join Positron, just below its crux. Do this, but then go straight up to a small corner and an excellent 'bucket seat' belay.

3 12m. 5a. Go up behind the flake to belay at the top of the slab, on Cordon Bleu. Finish up Alien.

★★★ Alien 93m E5   (1980)

A fine sustained first pitch, taking the obvious overhanging fault between Skinhead Moonstomp and Dinosaur, leads to a good finish in the top walls. Start in the cleft just right of Dinosaur.

1 37m. 6b. Climb up into the chimney, then break out onto the fault itself, and follow this until hard moves gain the corner above. Climb this more easily until it is possible to step right onto a good ledge, and belay, as for The Rat Race.

2 28m. 5c. Climb the chimney of The Rat Race for eight metres, then exit left, and climb a shallow groove, followed by a slabby rib to reach a large flake belay, on Cordon Bleu.

3 28m. 5c. Move right to the foot of the obvious crack system, and climb it to the top.

★★★ Alien/Positron Connection 67m E5

A brilliant way up the cliff is the combination of the first pitch of Alien (6b) with the third pitch of Positron (6a).

★★ Dinosaur 105m E5   (1966/1980)

A powerful and direct route up the right-hand of three chimneys in the steepest part of the face, leading to an interesting continuation groove above. Reasonably protected, but commitment is required for the crux. Start beneath the right-hand chimney.

1 30m. 6a. Climb up into the chimney and follow it to where it closes. Pull out left, very strenuous and bold, to reach the arête. Climb up, still strenuous, to a small stance and dubious belays.

2 30m. 5b. Step right and climb the long steep groove on reasonable holds, past a small ledge (Ordinary Route stance), peg, then ascend more easily to a block belay above.

3 45m. 5c. Go up right, and climb the short steep wall to reach the blank corner above (as for Cordon Bleu). Move out right and climb grooves in the arête, past a couple of ancient pegs, to an awkward exit up a shallow groove on the left. Scramble up the slope to belays in the rock wall on the left.

★★ **The Big Sleep** 62m E6   (1980)
Two contrasting pitches combine to produce yet another brilliant route, diagonally crossing this area of the crag. Start beneath the chimney just left of Dinosaur.
1 25m. 6a. Climb the straightforward chimney until it is possible to swing out left onto the arête. Climb this, peg, to reach big flat holds leading, strenuously, to the stance on Dinosaur. Dubious belays.
2 25m. 6b. Move down and right to hanging flakes, which are climbed with difficulty to a large foothold on the right, about four metres below the Positron overhang. Traverse right for five metres to join Positron, then go straight up the wall to the 'bucket seat' belay.
3 12m. 5a. Go up behind the flake to a stance on Cordon Bleu. Finish up Dinosaur or Alien.

Variation
2a 25m. 6b. A more direct way to climb the pitch. Follow pitch 2 to reach the large foothold below the roof. Climb slightly left, then right, to reach the roof, and turn this on the right to gain a crack. Go up to belay in the 'bucket seat'.

★★ **Wall of Fossils** 60m E6   (1980)
A strenuous route with fine climbing, taking the area of rock between The Big Sleep and Mammoth. Start as for Mammoth beneath the central chimney, which is actually a big left-facing groove.
1 30m. 6a. Climb the groove, as for Mammoth, to the roof and traverse right on undercuts to a junction with The Big Sleep, on the big flat holds above the arête. Go strenuously up to the stance on Dinosaur, dubious belays.
2 30m. 6b. Step left and climb through overhanging flakes, then continue passing a good spike to the ledge where Ordinary Route crosses. Very forceful climbing leads straight up the steep red wall above to a rounded exit onto the slab. Step right to a block belay. Finish up Dinosaur or Alien.

★★ **Mammoth** 62m E5   (1967/1984)
A compelling and strenuous route with a very difficult crux. Harder than Dinosaur, and virtually as good. Start beneath the middle chimney which is actually a big left-facing groove.

1 37m. 6b. Climb the back of the groove, passing a small ledge, and move up and left under the overhangs with increasing difficulty, good thread. Move left onto the arête, and make hard moves up the wall, past a couple of rotting pegs, to gain a shallow chimney on the left. Strenuously climb this and exit left from it, before climbing up to peg belays on the right of a narrow ledge.

2 25m. 5c. Climb up, past a small spike, and trend right to a larger, blunt, spike, before climbing back left to below a bulge, peg. Climb the bulge and continue up the easier groove above, moving right to belay on the huge flake at the top of the slab. Finish up Dinosaur or Alien.

Variation

★★ **Mammoth Direct** 33m E6 6b   (1984)

An excellent direct, and very strenuous, version which follows the big parallel-sided chimney left of the normal start, with perfect protection. Start on the raised flat-topped block beneath the chimney. Enter the chimney, and climb it past several surprising nut placements to a roof with a massive natural thread placement. Surmount the roof via the right-hand crack, then reach leftwards and gain an excellent weird jug in the left-hand crack. Pull up to join the original route, peg runner on the right. Go up strenuously to enter and follow the shallow chimney, exiting left to reach the belay. Continue as for Mammoth.

★★★ **Hunger** 90m E5   (1978)

The very impressive wall left of Mammoth Direct is split by a discontinuous rust-coloured crack. The first pitch utilizes this on a pitch of sustained difficulty, with more fine climbing above on the open wall, right of Citadel. Start on a high flat-topped block directly below the crack.

1 30m. 6a. Climb the crack for about six metres, then trend up left to a junction with Citadel, in the niche beneath the overhangs. Traverse right for three metres then breach the roof above, and continue for three metres, all very strenuous, before moving right to a stance, and good belays.

2 42m. 5c. Climb the wall above, fairly direct, then steeply up to gain a good flake at 12 metres. Traverse right for six metres, to a point just left of the groove on Mammoth, then head back up left to reach the remains of a flake. Go up right to a crackline, and follow this to a good stance beneath wider serrated cracks above.

3 18m. 5b. Climb the right-hand crack. After three metres exit left into easier, but looser, grooves and finish up these.

Variation

★★ **Ramadan** 40m E5   (1988)

A direct version of Hunger, pitch 2.

2a 45m. 6b. Follow Hunger to the good flake at 12 metres, and continue straight up past an overlap, with difficulty, to rejoin Hunger. Move two metres left and climb straight up to finish in a small groove, three metres right of Citadel. Belay at the top of the slab.

★★★ **Citadel** 100m E5   (1968/1977)
A magnificent route, reasonably sustained, apart from one very hard move on the first pitch. The second pitch is one of the finest at Gogarth, with a stamina-testing crackline in a superb position. Start a couple of metres left and down from Hunger, directly beneath a line of obvious undercut flakes.
1 40m. 6b. Climb up the wall to an old peg, then bear left to the start of the undercut flakes. Pull up and traverse right to a niche, good runners. Swing up left, and boulder out the short leaning wall, past an inverted peg, to reach a sloping ledge. Climb up right onto a long ledge, and belay beneath the fine upper crack.
2 35m. 6a. Climb the steep wall above the ledge, past a couple of old pegs, before a stride right gains the base of the crack. This leads eventually, strenuous and sustained, to a belay on the slab above.
3 25m. Climb the easy groove above to a good ledge and belay on large blocks on the left. An easy scramble leads up the slope to the path.

★★ **Graduation Ceremony** 92m E4   (1976)
A good route skirting its way up the left-hand side of the central overhanging section of the Main Cliff. Start a couple of metres left of Citadel, and below small overhangs which guard access to a little corner above.
1 37m. 5c. Climb up to the overhangs and enter the corner above with a tricky move. Pull up this before escaping left to a good hold, then move up to ledges above. Go up the short steep corner above and continue to a stance, on Big Groove. Go to the right-hand end of the ledge and belay beneath a steep quartzy corner.
2 30m. 6a. Follow the corner, then bear rightwards across the steep wall to a thin crack. Follow this, and the wider crack above to ledges, continuing in the same line over some bulges. From above these traverse right to belay on the slab, as for Citadel.
3 25m. Finish as for Citadel.

★ **Sebastopol** 98m E4   (1979)
Another impressive line up the left-hand edge of the central overhanging section of the cliff, taking the tower left of Graduation Ceremony in its upper section. Start five metres left of Graduation Ceremony.

Wen Slab area to the Main Cliff
Photo: Ken Wilson

1   43m. 5c. A short crack leads up to the left-hand side of a small roof. Pull out left and climb the wall, junction with Graduation Ceremony, then go left a little before moving up the continuation groove on the right to easy ledges. Traverse these rightwards and climb a short wall to belay beneath the steep quartzy corner, on Graduation Ceremony.
2   25m. 6a. Climb the corner, step left, then climb the wall moving leftwards to reach the arête. Make a strenuous traverse back right until a steep wall leads to a sloping ledge. Belay on the left at a thread in the crack.
3   30m. 5a. On the right is a groove. Climb this and the little wall above to reach sloping ledges and the top. Either scramble off left, or finish up the top pitch of The Tet Offensive.

★★ **The Tet Offensive**   122m   E5   (1979)
A good hard route, with a desperate start, and a second pitch that follows the fine arête overlooking Big Groove. Start about 12 metres right of The Big Groove and below an obvious overhanging crack, which is often wet.
1   37m. 6b. Climb the steep crack/faultline with great difficulty to reach the continuation groove, still steep, which leads to the large sloping ledge, on The Big Groove.
2   30m. 5c. Climb straight up the short leaning wall into the base of The Big Groove itself. From the two old pegs, step right to a foothold on the arête, and swing around to a crack, in a fine position. Follow the crack until a traverse leads right, on a ledge, to ascend a short wall and gain a sloping ledge. Belay on the left, at a thread in a crack, as for Sebastopol.
3   30m. 5b. Step left and climb the crack to a shallow cave, then take the groove on the right to reach a belay on a large ledge.
4   25m. 5a. Directly above the ledge is a pillar. Climb this to finish.

★ **The Wastelands**   100m   E4   (1978)
Another good route with exhilarating climbing in good positions, taking a direct line from the left of The Tet Offensive to finish up the arête left of The Big Groove. Start beneath another steep crack, midway between the starts of The Tet Offensive and The Big Groove.
1   35m. 5c. The steep crack leads to the ledge where the initial rising traverse of The Big Groove comes from the left. Bridge the corner of the wall of Pentathol, exiting rightwards with difficulty. A crack then leads directly to the large ledge, on The Big Groove.
2   40m. 6a. Trend up left on good holds to reach a huge flake (peg off-route to the left). Climb the steep wall on the right and pass another peg with difficulty. Move up to just

below a bulge, junction with Puzzle Me Quick, then step left to climb the left-facing corner. Move around the arête on the right and traverse into The Big Groove, for nut belays.
3   25m. 5a. Move back left and finish up the fine slabby arête, and the short wall above.

★★ **The Big Groove**   113m   E3   (1966)
This takes the huge left-facing groove, half-way up the cliff, which is difficult to see from below. Although not high in the grade, there are a number of tricky moves that command respect on this classic line. Start six metres right of the obvious large square block on the sea-level traverse, and beneath a line of flakes trending rightwards.
1   43m. 5a. Climb up to reach the flakes, and follow them rightwards across the face to a ledge below a short corner. Climb the corner for three metres, then move left into a left-facing corner, which leads to a ledge on the right. Climb the short corner above to reach a huge sloping ledge, with peg belays on the right.
2   18m. 5c. From the left-hand end of the ledge, climb over the bulge into a corner, peg, then go up right, with difficulty, to a sloping ledge at the bottom of the groove proper, old pegs. Move up and right, awkwardly, to gain and follow the steep small groove, and continuation crack, formed by a flake on the right wall. In turn, this forms a niche, from which a scrabbling finish is made onto a sloping ledge. Semi-hanging belay in the corner, pegs.
3   34m. 5b. Step left into another sustained groove, a little friable in places, with a harder move at its top. Holds then lead to a good stance around the arête on the left.
4   18m. Easy climbing leads up behind the stance to the top.

Variation
★★ **The Direct Finish**   28m   E3   (1969)
An excellent, fairly bold, and difficult pitch, starting as for pitch 3 of Big Groove.
3a   28m. 5c. Climb the wall behind the belay, then go up the arête to a jammed block. A step right, then moves up lead to a resting place, peg. Move up again and go right into the groove, which leads with less difficulty to the top.

★ **Puzzle Me Quick**   104m   E4   (1973)
Difficult and quite serious, this follows the groove that The Big Groove avoids on the right. Start as for The Big Groove.
1   43m. 5b. Gain the flakes, as for The Big Groove, and continue traversing right until forced to climb a very steep groove, which leads to the large ledge, as for The Big Groove.
2   43m. 5c. From the left-hand end of the ledge pull through the bulge as for Big Groove, and carry on up the

groove above, moving left beneath the overhangs. Continue up, then climb the short tricky wall to reach a small niche formed by a right-facing corner. Exit direct and follow cracks across the wall to a stance on the arête.
3 18m. Scrambling leads to the top.

★ **Pentathol** 98m Hard Very Severe (1964)
A popular introduction to The Main Cliff, taking the easiest way up this area of the crag. The first pitch is the most difficult, leading to more amenable climbing above. Start as for The Big Groove.
1 37m. 5a. Climb up to gain the flakes and follow them steeply across the wall, to gain a ledge below a short corner. Climb this for three metres then move left and into a left-facing corner. This leads to a large ledge with a good stance on the right. This pitch is shared with most of The Big Groove pitch 1.
2 15m. 4b. Descend a couple of metres, and step left into a wide crack. From the top of this follow a line of flakes diagonally up left, to belay below a long groove.
3 25m. 4c. Go straight up the groove, taking an awkward bulge, before gaining a good stance on the left.
4 21m. 4b. Easy climbing leads up behind the belay to the top.

Peepshow 100m E1 (1973)
Really a direct start to Jaborandi and nothing special. Start as for Big Groove.
1 30m. On the left is a steep crack. Climb this to reach a small cave underneath the overhang. Turn the overhang on the right then climb a wide crack to belay beneath the short chimney on Pentathol.
2 25m. Ascend the chimney then move right onto the wall, and climb this for nine metres to reach a crack, which is then followed to the ledge and belay on Jaborandi.
3 45m. As for Jaborandi.

Jaborandi 102m E2 (1966)
Rather scruffy and a little contrived. Start to the left of The Big Groove and a couple of metres right of the prominent square block marking the start of Syringe.
1 43m. 5b. Enter the short overhanging corner above then step out right to a good spike. Follow the ramp on the right, then stride left onto the lip of an overhang, and climb a short crack to a ledge. Step left into a deep crack and follow this to reach the flake traverse, on Pentathol. Move left and belay beneath the groove.
2 12m. 4c. Climb the bottomless corner up on the right to reach a belay ledge, pegs.
3 37m. 5b. Climb the short overhanging corner to gain a sloping ledge, and follow the ragged crack above until it is

possible to move up left to broken ground. A groove leads
to a large ledge and spike belays.
4 10m. Easy climbing leads to the top.

Morphine 86m E2   (1979)
Start as for Syringe, on top of the prominent square block.
1 25m. 5b. The right-hand crack is climbed steeply until
just below the sentry-box on Syringe, where a traverse right
gains a belay at the foot of a wide crack.
2 18m. 4a. Climb diagonally left to reach a smooth corner,
which leads to a stance on Pentathol.
3 43m. 5b. Five metres right of Pentathol is a thin crack.
Climb this over two bulges and continue in the same line,
exiting slightly rightwards to the top.

★★ **Syringe** 94m E3   (1966)
An interesting route with two fine and difficult pitches. Start
on top of the prominent square block.
1 45m. 5c. The grey wall above the square block leads to a
rest and runners under the overhang. Step right into the
sentry-box, and climb over the bulge with difficulty to gain
the groove above. This is followed, scary but without great
difficulty until a good ledge, pegs, on the left is reached,
just below the next overhangs.
2 28m. 5c. Move up the wall above, then step right and
take the overhanging crack to reach the groove above the
bulge. Follow this to a good stance.
3 21m. Easy climbing behind the belay leads to the top.

★★ **The Camel** 96m E4   (1974)
Another excellent route, with well-protected and very
strenuous climbing on the first pitch. Just left of the
prominent square block is an obvious corner, taken by
Hypodermic. Start two metres right of this.
1 45m. 6a. Climb the crack until three metres below the
overhang, and move left before pulling into a bottomless
closed chimney. Move right beneath a fang of rock and
follow the steep crack over the roof. The groove above
leads, peg, to easier ground and on to the top of a large
flake (on Hypodermic). Step down right to a good stance,
pegs, on Syringe.
2 30m. 5b. Regain the left-hand side of the flake, then bear
up left to the arête. Go up to a sloping ledge and take the
overhanging crack to reach easier ground.
3 21m. Easy climbing leads up behind the belay to the top.

★ **Hypodermic** 95m E2   (1968)
A good route with interesting climbing in fine positions.
Start beneath the corner, left of the prominent square block.
1 34m. 5b. Climb the corner for 15 metres before moving
out to the arête on the left. Cross the ledge on the left for

The Main Cliff – Left-Hand Section

six metres, then climb the steep wall bearing rightwards to a rib, and follow this for a couple of metres to the overhang. Move left then go back right to a ledge and belay, pegs, in an airy position.
2   40m. 5c. From the right-hand end of the ledge, climb up rightwards to the arête. Climb a crack for a couple of moves, then move up to the top of a large flake, where a bulge can be climbed to reach a groove on the right, on Syringe. Go up this to a stance.
3   21m. Easy climbing leads up behind the belay to the top.

★ **The Needle**   92m   E3   (1973)
An excellent sustained route, taking the impressive crackline in the front face of the buttress left of Hypodermic. Start beneath three steep cracks just around the arête from the corner of Hypodermic.
1   34m. 5b. Climb the central crack (often damp) to gain a ledge on the arête (junction with Hypodermic). Continue up the arête until moves left lead to the base of a short overhanging groove. Climb this directly, or turn it by moving left, then go back right up a deep crack, to reach the sloping ledge belay, as for Hypodermic.
2   37m. 5c. From the right-hand end of the ledge move up right and continue up the excellent crack directly, past a tricky move, and onto a sloping ledge. Continue with less difficulty to a good stance above.
3   21m. Climb the easy corner behind the stance.

Variation
Direct Finish   16m   Very Severe   (1978)
3a   18m. 4c. To the left of the huge block which leans against the cliff are two cracks. The right-hand crack provides an alternative finish.

★★ **The Assassin**   88m   E3   (1978)
A good route with an intimidating second pitch up the impending black wall right of Scavenger. Start three metres right of Scavenger at the foot of a wide flared crack.
1   30m. 5b. Climb the crack then bear rightwards to climb the steep wall leading to the left-hand side of a belay ledge, on Hypodermic.
2   40m. 5c. Climb diagonally leftwards up the wall, then surmount a bulge to the left of a corner. Move left into a crack, peg, then go diagonally right and continue up an open scoop. Go steeply up left to gain and climb a short right-leaning crack that leads to a good ledge. Climb a scoop before easier cracks lead to a huge ledge.
3   18m. 4c. Climb the left-hand of two fine cracks in the wall.

Hyena 88m E2 (1979)
This eliminate starts as for The Assassin.
1 30m. 5b. Climb the flared crack, as for The Assassin, then continue straight up the thin crack above to belay beneath the groove of Scavenger.
2 21m. 5c. Climb the wall between Scavenger and Scavenger Direct.
3 37m. Finish as for Scavenger, pitch 3.

★★ **Scavenger** 88m Hard Very Severe (1966)
A Gogarth classic on good rock following a series of grooves up the buttress left of The Needle. Start below a large ledge on the front face of the buttress.
1 8m. 4c. Climb steeply up the wall on good holds to a stance on the large ledge.
2 43m. 5a. Climb the corner above for ten metres then, gain a ledge on the right around the arête, and traverse right to the base of a cracked groove. Follow the groove to a ledge and belay.
3 37m. 4a. The continuation groove leads more easily to broken ground above. Either scramble up right to finish up Pentathol, or traverse off to the left and go up over grass to the top.

Variation
★★ **Scavenger Direct** 37m Hard Very Severe (1974)
A fine alternative middle pitch.
2a 37m. 5a. Climb the corner to reach the ledge on the right, then move back leftwards into the continuation groove and follow it to the ledge and belay.

★★ **Nightride** 72m E1 (1967)
A very good route which takes the arête left of Scavenger, with strenuous climbing on steep rock. A few metres left of Scavenger is a deep bay containing an overhanging chimney, Heroin. Start at the right-hand arête of this bay.
1 14m. 4c. Climb diagonally up rightwards to the large belay ledge, on Scavenger.
2 21m. 5b. Go up the corner to reach the obvious traverse line at three metres, and go left along this to the arête. Move up and right to the steep crack and follow this to a stance and belay.
3 37m. 4c. Move up and right to a wide crack and follow it to the top, finishing up easy ground, or go left into a corner which leads to more easy rock and the top.

Dream Seller 45m E1 5b (1976)
A bold pitch with some interesting climbing taking a steep line between Nightride and Heroin, starting as for the latter. A choice of starts lead up the wall, before trending up left to

Malcolm Howells on the 1st ascent of Phaedra.
Photo: Ken Wilson

gain the foot of a bottomless corner groove. Climb this moving right at the top to spike belays.

Heroin 55m Hard Very Severe (1966)
An interesting route based on the wide overhanging chimney in the back of the deep bay left of Scavenger. Start beneath the chimney.
1 45m. 5b. Climb the chimney until it becomes a cracked groove above the last bulge. Continue up the crack for a couple of metres, peg, before traversing left across the steep wall to a peg belay at a small block. It is also possible to climb directly up steep rock to the top from the peg in the crack.
2 10m. 4c. Follow the easier groove to finish.

Horse Above Water 52m E2 (1975)
This follows a second bottomless chimney, just left of Heroin, with the hardest climbing at the start. Start as for Heroin.
1 26m. 5b. Climb steeply up the groove and enter the chimney with difficulty. This leads more easily to a crack which is followed to a poor stance, with good belays.
2 26m. 4c. Climb the crack and corner above to finish.

★**Phaedra** 53m E1 (1966)
An enjoyable route which offers a technical start followed by fine open climbing above. The arête left of Heroin is split by three short grooves in its lower portion. Scramble up left to belay on a spike just right of central groove.
1 43m. 5c. Step left into the central groove with difficulty, and climb more easily up to the overhang. Go around the arête on the left to a wide chimney crack, and follow this on good holds in a fine position to a small stance and spike belay.
2 10m. 4c. Easier ground behind the belay leads to the slopes above.

Zed 45m Hard Very Severe 5a (1987)
A good pitch, bold in places. Start a little left of Phaedra. Climb up the blunt arête to reach the roof, thread. Step left, and go up the wall above for ten metres. Move right, around the arête, and follow a crack to the top.

The next route takes the groove in the front of the buttress to the left of Zed. Traverse 12 metres left from the start of Heroin to belay beneath a clean-cut groove.

★**Hud** 44m Hard Very Severe 5a (1966)
A fine steep and sustained route. Climb the groove to a point three metres below the overhang. Step right and

climb the steep wall to reach a crack on the right of the overhang, which leads to vegetated ground and the top.

A further ten metres left of Hud is a large open corner, taken by Hustler. The following routes begin by traversing across at low water (Hard Very Severe) to belay beneath this corner.

Mulatto   45m   Hard Very Severe   (1967)
Good climbing up the wall and arête right of the big corner, starting at the belay below the corner.
1   22m. 4c. Cross rightwards to the foot of a thin flake crack, and climb this until just below a ledge in the middle of the wall, then move right to a poor stance on the arête.
2   23m. 5a. Thin cracks above are followed for 12 metres, before finishing up a wider crack.

★★ **Mestizo**   43m   E1   (1970)
This direct line up the steep wall left of Mulatto offers a variety of interesting moves. Start at the foot of the big corner.
1   23m. 4c. Cross rightwards to the foot of the thin flake crack, as for Mulatto, and climb this direct to the ledge in the middle of the wall. Belay.
2   20m. 5b. The crack above the stance leads to the top.

The Three Musketeers   39m   E2   (1979)
A bold pitch taking the wall to the left of Mestizo. Start beneath the big corner.
1   18m. 4a. Go easily up the wall between The Hustler and Mestizo, to belay on the ledge.
2   21m. 5c. The wall on the left is climbed, mainly on layaways, to reach a thin crack, which leads to the top.

★★ **The Hustler**   40m   Hard Very Severe   4c   (1966)
A good route with sparse protection which follows the large corner, starting beneath it. Climb steeply up the crack in the right wall to a small ledge, carry on a couple of metres, then move left into a chimney above the overhang, which leads to the top. (The corner has also been climbed direct.)

★ **The Third Man**   43m   E1   5b   (1978)
A fine pitch up the wall left of The Hustler, starting at the foot of The Hustler. Climb the wall, then a short hidden crack, directly to the small right-trending corner at 12m. Follow this before moving left with difficulty to a break, on Gringo. Step back right to finish up an excellent crack.

★ **Gringo**   46m   E1   (1967)
A worthwhile route, with steep and strenuous climbing. Start as for The Hustler.

1   25m. 5b. Go up leftwards to a spike, then ascend again before stepping right to a crack in the wall. This leads to an obvious break which is traversed leftwards to a small stance on the arête.
2   21m. 5a. Climb the crack on the right of the arête, then move left to a crack above the stance, and climb this and the wall on the right to the top.

High Noon   36m   E1   (1979)
This takes the overhanging groove to the left of Gringo, starting as for that route.
1   18m. 5b. Follow Gringo until it is possible to traverse left to gain a hanging corner, which leads up to the stance on Gringo.
2   18m. 5b. Traverse right to a crack directly above the first pitch of Gringo, and finish up this.

Wrangler   48m   E2   (1967)
A difficult route which takes the strenuous wide crack left again from High Noon, starting as for The Hustler. A low tide is vital.
1   30m. 5c. Move left to the arête and go up to gain a runner at 6m. Return to sea-level, and traverse leftwards for ten metres until below an overlap, peg. Climb up with difficulty and gain the overhanging crack on the left, which is followed to a good stance.
2   18m. The groove is climbed more easily to the top.

GIRDLE TRAVERSES OF THE MAIN CLIFF

Although rather out of vogue, these routes provide exciting climbing in superb positions, and the first two also avoid the problem of high tides. They are worthwhile for the scenery they pass through alone, and the epic value of sea-cliff girdles is in a class of its own.

★ **The Girdle Traverse**   185m   Hard Very Severe   (1966)
A varied and exposed route with reasonable climbing, and a gripping abseil, provides a good outing. Start as for Cordon Bleu.
1   38m. 4a. As for Cordon Bleu, pitch 1.
2   37m. 4b. As for Cordon Bleu, pitch 2.
3   31m. Climb down to the left edge of the massive flake. Abseil from a block, down the overhanging wall (Mammoth) until ledges in the middle of the wall can be gained. Peg belay. Care should be taken to make sure the ropes can be retrieved!
4   12m. 4c. Traverse left to climb a short steep wall, past a large spike, to gain a big ledge, on The Big Groove.

5   6m. 4c. Descend to belay at the end of the first pitch of Pentathol.
6   15m. 4b. As for Pentathol, pitch 2.
7   25m. 4c. As for Pentathol, pitch 3.
8   21m. 4b. As for Pentathol, pitch 4.

★ **Trunk Line**   142m   E3   (1976)
A very sustained route crossing the superb central overhanging wall of the cliff. Start as for Resolution.
1   25m. 5b. Move left and climb the crack in the arête on the left. This leads to a junction with Gogarth, which is followed up and left to a good stance.
2   22m. 5a. Traverse leftwards, rising slightly across a broken area, until it is possible to gain a narrow ramp, which is followed down to a good stance below the chimney of The Rat Race.
3   18m. 5c. Step left and descend the corner (Alien) until an obvious traverse line leads leftwards. Follow this and move up to a resting place. Continue leftwards to reach the stance with dubious belays, on Dinosaur.
4   15m. 5b. Traverse left again into Mammoth and follow this to the stance.
5   15m. 5c. From the left-hand end of the belay climb the steep diagonal crack leftwards, until at 12 metres it is possible to move left over a bulge to belay on Citadel at a large flake.
6   22m. 5c. Follow Citadel up the sustained crackline, to belay on the slab above.
7   25m. Escape as for Citadel, pitch 3.

The Horizon   331m   E3 (3 pts. aid)   (1969)
An incredibly long and sustained girdle of the left-hand side of The Main Cliff and Easter Island Gully area. Initially done in sections, it has been completed in one day. Great care is needed with the ropes on many sections. Start on top of the prominent square block, as for Syringe.
1   22m. Climb the wall to the overhangs, and move left beneath these to cross the wall left of the groove. Move up onto the arête and continue left until it is possible to step down to a good belay ledge, as for Hypodermic.
2   37m. Climb the wall on the left continuing leftwards to beneath overhangs. Cross the smooth slab on the left and go around the steep wall into Scavenger. Follow the obvious flake to good ledges.
3   43m. From the end of the ledges go around left into Heroin, then climb the wall slightly left to the big overhang, and climb this. Move slightly left, then traverse left to a hidden peg under a small overhang. Descend nine metres to a small ledge in the middle of the wall. Move left across the top of the steep groove, Hud, and onto the arête where a crack leads to a good spike. Climb leftwards to the top of

a huge flake, in the middle of the wall right of The Hustler. and belay.

4 18m. Go left to a ledge, on The Hustler, then move left past the chimney crack and across the steep left wall (skyhook in horizontal crack to start). Reach the arête and move left again to a good belay ledge, on Gringo.

5 31m. From the left-hand end of the ledge, climb the wall to a peg, then step down and climb leftwards to spikes on the steep wall. Follow these leftwards, until using a rock fang, it is possible to gain a resting place on the arête. Go left again, on spikes, to take a hanging belay on the arête.

6 9m. Traverse left around the arête to the good ledge in the next corner, Big Gut.

7 31m. Cross left, through Rotten Gut, then semi-hand traverse beneath the obvious ledge, moving down to a good ledge, below the top pitch of Tape Worm.

8 12m. Drop down a little and traverse left, across the arête of Phagocyte, on a line of quartz holds to reach the top of a good crack. Carry on passing a further two cracks to a ledge and belay in the corner, on Volcano.

9 31m. Climb the corner above and move left into a small cave under the huge arch. Chimney down behind the arches until it is possible to move left into the corner at a pod, Exit Groove. Cross the wall on the left, with difficulty, to a point just short of the arête, and climb up (peg for aid) to a ledge. A long reach gains a crack above, on Sex Lobster, then step left to a hanging belay on the arête.

10 9m. Go down left to a spike on the arête, then descend into the steep corner, on Belial, and take another hanging belay at the foot of this.

11 12m. Descend again and move across to a crack on the left. Climb this until moves left gain the arête, on Drag. Hanging belay again.

12 12m. Move across the wall (skyhook tension) to gain a good flake, and continue more easily to large belay ledges, on Exit Chimney.

13 15m. Climb the chimney a little way, then take the steep wall above to a good flake in the right-hand corner. Traverse left to a small corner and move down to a ledge. Move around the corner, peg, to belay in the chimney, on Ormuzd.

14 18m. Move left and go up, peg, before climbing down and across to thin flake ledges on the wall. Move left to a spike on the arête, and climb up and then leftwards to belay ledges, on Ahriman.

15 31m. Go leftwards up the wall and follow a line of shelves, slightly leftwards, to the top. (Or reverse the route!)

Above the routes at the left-hand side of The Main Cliff is an upper wall of more broken rock. At its highest point two easy routes provide worthwhile exits from The Main Cliff. Directly above the finish of Mulatto a scramble leads to a wall, with an obvious crack in the centre, right of a big corner directly above The Hustler.

The Fast Buck   37m   Hard Severe   (1978)
The obvious big corner on the left is the line of Minnesota Fats. Right of this is an easier corner, followed by a steeper wall containing a wide crack starting at five metres. Take a short corner for five metres, then go two metres left to reach the crack, which leads to a platform. A continuation crack then leads to a second sloping platform. Go into the corner and climb the crack to finish.

Minnesota Fats   30m   Severe   (1978)
This big corner provides an obvious and direct way off from this area of the cliff. Scramble up to the base of the corner and enter it from the left. This leads pleasantly to the top.

The Finisher   30m   E1   5b   (1983)
This is the crack around the last arête of the previous route, exiting right onto a slab and finishing up a wall at the top.

Easter Island Gully Area

The Easter Island Gully cliffs are actually the left-hand continuation of The Main Cliff, reaching to the entrance of Wen Zawn, but is considered a separate area due to the difficulty of access from either side. Although not as high as The Main Cliff, this is an area well worth a visit from any team, with many fine and varied routes across the grades. It is eminently possible to climb a number of routes in a visit, once the abseil has been located and equipped.

To reach the routes descend the gully (which is the next one south from the Wen Zawn approach) as far as an obvious pinnacle, whose resemblance to the real Easter Island statues provided the name of the area. Go down steeply to the right of this (facing out), on unpleasant grass steps to reach, with relief, a small rock platform containing several rotting pegs. It should be noted that this gully is a serious proposition when the ground is damp, and many teams use a back-up rope on the upper part. An abseil can be arranged 30 metres down the wall (taken by Supercrack) into the bed of Wonderwall Zawn, (Wonderwall is the leaning wall opposite the abseil). An extra rope to leave the abseil in place should be considered by any party not totally convinced of their ability to climb back out again! Access to most routes is by an easy sea-level traverse; this is however tidal, and it is not possible to get out of Wonderwall Zawn at high water, or if a swell is running.

If the sea is up then it is possible to abseil down the opposite (north) side of the buttress to routes on the left-hand side of the cliff.

To reach the first routes, traverse right from the Wonderwall Zawn at barnacle level, until just before the point where the cliff juts out and the traverse peters out.

Watership Down   34m   Very Severe   4c   (1978)
A fun route which is to be found just to the right (looking out) when descending the upper part of the approach gully en route for the Easter Island climbs. Start at the foot of the buttress where there is a slab on the right. Climb a steep crack in the slab to an overhang at six metres, then move left and make a hard move right to enter a chimney groove which is climbed more easily then go up leftwards to a ledge on the nose. A tricky step up right on dubious holds gains the finishing groove.

★★ **Swastika**   62m   E1   (1969)
A steep, committing climb on good rock, with one tricky move to start. Start beneath the obvious groove immediately before the wall projects out and becomes very hard to traverse.
1   15m. 5c. Drop down a few mtres and traverse onto the front of the buttress. Bear rightwards up to a flake then make a descending traverse right to a stance and belay.
2   10m. 5a. From the base of the chimney (Praetor) move onto the right wall and ascend to a flake. Go up rightwards from this to a ledge and peg belay.
3   15m. 5a. Go straight up then right to a ledge on the arête, then carry on to a second ledge, and from its left end pull over the bulge and ascend leftwards to a peg belay (as for Praetor).
4   22m. 5a. Traverse left for three metres and pull onto a small slab and climb the steep crack above, moving right to finish up a short corner.

Praetor   57m   E1   (1967)
Another committing proposition, again with one tricky move at the start. Start as for Swastika.
1   15m. 5c. As for Swastika.
2   21m. 5a. Gain the shallow chimney and follow this and the crack above to a peg belay.
3   21m. 5a. Continue, following the obvious line to the top.

★★ **This Year's Model** 61m E3   (1978)
A superb route taking a steep and exposed line up the black
wall right of Hombre. Start as for Swastika.
1 40m. 5c. Follow Swastika, around past Hombre, then go
up a shallow crack/groove bearing leftwards until a line of
holds leads up rightwards across the steep wall to slabs.
Belay at the base of a ramp.
2 21m. 5a. Take the obvious crack between Swastika and
Praetor.

Boil All Irishmen 60m E5   (1986)
This again follows the wall to the right of Hombre, starting
as for that route.
1 30m. 6b. Climb the wall right of Hombre, by two thin
seams, to reach a dubious hold. Span right and move up to
a sloping ledge and belay.
2 30m. 4c. Step left and follow the groove, on its right
side, aiming for a crack and finish up this.

★★★ **Hombre** 64m E1   (1967)
A brilliant and popular route with excellent climbing at its
grade, good protection and solid rock. Start as for Swastika.
1 15m. 5b. Climb up into the corner above until quartz
holds lead right to the arête, then go strenuously up a small
groove to reach a ledge and belays on the right.
2 37m. 5b. Climb the groove then the steep crack above.
3 12m. Easy cracks lead to the top.

★ **Big Gut** 52m Very Severe   (1967)
A varied and interesting climb, reasonable for its grade.
Start as for Swastika, beneath the groove.
1 15m. 4c. The groove leads pleasantly to a ledge.
2 10m. The broken corner on the left leads to a ledge.
3 27m. 4c. Climb the slabby groove to a small ledge, then
take the broken corner to reach the top.

Rock Island Line 45m Hard Very Severe   (1978)
This climb takes the obvious arête between Big Gut and
Crossover. To the left of Big Gut is an obvious break of
yellow rock that trends slightly right. Start at the foot of a
groove immediately right of this yellow break.
1 23m. 5a. Go right and climb the fine open arête to a
ledge, then take the short corner crack, as for Big Gut, to
the ledge.
2 22m. 5a. Take the thin flake crack in the wall left of Big
Gut until an easier wide crack leads to the top.

Crossover 50m Very Severe   (1967)
Start as for Rock Island Line.
1 15m. 4b. Climb the groove to belay on a good ledge on
Big Gut.

2 10m. 4c. Take the crack in the right wall, then the shallow groove which leads back into the main corner, to belay as for Big Gut.
3 25m. 4b Climb steeply up the slab on the right of a thin crack in the right wall, then take the groove and a flake on the right to finish.

Rotten Gut 45m   Hard Very Severe   5a   (1967)
A disgusting-looking route which goes through the yellow break. Start directly beneath the break and climb the groove by its right wall to reach the overhang. Step right then go into the break on the left above the overhang. Finish more easily above.

Fluke 50m   Hard Very Severe   (1967)
Strenuous climbing up the wall between Rotten Gut and Small Gut. Start beneath a groove, a few metres right of Tape Worm.
1 15m. 4b. Climb the overhanging groove diagonally rightwards to a small ledge, then move left to climb a short crack to reach a belay ledge on the left.
2 20m. 5b. Move back right and go up the wall to a short overhanging crack. Go over the bulge above then step left and ascend to another ledge. Belays higher up.
3 15m. 4a. Step right (as for Small Gut) to climb a crack which leads to the top.

Small Gut 60m   Hard Very Severe   (1967)
Start as for Fluke, beneath the groove a few metres right of Tape Worm.
1 20m. 4a. Climb the groove to a ledge with spike belays.
2 10m. 5a. Take the clean-cut groove above.
3 30m. 4a. Go right along ledges for 12 metres then finish up a thin crack.

★ **Tape Worm** 50m   Hard Very Severe   (1967)
A direct line up the groove just right of the arête, with a steep top pitch.. Start beneath the clean-cut groove just right of the arête.
1 10m. 4c. Climb the groove to a stance on a sloping ledge.
2 12m. 4c. Follow the thin diagonal crack on the left to a small ledge, then step right to another ledge and spike belay.
3 28m. 5a. Steeply climb the cracked wall, to the left of the clean-cut groove of Small Gut, straight to the top.

★ **Merchant Man** 45m   E1   (1978)
Well-positioned climbing up the airy arête between Tape Worm and Phagocyte leads to a rather gripping pitch above. Start just right of the arête.

Easter Island Gully Area

1   20m. 5b. Climb the wall just right of the arête to where it steepens, then climb the flying arête itself to a cramped stance (as for Phagocyte).
2   25m. 5a. Move up right then climb the true arête which leads, thankfully, to easier rock and the top.

★★ **Phagocyte**   45m   Hard Very Severe   (1967)
A good hearty route up the left-hand side of the right arête of the Wonderwall Zawn. Start beneath an obvious crack just left of the arête.
1   20m. 5a. Climb the crack strenuously until a step right leads to a cramped stance on the arête.
2   25m. 5a. Go up right and climb the steep groove before moving left to the arête and finishing up this, easing towards the top.

★★ **Wonderwall**   45m   E3   6a   (1969/1974)
A fine sustained pitch up the impressive leaning wall directly opposite the abseil. Start at a pillar, beneath a crack in the middle of the wall. Climb the crack then transfer to the parallel crack on the left and follow it to the overhang. Pull over this then go rightwards to the base of a groove. Ascend this with difficulty to reach good holds leading leftwards to a narrow ledge. Gain the arête on the right and climb this to finish.

Variation
★★ **I Wonder Why**   40m   E5   6a   (1986)
A difficult direct finish to Wonderwall. Follow Wonderwall to where it steepens, climb over the overhang and go straight up the thin crack to ledges and finish up cracks above, moving left to belay. A very good pitch.

Volcano   45m   E2   (1967)
A strenuous route which follows the overhanging crack in the corner at the back of the zawn before crossing the upper part of Wonderwall, unfortunately loose in the upper part. Start beneath a short crack and to the right of the base of a groove.
1   8m. 5a. Climb either crack to a ledge and belay.
2   37m. 5c. Gain the overhang and carry on to gain the thin crack, and follow this, over another overhang, peg, for a couple of metres before trending right across Wonderwall to finish up the arête.

Wandering Wall   48m   E2   (1 pt. aid)   (1978)
A curious route taking the back wall of the Wonderwall zawn. Start beneath a chimney, at the back of the zawn.
1   15m. 4b. Go up the inside of the chimney for ten metres to reach an overhang, then using 'a weighted line', thread a

rope through the hole above and use this to gain a small stance!

2   8m. 4b. Traverse left beneath the overhang to belay in Exit Groove.

3   25m. 5b. Climb the crack for a couple of moves then make a rising traverse rightwards to reach a small ledge. Step right then go up a couple of metres before moving left onto the wall and climbing straight up the centre of it to the top.

Exit Groove   30m   Hard Very Severe   5a   (1967)
A steep route up the back, left-hand corner of the Wonderwall zawn, starting beneath the corner. Climb the chimney in the corner then move left to a crack, which leads to a vertical slot. Step left to a niche beneath a corner crack and climb this to reach the abseil point.

Variation
Shagger's Start   30m   Hard Very Severe   5b   (1989)
A much better way to do the route, starting at a crack a little way right of Supercrack. Climb the crack, moving across to finish as for the original way.

★★ **Supercrack**   30m   E3   5c   (1974)
A deservedly popular,. and strenuous pitch which takes the obvious crack directly up the abseil wall. Climb the crack, the initial ten metres being very steep. Above, the crack narrows and becomes technically very interesting, before a tricky move left just short of the top leads to an easy finish.

Sex Lobster   30m   E3   (1986)
This takes the arête left of Supercrack, starting directly below it.

1   12m. 5c. Climb up past a peg to reach large pockets. Go left around the arête and gain a belay.

2   18m. 5c. Cross back right, past an undercling, to gain a fine crack in the wall left of Supercrack, and climb up to the top.

The next route takes the steep front face of the buttress left of the Wonderwall zawn. Moving left again is another zawn whose right and left corners are taken by Exit Chimney and Ormuzd respectively. The wall left of Ormuzd is taken by Ahriman and Gazebo.

Belial   30m   Hard Very Severe   5a   (1967)
An interesting route to and up the overhanging groove in the front face of the buttress. Start below this, on a platform, and climb up to the base of the groove. A few airy moves up this lead to easier ground and the abseil point.

Pequod 30m E3 5c   (1978)
Takes the obvious steep crack in the scooped wall to the
left of Belial, and gives a few serious and difficult moves.
Start to the right of the arête on the left of the scoop. Climb
the wall to reach the flake crack in the middle of the scoop,
and follow this to the bulge, and continue up the steep
right-trending crack to reach easier ground and the top.

Drag 30m Hard Very Severe 5a   (1968)
Steep climbing up the obvious thin crack right of Exit
Chimney, starting as for Pequod, taking care with the
ropework. Ascend the short wall then go up left onto the
arête. Move up and around this to reach a crack on the left
which leads to the top.

Vicious Fish 30m E3 6a   (1988)
This worthwhile climb takes the arête right of Neutrino
direct, starting slightly left, and moving up right to finish up
the arête proper.

★ **Neutrino** 30m E1 5b   (1976)
This takes the thin crack between Drag and Exit Chimney,
starting left of the arête, to join Drag directly.

Exit Chimney 30m Very Severe 4c   (1968)
This route follows the obvious slabby chimney in the rear
right-hand corner of the zawn, on rock that leaves a little to
be desired. It is the easiest way out of the area. Start by a
short scramble up to the foot of the chimney, then follow
the slab to the overhang and move right to easy ground,
which leads to the abseil point.

The Real Keel 23m E5 6b   (1988)
This is the hanging prow to the right of Annihilator. Start up
Exit Chimney, and from six metres up it make an obvious
traverse to gain the keel. Climb up it, peg, to a rest on a
plinth, before taking the wall direct past two portholes to a
big spike, belay. Abseil off, or scramble up to the top.

★ **Annihilator** 30m E5 6a   (1975/1986)
Fine steep climbing up the leaning wall left of Exit Chimney,
starting on the ledge reached by scrambling up, as for Exit
Chimney. Surmount the bulge leftwards and move up to a
resting place in the main crack, where the wall steepens.
Difficult moves up the right wall gain a step left to the
groove, which is followed to easier ground and the top.

Variation
For Madmen Only 30m E5 6a   (1986)
Follow Annihilator to the resting place, and swing wildly left
into a flake line. Layback heading for a keel, then make a

hard move onto on a sloping ledge, and finish just left of Annihilator.

★★ **Ormuzd**   33m   E4   (1967)
An excellent route up the big overhanging chimney with a roof at its top and an airy continuation above. Start from a small ledge below the steep wall left of the chimney.
1   18m. 5b. Climb the left-hand side of the wall for a couple of moves then go right across the wall into a shallow groove. Go up this a little way before entering the chimney on the right, above the lower overhang, and climbing up to a good stance, pegs.
2   15m. 5c. Carry on up the chimney, then bridge out across the roof, in a fine position, peg, moving out onto the front face. Finish up the wide crack.

★ **The Red Sofa**   37m   E5   6b   (1987)
Interesting climbing on good rock. Start as for Ormuzd, and climb up the continuation groove left of the chimney of Ormuzd, until a difficult traverse left gains a hand-and-finger crack. Finish into a flake line, then go out right to a crack on the arête. This leads to the top.

The Ancient Mariner   37m   E5   (1986)
This route takes the wall and groove between Ormuzd and Ahriman.
1   15m. 5c. Climb up the wall then traverse leftwards, past an old wire, to gain the arête and move left again to the belay on Ahriman.
2   22m. 6b. Move back right and climb up into the groove with difficulty, then using a pocket near the top of the left arête swarm onto a ledge. Finish up Ahriman.

★ **Ahriman**   37m   Hard Very Severe   (1967)
A nice route, with a good second pitch up the obvious groove in the arête left of Ormuzd, starting well to the left of Ormuzd, at a left-trending crack.
1   12m. 5a. Climb the wall until holds lead right, around the arête to ledges and a belay beneath the groove.
2   25m. 5a. Climb the bulging groove and continue to the top.

★ **Gazebo**   30m   Hard Very Severe   5a   (1968)
A good route with fine positions which takes the wall left of Ahriman. Start as for Ahriman, below the diagonal crack and follow it for eight metres before moving right to a spike. Gain the bottomless groove above and follow it to a short corner. Go up again to a ledge below a second corner, swing left onto the wall and finish up this.

Tumbling Dice 30m E3 6a   (1978)
An enjoyable steep pitch on good rock, starting as for
Ahriman. Follow the crack to a series of holds which leads
up right to the small overhang in the middle of the wall.
Surmount this with difficulty and after a further move up left
head up right to a flake. Step left and climb the steep open
corner, finishing up a final short corner/crack.

An Unimportant Wave 30m E4 6b   (1988)
This takes the overhanging wall, and crackline, left of
Tumbling Dice.

Perpendicular 33m Very Severe   (1978)
A contrived but reasonably interesting route, starting as for
Ahriman.
1 15m. 4b. Follow the crack until it is possible to move left
to a ledge on the arête.
2 18m 4b. Go left into the groove on Diagonal, then take
the obvious flake crack out across the left wall and finish
straight up.

Belvedere 30m E2   (1978/86)
This route follows the obvious arête left of Perpendicular,
starting at its base.
1 15m. 5c. Climb the arête, using the thin crack on its
left-hand side, to a good ledge and belay.
2 15m. 5b. Follow the groove directly above the belay to
finish up a crack in the arête.

Diagonal 30m Very Severe 4c   (1967)
Start beneath the shallow groove left of Belvedere, and
climb it to finish up the wall on the right near the top.

Diatom 30m Very Severe 4c   (1978)
Start as for Diagonal. Climb the groove of Diagonal for six
metres then take the lower line of holds leading diagonally
left to the arête. Climb the arête on its right side to join and
finish up the last few moves of Perpendicular.

Micron 28m Hard Very Severe 5a   (1976)
This follows the diagonal crack left of the groove of
Diagonal, and gives a short section of strenuous climbing.
Start as for Diagonal and take the crack up leftwards to
reach easier ground, and thus gain the top.

Microdot 28m Hard Very Severe 5a   (1978)
A short, sharp problem taking the crack left of Micron, over
a bulge at half-height to finish up a short easy corner.

Wen Slab Area

Wen Slab is the stupendous 90-metre slab rising steeply straight from the sea, and forming the south side of the large zawn between Easter Island Gully and North Stack wall. The climbs on this slab are, virtually without exception, very worthwhile. A Dream of White Horses in particular is an outstanding expedition of great character. The slab is well viewed from the promontory opposite, although it should be noted by the nervous that, in places, the slab is not quite as steep as it looks.

The slab curves over to the left, above the steep wall taken by T. Rex. The back overhanging wall of the zawn holds potential for the future while to the left a huge natural arch, taken by Conan the Librarian, is bound on its left by the big slabby Uhuru Wall. The left side of the entrance to the zawn is in the form of a buttress, taken by The Trap, while just round to the left of this is the marvellous steep and hold-plastered face of Spider Wall. The left-hand side of this wall re-forms as the through side of the huge natural arch opposite T.Rex. The inside of this arch provides the setting for fun and games on Spider's Web, while left again the walls extend around towards North Stack, not as high, but still with a number of interesting routes.

The routes on Wen Slab are reached by two means – depending on the state of the tide.

At low water abseil down the Uhuru Wall from blocks at its top to reach the bed of the zawn (access to the Uhuru Wall routes) and boulder-hop across to the base of the slab.

At high water, or in rough seas, the initial pitches have to be avoided. Scramble across, on a narrow path, above the top of the slab to gain broken rocks on the ridge on the right, and descend this for a short section to further blocks on the edge of the slab. (The loose ground hereabouts should be treated with respect, as any dropped blocks cascade down the slab on to teams below.) From this point abseil diagonally down a line of flakes to ledges, about 20 metres above the sea, then traverse easily left or right to belay as appropriate for the chosen route. The left-hand end of the ledges is the first stance of Wen.

To gain the alternative start to A Dream of White Horses, carry on down the ridge with great care, from the abseil point, to reach block belays at an obvious notch on the arête, where a short groove leads down onto the slab.

Wen Slab.
Photo: Ken Wilson

For routes adjacent to The Trap and those on Spider Wall, an abseil can be arranged down a chimney (The Trap), on the seaward end of the promontory, past ledges to the foot of the buttress. Step around left to reach Spider Wall. It may be wise to leave a rope in place here as The Trap is well-named; pulled through abseil ropes often snag in the chimney.

To reach Spider's Web and the routes in the Ipso Facto area, follow a faint path leftwards around a spur, from above the promontory, and into a steep grassy gully. Follow this down with great care until a steep rocky section is encountered, it is best to abseil down this section, from spikes, to reach good ledges at sea-level. It is possible to downclimb this section by going along a ledge rightwards (facing out), then down a short groove to a ledge, and finish down a shallow groove below the upper part of the gully.

Hydrophobia 45m Hard Very Severe 5a   (1981)
An alternative approach to the upper slabs of Dde. Start at sea-level round the arête right of Dde, at the foot of a square-cut chimney. Climb the chimney and exit right at its top. Move left onto the right-hand edge of Wen Slab then go up left into Dde up which the route finishes, belaying as required.

★ **Dde** 105m Hard Very Severe   (1966)
A long enjoyable climb up the right-hand side of the massive slab to finish via the obvious layback crack. Low in its grade. Start, at sea-level, at a boulder beneath a steep groove capped by an overhang, and just right of the obvious chimney of Wen. At high water start from the first stance of Wen.
1 45m. 5a. Move right and climb a thin crack to a good ledge 5 metres short of the arête.
2 15m. 4c. Climb the slab to a sentry-box and a belay.
3 45m. 5a. Follow flakes up to the left to below a small overhang, where an awkward move up around the corner gains a groove, which is followed to finish with care onto the approach path.

Variation
1a 35m. 4c. From the first stance on Wen go right along easy flakes and ledges then climb a thin crack to a good spike. Move right and go up to the sentry-box belay.

★★★ **A Dream of White Horses** 150m Hard Very Severe (1968)
This brilliant route traverses Wen Slab from bottom right to top left offering a wealth of fine atmospheric situations. Although the climbing is of a reasonable standard, the situations are exposed and serious. A fall from the final

Wen Slab Zawn

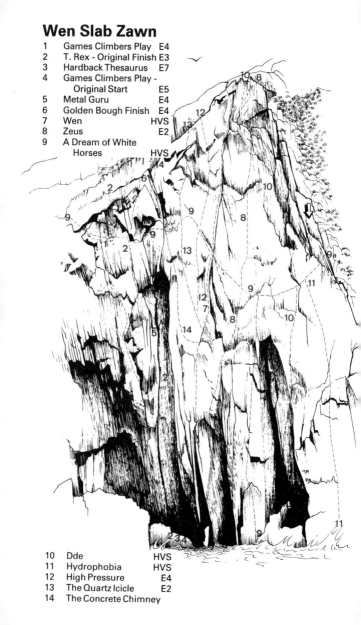

pitch would leave a climber hanging free 70 metres above the sea. At low water start as for Dde, below the groove. At high water, or in big seas, start from the arête, as described, taking pitch 2a.

1 45m. 5a. Climb the left-hand edge of the groove to reach the ledges on Wen. Continue directly above to a good spike, then head up right to a small corner and belay.

2 25m. 5a. Follow the horizontal line leftwards, past a couple of rusty old pegs, to a difficult move which brings better holds and a hanging belay in the crack of Wen.

2a 35m. 5a. Climb down the groove, from the notch on the arête, and out onto the slab. Follow the traverse line leftwards across the slab, past the rusty pegs, to gain the crack of Wen after a couple of difficult moves. Hanging belay.

3 35m. 4c. A line of flakes leads up left, past a good ledge at 15 metres, to where they peter out. Climb across and down, past a short broken chimney, to reach small ledges and peg belays in The Concrete Chimney.

4 45m. 4c. Step left, trying to feel brave, and clip an old peg under a small roof. Descend leftwards until a step around a rib gains better holds. Continue up then left, past good spikes, to reach the final slab, which is crossed delicately to reach the foot of a short bottomless groove, in a superb position. Climb the groove and exit leftwards to belay on large boulders a long way back. If the runners on this pitch are not extended, considerable rope drag or pulled out protection will result, providing extra excitement for the second. An outstanding pitch.

Echo Beach 80m E2 (1980)
Bold but pleasant climbing. Start at the belay at the top of pitch 1 of Dream etc.

1 40m. 5b. Follow a quartz band up and across Zeus to a hanging stance in Wen; protection scarce.

2 40m. 5b. Go up left under a roof, then cross High Pressure, and keep going leftwards to finish up the Direct Finish to The Quartz Icicle.

If 62m HVS (1969)
Another bold route taking the slab right of Wen, starting as for Dream etc. pitch 2a, at the notch on the arête. The exact relationship between Echo Beach and this route is not clear, and they may share a portion of the climbing.

1 40m. 5a. Climb down the groove and across the traverse line for a little way, then follow quartz holds diagonally leftwards, into shallow scoops, to climb over the small roof on Zeus at the left side. Follow a crack up then go right to belay on a ledge a few metres right of the upper part of Wen.

Lawrie Holliwell leading T. Rex.
Photo: John Cleare

2 22m. 5a. Climb up and right to gain the bottom of the final groove of Dde, and finish up this.

★ **Zeus** 85m E2   (1970)
A good route, both bold and delicate for the grade, taking the slab between Wen and Dde. Start at sea-level below a groove, immediately right of the chimney to Wen, or from the ledges of Wen at high water.
1 25m. 5a. Move left onto the wall and go straight up to where it steepens. Move left to a small niche then move up and bear rightwards to good ledges just right of Wen.
2 45m. 5b. Climb the line of cracks behind the stance to a bulge at ten metres. Cross this rightwards, tricky, then go up to a junction with Dream etc at a rusty peg. Continue bearing up to the left for a further ten metres until it is possible to move right, and then go up to a line of small roofs. Step right and pull through these at the widest point, then go straight up, to a poor stance and dubious peg beneath the final wall, junction with Dde.
3 15m. 4b. Go up right and climb a friable thin crack to the top.

★★ **Wen** 100m Hard Very Severe   (1966)
A fine and popular route following the large central crack splitting the slab. Start directly below the initial chimney at sea-level, or the good ledges at the top of pitch 1 if the sea so dictates.
1 25m. 5a. Climb the chimney, through a natural hole, then ascend the shallow groove above to reach good ledges, peg, just right of the crackline.
2 40m. 4c. Gain the crack and follow this, nicely sustained, to a hanging stance where the crack is widest.
3 35m. 5a. Climb up and pull through the bulge on the left, to gain a cracked corner leading up and left. An awkward move gains a ledge on the left, then traverse along this to good belays in the back wall. The crack/ chimney can be followed directly, but this is loose and will cascade stones down the slab.

★ **High Pressure** 55m E4   (1976)
A good eliminate with some very serious climbing, taking the slab between Wen and The Quartz Icicle. Start from the good ledges of Wen.
1 30m. 5c. Climb diagonally left, as for The Quartz Icicle, to a peg (sometimes) above the crack. Step right and boldly climb straight up the pink slab above to reach a good ledge, mentioned on pitch 3 of Dream etc. Belay.
2 25m. 5b. Follow the flakes for three metres then climb straight up to a prominent crack, and climb this to where it closes. Step right to a second narrow crackline and follow this to an undercut section. Pass this to join the top ledge

traverse on Wen, a couple of metres right of The Quartz Icicle, and belay as for that route.

★★ **The Quartz Icicle**   62m   E2   (1968)
Another excellent eliminate, varied and bold, especially on the first pitch. Start as for the previous route on the good ledges on Wen, top of pitch 1.
1   37m. 5b. Go up left to the quartz vein and climb it to a peg (sometimes) then a few tricky moves lead to where the quartz vein opens into a crack. Follow this, peg, to belay, pegs, in the broken chimney, some six metres right of The Concrete Chimney.
2   25m. 5b. Go up diagonally rightwards, through Dream etc. then traverse right to a small curving groove containing a crack. Climb this and exit right into a thin diagonal crack to the right of the smooth slab, then head up left to finish up a crack leading to the final traverse of Wen, and belay as for that route.

Variation
The Original Finish   25m   E2
2a. From the belay go straight up then move left into a crack. This leads to a jutting overhang and a step left onto its lip. Carry on up the slab, move right and take the crack to the top. A slightly easier finish, that some may find less trying to find.

★★★ **The Concrete Chimney**   70m   Hard Very Severe   (1967)
To the left of Wen is a prominent rubble-filled chimney cleaving the slab. This excellent route follows the arête to the right of the lower section before crossing the chimney to finish up bulges to the left. The first pitch is the finest of its standard here, although the protection takes skill to find. Start as for the last route.
1   45m. 5a. Take an obvious line rising leftwards to the arête, then climb steeply up the slab to a thin crack (runners). Climb the wall, in a fine position, on good holds before moving left a little and climbing up the slab and short crack to belay in the rubble filled chimney, as for Dream etc.
2   25m. 5a. Climb up and cross overlapping slabs leftwards to reach an overhanging groove. Follow this to join the very top bulge of the chimney, and scramble up to belay on the ledge, as for Wen. The chimney direct has been climbed, but is atrocious.

★★ **Games Climbers Play, Original Start**   30m   E5   6a
                                                      (1970/1979)
This fine and strenuous pitch follows a streak of unusual bubbly rock, and is probably best described as a hard alternative start to T.Rex. Start up the bubbly rock a little left

of the true base of The Concrete Chimney. Climb straight up, past a peg, to reach the slab below the first belay on T.Rex. Belay as for that route. A strenuous, sustained pitch.

★★ **Hardback Thesaurus** 30m E7 6b (1988)
Desperate climbing up the wall between the previous route and T.Rex, starting at a tiny flake groove. Go on a diet for this one! Climb the groove and trend diagonally out left then right to an orange break. Carry on up left to the overlap, traverse right and pull over onto the slab, then take twin ramps up rightwards to a hidden pocket. Traverse right to belay, pegs, as for T.Rex.

★★ **T. Rex** 115m E3 (1969)
A superb route with a variety of climbing, strenuous and delicate, sustained but never desperate. A great piece of route finding, it threads its way through some very steep ground to generally follow the large flake/corner at the bottom left of Wen Slab. Some large gear is handy for the initial few metres. Start beneath the corner, ten metres left of the true base of The Concrete Chimney.
1 40m. 5c. Thrutch up behind the flake until forced to layback up to a small overlap, good runner, and continue, much more pleasantly, up the corner to a break, with a scattering of pegs on the left. Step down right, and traverse in a great position on good, but friable, holds to reach a stance and pegs on the slab.
2 35m. 5b. Move up left and climb the steep short wall to a slab. Follow cracks on this to below the big overhangs, peg, then move down to the edge of the slab and step awkwardly around the corner before moving up and left more easily to a good stance in the corner. Care should be taken to protect the second on this pitch, especially if the peg is missing.
3 40m. 4c. Move up to reach the traverse on the last pitch of Dream etc. and follow this to the top. Boulder belays well back.

Variations
★ **Metal Guru** 40m E4 6a (1989)
1a Climb the corner as for the usual way, but instead of traversing rightwards from the pegs, continue up the corner above direct, peg, to eventually reach the stance at the end of pitch 2. A strenuous pitch.

If combined with The Golden Bough Finish this gives a fine and direct line which is sustained at the grade.

The Original Finish 35m E3 5b.
1a Climb up to the traverse on Dream and move left along this a few metres, then take the steep groove above before

stepping out right onto the wall. Follow a vague right-trending crack to a ledge in a niche. Poor rock leads to the top. Not as good as the Dream finish.

3b The Golden Bough Finish 25m E4 5c.

Move up to the Dream traverse and climb the golden-coloured groove above, moving slightly left, then exiting right onto the easy finishing slab. A strenuous, and somewhat loose, direct alternative.

Games Climbers Play 72m E4 (1 pt. aid) (1970/1977)

A strenuous climb taking the obvious flake/groove system left of T. Rex although the rock in parts is dubious. The direct start has been combined with the original finish to provide the most logical route. Start in the groove just left of T. Rex.

1 20m. 5c. Follow the groove to the overhang, then pull over this to holds leading up left to a spike. Enter the groove above and step right to a small ledge and belay.

2 30m. 5b. Climb steeply up the cracks on the left to reach an obvious niche. Carry on up, past the roof to a small rib, peg, and climb the steep wall above to a ramp which is followed leftwards to small ledges, pegs.

3 22m. 5a. Use a sling for aid to gain the final slab on Dream and finish up this.

The original start took a skyhook pitch up the wall right of T.Rex, now free and described earlier, before climbing up left on hooks and spikes and penduluming down, from a corner, a long way to the niche on pitch 2 and then following the rest of the route as described. This has no contemporary merit.

To the left of the back wall of the zawn is a huge natural arch. The next route takes an amazing left-to-right sweeping line across this.

★★★ Conan the Librarian 95m E7 (1986)

A stunning adventure, the line that hundreds of climbers must have eyed from Wen Slab. Difficult climbing, combined with friable rock, make this a route for a strong team. Start at the foot of the obvious open corner at the base of the arch.

1 28m. 6b. Climb the crack, just right of the corner, diagonally up right, then use this and the arête until the hanging corner on the right, peg at base, can be gained. Climb this to a peg then traverse right and go up to a hanging stance in a groove.

2 45m. 6b. The Janitor Finish. Climb the groove, four pegs, to its top then go rightwards along a ramp, two ice pegs, to eventually join T. Rex.

3 22m. 5c. The Golden Bough Finish to T. Rex.

Variation
2a 36m. 6b. The route was first climbed by finishing up leftwards from the top of the groove, requiring a peg for aid.

The Unridable Donkey 60m E7   (1987)
A stubborn little number, taking the huge corner groove just left of Conan The Librarian, with some desperate climbing and a portion of suspect rock thrown in for good measure. Start at the base of the groove in a sort of cave area.
1 38m. 6b. Climb up into the groove proper and follow it, and the slab, to the overhangs. Desperate moves past three pegs, poor, gains a niche and a rest on the left. Move back to the lip of the second roof and climb the groove again to an ice peg below the third roof, before exiting left to a rubble-covered ledge and belay.
2 22m. 5c. Climb huge wafer flakes right of the belay until diagonal progress can be made to the base of a hanging groove, where the two walls of the zawn meet. Finish up the talc groove in a fine position. A serious pitch, part of which fell into the sea some time after the first ascent, although not apparently affecting the climbing!

The following two routes appear to share much common ground, and their relationship is not totally clear.

Igdrazil 53m E2   (1969)
This follows the steep wall opposite Wen Slab, crossing Uhuru at half-height, and starts at a group of isolated pinnacles at the base of the wall.
1 28m. 5c. Head up rightwards towards a cave then go straight up a groove for six metres. Go left then up the wall, peg, then trend up leftwards to a ledge and peg belay, (shared with Uhuru).
2 25m. 5b. Work left a few moves, then climb a short groove and ramp back up right until above the belay, and continue straight up the wall passing a peg half-way to the top.

Broken Mirror 45m E3   (1976)
Serious climbing up the middle of the Uhuru wall, starting at a ledge at the centre of the base of the wall.
1 25m. 5c. Climb cracks bearing slightly rightwards to a ledge on the right after ten metres, step left and climb up to a peg belay, (shared with Uhuru).
2 20m. 5c. The obvious crack leads directly to a ramp. Cross this then climb thin cracks to the top.

Uhuru   60m   E1 (1967)
The climbing is well positioned, but marred by a loose and serious top pitch. Start at a small stance, with a big flake, about six metres above the boulders.
1   30m. 5a. Move right and climb diagonally, as the line dictates, to gain a small ledge on the right. Move up, then go back left to regain the slanting line and follow this to a stance with peg belays.
2   30m. 4c. On the right is a shorter corner. Ascend this, exiting left to climb the loose groove, moving left just below the top.

Boogie Woogie   45m   Very Severe   4b   (1988)
Start right of Thor. Climb the sharply defined rib, and the overhanging flakes above.

Thor   56m   Very Severe (1967)
This route takes the slanting diagonal break on the left-hand side of the wall, and starts from the nose to the right of The Trap, or from the bottom of the chimney. The top pitch has some loose rock.
1   28m. 4c. Go around the arête on the right to the start of the wide chimney. Climb this to a small cave, then take the steep crack on the right, and go up a short chimney through the overhang to a stance and peg belay.
2   28m. 4b. The obvious crackline, trending rightwards, leads to the top.

For the next four routes, bridge into the rift behind Thor, very atmospheric, for ten metres, to a ledge on the right.

The Escapegoat   15m   E1   5b   (1987)
Start at the near end of the ledge, and chimney up until forced deeper into the rift. Continue up to the boulder choke. Scramble off.

Agrophobia   60m   E4   (1986)
Interesting positions on this route, which samples the atmosphere of the rift.
1   15m. 5c. Strenuously climb the leftward-slanting crack to gain a block, lunge out right to hidden leftward- slanting flakes and follow these to a hanging belay.
2   9m. 4c. Traverse right then bridge across the zawn top to a boulder choke and belay.
3   18m. 5c. Climb the wall on the right, initially hard and serious, to a thread. Continue easily straight up the crack and belay below an overhang.
4   18m. 5b. Go round right up blocks to the top.

★ **Dislocation Dance**   27m   E3   (1986)
Interesting climbing, starting as for Agrophobia.

1 18m. 5c. From the middle of the ledge at the base of the rift, step down to a square foothold, then cross the zawn, and climb easily up holes and flakes to a chimney formed by a huge thin flake. Climb up the back slab of this to a roof. Move around the right-hand side of this, and into the continuation. Step down and right to a foothold on the rib, and lean across the zawn using a down-pointing spike as a balance, to gain holds and swing wildly across and climb to a belay, as for Agrophobia.
2 9m. 4c. As for Agrophobia, pitch 2. Scramble down to finish.

★ **Evidently Chickentown** 35m E5 6b   (1986)
This goes up inside the Cryptic Rift, as the cleft has become known, in some amazing positions. Start as for Agrophobia, on the ledge in the zawn. Climb down from the inside end of the ledge and traverse at sea-level, to gain and cross a boulder-dam leftwards, only possible at lowish water. Climb diagonally outwards and up to gain a flake chimney, below Dislocation Dance, and climb this to the roof. Neck and foot, (this bit's wide!), rightwards and inwards until it is possible to layback around the roof to an apparent rest on an apparent slab! Step up left, outwards, and lean against the underside of a protruding slab behind. Swing up backwards, right, to gain a good rest in a huge niche. Step right, outwards, to gain the hanging stance as for Agrophobia.

Minute Man 50m Hard Very Severe   (1970)
This follows the nose of the buttress between the clefts of The Trap and Thor. Start at the base of a groove in the front of the buttress.
1 25m. 4b. The groove leads to a large ledge with peg belays.
2 25m. 5a. Go right and up to an overhang. Traverse right below this to gain a chimney, which is followed a little way before stepping onto the right wall and going up to the top.

Sprung 45m Hard Very Severe   (1978)
Start beneath the arête, right of the start of The Trap.
1 25m. 5b. Climb the steep wall, keeping just left of the arête and move right near the top to the good stance on Minute Man.
2 20m. 5a. Climb the groove of Minute Man to the overhang. Move left, surmount the overhang and finish up the arête on the right.

The Trap 40m Hard Very Severe   (1967)
This is the left-hand of the two chimneys on the end of the promontory, down which the abseil approach is made. Bold

for its grade, the exit from the chimney lurks, drooling for a lycra-clad ascensionist.
1   25m. 4c. Enter the chimney and levitate up to the overhang before tackling the narrow vice above. Thankfully gain the wider section above and move left to a good belay ledge.
2   15m. 4a. Climb up the shattered groove on the right and finish up the final wide cleft.

Star of the Sea   40m   E2   (1970)
This route follows the outside of the chimney of The Trap.
1   25m. 5c. Climb the outside of the chimney and crack moving left to the large sloping belay ledge.
2   15m. 5a. Take the groove on the left to join and finish up the final few moves of Britomartis.

Gobbler's Arête   40m   E3   (1977)
Follows the wall and arête left of The Trap. Start just left of The Trap.
1   25m. 6a. Gain a diagonal ramp on the wall from the left, and follow it to the foot of a short wall, which is climbed to gain a series of diminishing steps below twin cracks on the left. Climb steeply up the cracks to the good sloping ledges.
2   15m. 5a. Climb the crack on the left to join and finish up Britomartis.

Vend-T   55m   E2   (1980)
A good addition that takes a parallel line of weakness across the wall above Britomartis. Start as for Gobbler's Arête.
1   37m. 5b. Swing left around the arête onto the wall right of Britomartis, just above a small overhang, and make a bold move to gain huge holds at the start of a line of craters leading up leftwards. Follow these to the left-hand end of the large sloping belay ledge.
2   18m. 5a. Move right and climb the steep crack to the top.

★★★ Britomartis   58m   Hard Very Severe   (1967)
A wonderful route up the fine seaward face round to the left of The Trap, steep but with many huge holds. Start as for Gobbler's Arête, unless low water permits a belay at the foot of the groove.
1   36m. 4c. Swing down left and traverse awkwardly into the bottom of the diagonal groove. Move down to the left and make an awkward traverse left into a shallow groove. Follow this, past some unusual holds, and the crack above in the same line to gain a small stance, pegs, in a fine position.

2 22m. 4c. Move up right and pull over the bulge to a good ledge, then go round right to finish up an easy final groove.

★★ **Toiler on the Sea**   62m   E2   (1980)
A fine route, with some strenuous, and bold, climbing on good holds. Start as for Britomartis.
1 37m. 5b. Traverse left at sea-level, past the groove, to the edge of the wall before climbing steeply up the wall to reach footholds at the base of a straight crack. Climb this directly to the Britomartis stance.
2 25m. 5b. Climb the thin crack behind the stance to a peg, and go up left, then back right across the upper slab to easy ground and the top.

★★ **Spider Wall**   60m   Hard Very Severe   (1969)
A marvellous climb on good, but often hidden, holds. Start as for Britomartis.
1 45m. 5a. Move up Britomartis a couple of metres then climb diagonally up and left, on the steep wall, to reach footholds at the base of the steep straight crack above the arch. Climb the crack for a few metres until holds lead left then right and into a groove which is followed to the Britomartis stance.
2 15m. 4c. Climb leftwards across the wall into a groove and follow it, some loose rock, to a good ledge and peg belay on the left.

★ **The Bluebottle**   80m   E2   (1969)
A worthwhile route which goes across the top of the arch in a fine position, before finishing direct. Start as for Britomartis.
1 45m. 5a. Follow Spider Wall as far as the footholds below the steep crack, above the arch, then carry on traversing to reach a small stance and pegs, shared with Spider's Web.
2 35m. 5b. Move up to the roof and climb round it to the right to gain the crack above. Follow this to the groove above and finish up the steep crack.

The next routes are situated to the left of the huge arch (taken by Spider's Web), left of the Britomartis wall. From the ledges at sea-level below the gully (see approach description), ledges can be traversed fairly easily left or right to gain all the routes in the following section.

★★ **Spider's Web**   73m   E2   (2-5 pts. aid)   (1968)
A classic expedition, involving both free and aid climbing, going up inside the huge arch before gaining the lip and finishing up the outside in a fine position. Double ropes are vital. Both members of the team should carry ascendeurs,

Joe Brown on Spider's Web.
Photo: John Cleare

or prussik loops, and it would be handy if the in situ pegs were replaced from time to time. Start by traversing rightwards, in towards the arch, from the descent, crossing a small channel to reach a sloping ledge on the arête, opposite Spider Wall.

1   15m. Traverse round right, at sea-level, to belay at the big chimney. (The same point can be reached at high tide via the first pitch of Archway, and descending the big chimney.)

2   18m. 5b. Move right around the bulge and go up to a shallow groove, then go two metres right and climb the steep wall, with difficulty, moving right at the top into a small cave and belay.

3   25m. 5a/A1. Climb up and chimney out above the sea, peg, to reach a cluster of pegs at the top of the chimney. From these pegs, descend on one of the ropes, which has been pulled through, clipping another peg on the way. Continue descending on the rope until it is possible to place a nut behind the overhang, which enables the outside lip, pegs, to be gained. Climb up, aid nut, to a small stance and peg belay. Great care should be taken to avoid the ropes becoming jammed on the lip. It should be possible for the second to descend on a rope similarly to reach the lip, where the rope can be retrieved and pulled through to be used as normal. Needless to say, the second should be as confident with the ropework as the leader.

4   15m. 4c. Step down right and climb back up a short crack, then move left to another crack and take this to reach easy ground.

★ **Archway**   48m   E2   (1967)

This complex and atmospheric route takes a chimney below the arch of Spider's Web, before crossing leftwards beneath the overhangs, and is equally trying for both members of the team. Start at the sloping ledge on the arête, as for Spider's Web.

1   15m. 4a. Go around right into the chimney, move right again then bear up rightwards to gain the chimney below the overhangs and a good stance.

2   18m. 5b. Climb down for three metres before climbing up leftwards to the overhang. Move left to the arête and a poor stance.

3   15m. 4c. Take the wall above before going rightwards and over a bulge to easy ground.

Blowout   45m   E2   (1977)

Start as for Spider's Web at the sloping ledge on the arête.

1   30m. 5c. Climb the overhanging groove immediately right of Genuflex to the overhang, then step right and cross the slab to its right edge. Gain the roof above and cross it

rightwards to a steep crack leading to the belay on Archway.
2 15m. 5a. Go up right into the groove and climb this until it is possible to move right onto the arête. Climb this easily to a belay overlooking Spider's Web. Some loose rock is encountered on this pitch.

Genuflex   40m   E2   5b   (1967)
A tricky wide crack provides the meat of this route, taking the edge of the wall left of the arch. Start as for Spider's Web, at the sloping ledge on the arête. Go around the corner into the deep chimney and climb this past the overhang, to reach, and follow, steep cracks to below loose bulges near the top. Go right and over a bulge to easy ground.

(Will Mawr gets the) Vulcan Lip Lock   40m   E4   6a
                                                    (1988)
Right of Genuflex is a wall, ochre-coloured in its upper part. Start below it. Climb the wall, difficulties variable, and go over the roof above a little niche. The remainder is somewhat loose.

Ipso Facto   30m   Very Severe   4c   (1967)
A pleasant route, although not overly protected, which takes the wall to the left of a shallow groove, about 15 metres left of the huge arch, and just to the right of the descent, starting below the wall. Take the crack in the wall until the right-hand arête can be gained and followed, some suspect rock, before stepping left to climb an obvious crack to the top.

Mustang   30m   Very Severe   4b   (1970)
Steep climbing, but low in the grade, up the wall to the left of the descent. Start below the first groove along the ledges, and climb it to the top.

Mr. Seal   30m   Very Severe   4c   (1981)
Nice climbing, although bold in places. Start left of Mustang, at the next groove along the ledges. Climb the groove/ramp, on big holds at first, until a couple of trickier moves lead to a ledge. The small wall on the right is then crossed to gain a triangular slab, and a finish is made up the groove at the back.

The Tail   32m   E2   5c   (1978)
Start at a pointed block on the traverse along the ledges, left again from Mr Seal, and beneath the second groove. Climb the groove direct to the top.

Miura   37m   Very Severe   4c   (1970)
An easier way of climbing the previous route. Start as for
The Tail. Follow the groove until it gets hard, and leans
leftwards. Traverse left and go over a bulge, and up, loose,
to a small overlap which is passed on the left. Climb up
leftwards and then rightwards to the top.

Maverick   52m   Very Severe   (1970)
A good little route, the longest on the wall. Start where the
ledge traverse peters out, just left of Miura.
1   30m. 4b. Climb up and left, on unusual rock, before
moving up more steeply and left again into a steep groove.
Belay.
2   22m. 4c. The groove is climbed with some interest to
the top.

Annie's Arch   92m   E2   (1970)
A girdle of the cliffs between Ipso Facto and Britomartis,
crossing over the huge arch of Spider's Web on the way
and providing some well positioned climbing on
intimidating ground. Start as for Ipso Facto.
1   25m. 4c. Follow Ipso Facto to the arête, which is climbed
for three metres before swinging right around into a groove
to belay at some pegs.
2   12m. 5b. Step down right and go across the wall to a
peg. Carry on to the arête and step up to a small cave, then
move down and right to a green slab which is descended
for three metres to a belay.
3   18m. 5a. Go down right across the slab to a corner, and
move up onto the right wall to gain the arête, peg. Step
down and traverse to a large fin, which is climbed to a peg,
before descending across for five metres to the corner and
a belay, on Spider's Web.
4   37m. 4c. Enter the flake crack down on the right and go
up this for three metres, then make a descending traverse
to an obvious flake. Move up to a good spike and traverse
across the wall to a junction with Britomartis. Descend this
a little until a traverse gains a huge ledge, and good belays
at the top. Finish up the wide crack at the top of the ramp.

Flytrap Area

Hereabouts the cliffs lower slightly in height, and are made
up of narrow walls and buttresses divided by deep and
fascinating sea caves. Although rather a backwater, two or
three very good routes make a visit worthwhile.

For the initial routes here, abseil down Prom buttress. This
is the promontory which forms the north side of the zawn,

North Stack – Flytrap Area

1	Holyhead Revisited	E5	5	Mordor	HVS
2	Arachnid	E4	6	Seal's Song	E5
3	Arachnid Variation	E4	7	Hash	HVS
4	Flytrap	E2	8	Bullitt	HVS

9	Miura	VS	13	Spider's Web	E2
10	Ipso Facto	VS	14	Britomartis	HVS
11	Genuflex	E2	15	The Trap	HVS
12	Blowout	E2	16	Thor	VS

north of Wen Slab, just beyond the routes in the Ipso Facto area.

Bullitt   45m   Hard Very Severe   5a   (1969)
Reasonable climbing, but the quality of the rock is not good, taking a line of grooves up the right-hand side of the buttress. Start right of the foot of the abseil, at a small cave. Gain the slabby groove, via a steep initial crack, and move up this to the overhang. Move up into a second groove on the right then exit left onto a ramp. Ascend this then go left round a small overhang and go up to the top.

Prom   47m   Hard Very Severe   (1968)
The route is quite often damp, and as with the previous route, the rock could be better. The route follows the crest of the buttress and is gained by an abseil to the foot of the rib.
1   17m. To the left of the rib is a groove which leads to a stance.
2   30m. Move left then go up for five metres until moves can be made to gain the obvious groove to the right of the rib. This leads to the top.

The Dope   47m   Hard Very Severe   5a   (1981)
Follow a shallow V-groove in the arête between Prom and Hash.

Hash   48m   Hard Very Severe   (1969)
Another fairly loose climb, this time following a groove-line above a large cave on the left-hand side of the Prom buttress. Start at the left-most side of the buttress.
1   10m. 5a. A scramble leads to a good stance overlooking the cave.
2   38m. 5a. Go leftwards across a short wall then ascend a steep slab to a short wide crack. Climb this and the broken groove above, stepping right to finish over broken ground.

To the left of the Prom buttress is a steep cracked wall, containing much sea grass, above a cave. Descend a short gully on the North Stack side of this wall and scramble down broken ground to a platform containing some blocks. Abseil 45 metres down to sea-level, then traverse right to reach a chimney slanting from right to left. The next route starts at the base of this chimney.

Mordor   68m   Hard Very Severe   (1968)
1   43m. Ascend the left wall of the chimney until over an overhang the wall steepens. Climb this wall to a flake then go up right to a crack in the overhang. Climb this to a stance and belay.

2 25m. Go left for three metres to reach left-trending cracks that lead to the top.

Variation
Mordor Newydd 45m E3 5c (1986)
A strenuous alternative way of climbing the previous route. Start up Mordor, then climb the overhanging squeeze chimney/crack to rejoin Mordor at 25 metres, and finish up this.

Seal's Song 50m E5 (1988)
A strange route, strenuous but not technically desperate, apart from the flight across the zawn which can only be described as a 'turbo glide'. Start to the right of the previous route.
1 20m. Climb the zawn for six metres until opposite a collection of jugs, then launch across the zawn to gain these. If you do, move around the overhanging arête, and belay.
2 30m. 5b. Climb over the roof above at the easy left-hand section and travel right to a good crack, loose in places, and follow it to the top.

Colditz 30m Very Severe 4c (1982)
A useful escape route starting at the base of the Mordor abseil. Go up the crack to a break, traverse this leftwards onto the arête, then climb this and a flake before scrambling up to the top.

To the left of the Mordor buttress is another large cave. The next route makes a traverse above this cave. Abseil down and climb to a ledge on the arête on the left of the Mordor wall.

Mistaken Identity 35m Hard Very Severe (1973)
1 10m. Go left along the ledge, almost to a cave. Belay.
2 25m. Go to the back of the cave and chimney down to a ledge. Climb out to the front of the wall at the end of the ledge. Step down left and hand-traverse six metres left to a peg in niche. Go up over a bulge then follow a groove to a peg belay at the top.

★★ **Flytrap** 82m E2 (1978)
An excellent adventure, which ideally involves equal ability in both members of the party. A lowish tide is advisable, as is a calm sea. The route passes through some damp areas of rock, but is graded accordingly. Start about ten metres left of the base of the Mordor abseil, and at the foot of a pinnacle.
1 12m. 4a. Go up left on big holes to a ledge and belay. (This can also be reached by abseil.)

North Stack with its long wall and Parliament House Cave.
Photo: Geoff Milburn

2 25m. 5a. From the left-hand side of the ledge descend for five metres and make a slightly descending traverse on small, but positive, holds to the foot of a black groove.
3 25m. 5b. Climb the groove, often damp, until an obvious rightwards traverse is reached. Follow this with ease, in a superb position, until it steepens, then pass the peg with difficulty to reach good holds on the front of the massive jammed chockstone, at the head of the cave. Pull out over this to a stance and belays.
4 20m. 4b. Ascend the right-hand wall for six metres then traverse right for six metres to an obvious crack up which the route finishes.

★★ **Arachnid** 30m E4 5c   (1988)
An excellent, strenuous, but well-protected, pitch at the lower limit of the grade, through the roofs ten metres right of 20,000 Leagues. Best reached by abseil. Climb the arête and steep crack system leftwards through the roofs to easier ground.

Variation. E4 6a/b. Finish up the crack out right from the deep crack.

Holyhead Revisited 35m E5 6a   (1988)
An interesting route which starts just right of 20,000 Leagues, below a steep groove. Climb the strange groove to gain a ledge on the left, below an obvious nose. Move up the wall on the left, step into a slabby groove, and follow this to a break where the difficulty eases and the groove can be followed to the top.

★★ **20,000 Leagues Under the Sea** 30m E4 6a   (1987)
This takes the prominent arête at the seaward end of the wall opposite North Stack Wall. Gain the start by traversing round from Parliament House Cave at low tide, tricky in places. Climb the groove and overhanging crack in the arête, to the left of the cave, to reach broken ground. Belay well back.

The Hitcher 30m Hard Very Severe 5a   (1988)
A pleasant route starting six metres left of the previous route, below an obvious crack. Climb the crack and groove onto the slabby wall, which leads via cracks to the top.

Oijee Wall 45m E1 5b   (1988)
Not a great route, but easier than it looks due to numerous hidden jugs. Start some 20 metres left of The Hitcher, at a high point on the traverse in from Parliament House Cave. Climb up to the large lump of odd rock, then go up rightwards on good holds through a bulge to follow a

slabby wall up to a large ledge. Carry on up a crack, right of a chossy corner, and belay well back.

The Walls of Jericho   73m   E1   (1988)
This follows the arête above the hard section on the traverse around from Parliament Cave. A good first pitch, followed by steep rubble. Abseil off after pitch 1 recommended.
1   28m. 5b. Climb the rib directly to a ledge.
2   45m. 4b. Deadly scrambling remains to gain the top.

Route 66   82m   Very Severe   (1967)
A girdle of the wall opposite North Stack Wall, essential for lovers of bird-covered rubble, but otherwise not recommended. Start by descending the short gully at the top of the buttress as for Mordor, then scramble down grass to the start of the traverse line.
1   30m. Traverse the ledge, over much guano, to belay in a large recess below a steep crack.
2   15m. Move down and follow a narrow ledge to where it peters out below an overhang. Carry on a few more moves then bear leftwards up the steep wall to belay in a grassy bay.
3   37m. The obvious diagonal break has some loose rock and leads to the top.

Point Blank   40m   Very Severe   (1967)
Takes the middle of the wall opposite North Stack Wall, hard for its grade. Descend as for Route 66 and follow the first pitch to the belay in the large recess. Abseil from this point to ledges and a belay at sea-level, or traverse around from Parliament House Cave at low water.
1   25m. 5a. Climb the crack up left to a flake then go up right to a good crack in a shallow groove. Climb this to a ledge and move right to the abseil point in the large recess.
2   15m. 4c. Go right, into the corner, and climb the crack to the top.

North Stack Promontory

Beyond The Flytrap area a big vegetated wall bears round to the right and forms the right-hand wall of Parliament House Cave. The left-hand wall emerges from the very bowels of the hillside to protrude a long way out, and at right-angles to the main cliff. This is North Stack Wall and it offers several brilliant, one-pitch routes on a blank-looking and just off-vertical wall, immediately below the North Stack Fog Warning Station. The cave is so named from the constant chatter of sea birds, said to resemble the House of Commons.

To enter the zawn, simply abseil 40 metres from the obvious telegraph pole, next to the white wall, down a short groove, onto a slab, and down the line of Birth Trauma. Alternatively, on the north side of the promontory, and at sea-level, is a tunnel which passes through the headland to emerge at the rear left-hand corner of Parliament House Cave. This second approach assumes the party will wish to swim or wade a few metres, however it does provide an emergency escape route. Several massive ring belays can be found on both sides of the white wall, but these are old and should be used with some consideration of their age.

PARLIAMENT HOUSE CAVE

The artificial grades for the Big Overhang routes are dependant on the amount of fixed gear in place at the time of an ascent. With less gear in-situ the routes will obviously become more difficult.

★ **Black Rod**   55m   A4   (1975)
Takes a line through the vast roof just right of centre. Some of the rock is dubious and needs careful handling. Start at a pedestal, to the right of the start of The Big Overhang.
1   18m. Climb the pedestal and wall to a hanging belay at the roof.
2   25m. Follow the obvious line across the roof to reach the lip and belay in a hanging corner.
3   12m. Go round the lip and up to an ice peg. Free-climb to the top.

★ **L'Affreuse**   58m   A4   (1982)
Another long and difficult aid route through the huge ceiling of the cave.
1   18m. As for Black Rod.
2   40m. Go straight up and across the roof to the obvious hanging slab midway out. Follow this to its end, over a bulge and gain an upside down groove. Continue for six metres to a possible hanging stance on the lip, and climb the wall rightwards to the top.

★★★ **The Big Overhang**   55m   A3   (1967)
An excellent expedition, full of character and excitement for those who are not used to swinging about on gear. Many pegs are usually in place but it does tend to vary. The rock could be better on the first ten metres or so, but the rest is not as bad. Long slings are needed to prevent rope drag. Start beneath a buttress in the back wall of the cave.

Parliament House Cave Area

GREG 87.

6

1   12m. Free-climb the buttress, via a crack, to a shattered stance beneath the roof.
2   43m. Aid up to the roof and follow two vague parallel cracks through the roof to the lip and a possible stance. Climb the final headwall to finish.

NORTH STACK WALL

This wall, along with Left Hand Red Wall, contains some of the most serious routes in this guidebook. Ability, and a steady head are invaluable assets, while 'red point' doggers need not apply.

The routes left of The Cad have starts that are affected by high tides. A potentially wet traverse can be made to some routes, or better, if you really must do the routes that day, is to take a hanging stance just above the sea from abseil; water wings optional.

Wall of Horrors   45m   E2   5b   (1970/1978)
This takes the wall left of the huge cave entrance, and is serious in the easier upper part. Start at the foot of the arête which comes down from the left side of the lip of the huge roof. Climb the arête rightwards and onto the face. Go up to a small ledge, peg, then move up into the yellowish groove above to a second peg. Step right and climb the wall until moves back left over the top of the groove lead to the large flake crack above, then go up the groove to exit left onto the upper slab. Ascend leftwards over this to a niche then move left on flakes and finish up a groove at the top, loose, as for The Whip.

Birth Trauma   43m   E6   6a   (1984)
A serious proposition due to poor, spaced protection and some dubious rock. Start six metres left of Wall of Horrors, a couple of metres left of a small cave. Go steeply up a short flake to a 'handrail'. Traverse right to a peg then follow the obvious thin crack up the wall, transferring to a second crack on the left, peg, and climb this to finish up an easy slab and wall.

The Whip   44m   E1   (1968)
The long groove to the left of Birth Trauma, friable and bold. Start on the sloping platform at the foot of the groove.
1   22m. 5a. Go up into the groove and climb it to a stance on the right.
2   22m. 5a. Continue up the groove, avoiding a block on the right, to the top. Poorly protected.

Headbutt   40m   E6   6a   (1986)
An uninspiring pitch on dubious rock. Start a couple of
metres left of The Whip. Climb up leftwards to a peg at ten
metres and pass this before stepping left after three metres.
Ascend the open scoop passing a poor peg to gain
progressively easier climbing up to a shattered roof. Climb
through this leftwards, dangerous, and finish on creaking
holds.

Tom's Shredded Slippers   40m   E4   6a   (1986)
Start beneath the slim groove just left of Headbutt. Climb
the groove and a thin crack, loose in places, to join
Headbutt. Move left into Green Gilbert and finish up this.

Green Gilbert   40m   E1   5a   (1970)
Start to the left of Headbutt, beneath a long flake crackline.
Poor protection, although perhaps not as bad a route as
previously suggested. Reach the crackline and climb it
straight to the top.

Art Groupie   40m   E6   6b   (1984)
A serious pitch between the grooves of Green Gilbert and
Blue Peter. Start a couple of metres down left from Green
Gilbert and below the right-hand side of a slanting
overhang. Climb up to the overhang and surmount this to a
peg in the wall above. Make a hard move up rightwards
from this to a line of small flakes trending very slightly
rightwards. Follow these to a hard move up left which leads
to the ledge just below the top of the groove of Blue Peter.
Finish up this.

★★ **Blue Peter**   40m   E4   5c   (1978)
A very good route, with only just sufficient protection,
taking the crack/groove line left of Green Gilbert. The pitch
is not technically hard but the gear is poorer than it looks
thus making quite a serious lead. Start as for Art Groupie.
Climb boldly up to, and make strenuous moves over, the
roof to a peg in the wall above (as for Art Groupie). Move
up left and make a few tricky moves left into the crackline,
which is followed, dubious protection, to a small ledge just
below the top. Finish up the short groove on the left.

Variation
Sarah Green   37m   E4   5c   (1983)
The obvious direct entry into the groove of Blue Peter
provides an excellent variation, although it is now the start
to other harder routes. Start directly beneath the groove.
Climb the groove to a junction with Blue Peter where it
comes in from the right. Finish up this.

North Stack Wall

CREZ 87.

★ **The Angle Man**   45m   E7   (1988)

A rising counter line to Stroke of the Fiend, taking in much fine, but little independent, climbing. Start as for Blue Peter.
1   25m. 6b. Follow Blue Peter then Wreath round onto the wall to traverse across past the peg on The Bells! (crux) to belay on the Cad's bolt (abseil rope back-up).
2   20m. 6b. Climb The Cad for a little way, before traversing left from the large foothold above the bolt. Climb up to a runner then traverse left, reversing the crux of The Long Run to finish up the obvious direct finish.

★★ **Flower of Evil**   37m   E7   6b   (1986)

A big serious pitch which takes the arête and wall left of Blue Peter. Start as for Sarah Green and climb it to a junction with Blue Peter. Ascend for a couple of metres, then undercut out leftwards onto the arête. Move up, then bear left, to reach the upper traverse on The Bells! at the right-facing blunt flake. Go straight up with difficulty, then slightly rightwards to a sloping ledge and the top. Gripping!

★★ **A Wreath of Deadly Nightshade**   40m   E7   6b   (1988)

A very sustained and bold pitch, a fine eliminate on this part of the wall. Start as for Sarah Green. Climb directly into the groove of Blue Peter, as for Sarah Green, then follow hanging flakes out left to move blindly, and with difficulty, around the arête and onto the edge of the wall. Climb straight up, left of the arête, to reach the small shield of The Bells! Finish straight up as for Flower of Evil.

★★★ **The Hollow Man**   43m   E7   6b   (1986)

This very direct line takes the strenuous Clown start as far as The Bells! then goes straight up through the line of this offering immaculate fingery climbing with virtually non-existent protection. There is no margin for error, so either a strong will to survive, or better still a blatant disregard for life, will prove helpful. Start left of Sarah Green beneath a left-facing flake crack with twin overhangs at eight metres. Climb the flake, moving left at its top, then reach right to a peg beneath the first roof, Friend. Surmount this to a standing position below the next roof, then pull out left onto the wall and move up to good holds at the end of the initial traverse of The Bells!. Move up to small holds (down right of the peg on The Bells), then go up left passing the peg and straight up to good incut holds in the quartz break. Pull up left to the base of a thin flake crack and climb this to final big holds rising rightwards to reach the sloping ledge just beneath the top. Climb the short back wall to the top. Congratulations.

★★ **The Clown**   45m   E7   6b   (1984)
Another fine, sustained and serious pitch taking a big
sweeping line across the face. The section leaving The Cad
is quite brilliant climbing. Start as for The Hollow Man, and
follow it, through the roofs and out onto the face, to reach
the good holds at the end of The Bells! traverse. Go left
along this, then up left to the undercut flake on The Cad,
Friends. Move out left onto the wall and make blind moves
up to undercuts beneath a small bulge, where a hard move
leads to a good hold and a standing place above. Go up
again to join The Long Run at its final traverse, follow this
over the final bulge, then head up left to the top.

★★ **The Bells! The Bells!**   45m   E7   6b   (1980)
An undeniably worrying pitch, taking a counter diagonal
line to The Clown, with extremely sparse and uninspiring
protection. Total commitment obligatory. A climb truly
ahead of its time, which along with its maker, has directly
inspired the creation of many more routes of this ilk. Start
about ten metres left of The Clown, beneath a faint cracked
groove leading on to the upper wall, below an obvious
undercut flake at half-height. Climb the crack at the start and
trend up right to a trio of spike runners at eight metres, one
above the other. From the middle spike make a long
traverse out right to good holds after six metres. Move up
to small holds on the right, then where it steepens climb up
leftwards to a protruding blade peg, poor. Go straight up for
about five metres to good incut holds in a quartz vein. Rock
up to the right and traverse right above the vein, past a
right-facing blunt flake and small shield to a comforting
ledge on the arête. Step right and climb the short groove to
the right-hand end of the sloping ledge just beneath the
top. Climb the short back wall to the top.

★★★ **The Cad**   37m   E6   6a   (1978)
An absolutely superb wall climb - one of the best in Wales.
Continuously interesting with a very serious and sustained
runout up the top wall. A good grade easier if the bolt is
clipped. A few thin slings will be found comforting on the
initial section. Start as for The Bells! and follow the crack at
the start, then go up the wall to a trio of spike runners. From
the top spike climb up and right to reach the undercut flake
(Friends). Step left then a series of trickier moves leads up
rightwards across the flake to a good standing place at a
bolt beneath the upper wall. Boldly go straight up passing a
break, (don't lunge!), to a ledge where easier climbing
above leads to the top.

Direct Start   E6   6b   (1988)
The crux moves at the flake can be gained directly by
starting a couple of metres left of the start of The Clown,

and climbing over the overlap with difficulty to gain the wall above and join the parent route.

★★ **The Long Run**   38m   E5   6a   (1979)
A fine counterpart to The Cad up the obvious streak between The Cad and South Sea Bubble. The seriousness of the route is well felt. Start as for The Cad, and follow it for about five metres then pull out left, and go up to the start of a thin flake crack in the wall. Climb this and the wall above to good holds where the wall steepens. Hand-traverse right for three metres and pull over the bulge on small holds, then head up left more easily for the top.

Variation
The Long Run Direct   35m   E6   6b   (1988)
This is a hard eliminate on the previous route. Start left of The Cad and climb up to the roof, pulling over it to join the original line. Follow this to the point where The Long Run moves right, and climb straight up to finish direct.

★ **Stroke of the Fiend**   40m   E7   (1986)
A sustained and serious girdle going from left to right across the face, with some superb delicate climbing. Start as for South Sea Bubble.
1   20m. 6b. As for South Sea Bubble for about five metres then go rightwards across the wall and up to The Cad flake. Pass this to a hanging stance on the bolt above; an abseil rope back-up would be prudent, if not essential.
2   20m. 6b. Traverse directly rightwards on a vague break, which is three metres beneath the upper traverse of The Bells! This leads to the arête of Flower of Evil, wire runners. Step down and reverse the traverse of Flower of Evil, descending slightly, to reach the sanctuary of Blue Peter. Finish up this.

★★ **South Sea Bubble**   35m   E3   5c   (1978)
A lovely route taking the fine flake crack to the left of The Cad. Start beneath the flake, and under a small overhang. Climb up to the overhang and boldly pull leftwards across this to gain the base of the flake. Follow this past a tricky couple of moves to a good ledge just short of the top. Move left and awkwardly climb the short wall to the top.

★ **The Demons of Bosch**   35m   E7   6b   (1984)
A very sustained, fingery and serious line taking the wall between the cracks of South Sea Bubble and Nice 'n Sleazy. Start between the crack, and beneath a small overhang at five metres. Go up to and over the overhang, then up the middle of the wall for eight metres. Pass a poor peg above, before embarking on a very sustained few metres, which

lead to an exit rightwards onto the sloping ledge, just below the top. Finish up leftwards easily.

Nice 'n Sleazy 35m E1 5a   (1978)
Very pleasant climbing up the crackline seven metres left of South Sea Bubble, a good introduction to the easier routes on this wall. Start beneath the crack. Start easily and continue as the crack steepens, past a move left to a good flake, to where the angle and difficulty ease to reach the top.

★★ **Talking Heads** 37m E2 5b   (1978)
Another good route which requires a fairly low tide to reach the start, a couple of metres left of Nice 'n Sleazy. Traverse left just above the lapping sea until directly beneath an obvious overhang high up. Climb the wall and then a crack to below the right-hand side of the overhang. Surmount this, awkward, and make a big bold stride left to reach the final crack. This has a few tricky moves, but the difficulty is short-lived.

Live at the Witch Trials 38m E6 6b   (1988)
A hard route, filling a gap between two older routes. Start as for Talking Heads. Step left and climb direct to the left side of the large roof above, cross this on undercuts, then climb straight up the wall, sustained and poorly protected, to reach a good break three metres from the top. Move right a metre or so and climb a short crack to the top.

★ **Not Fade Away** 40m E4 5c   (1978)
A sustained pitch, serious in places, up the wall left of Talking Heads. Start as for Talking Heads, tide allowing. Traverse left, just above the water, until below the top crack of Talking Heads. Climb the wall on the left for about eight metres then traverse left (not obvious) with difficulty, for three metres to reach the arête. (Big roofs down left of here.) Ascend steeply to a peg beneath the bulge above, move up left to a flake then bear up leftwards again before moving back up right to a flake crack. Climb this, moving rightwards to good footholds and finish direct up some cracks in the wall.

Penelope Undercling 35m E5 6b   (1987)
A direct approach to Not Fade Away, starting from the foot of the groove below the roofs to the left of that route, gained by traversing in, or by abseil. Climb the groove towards the roofs until desperate moves right and up, passing the remains of an RP, lead into Not Fade Away and finish up this.

Le Bon Sauveur   30m   E3   5c   (1984)
Start 12 metres left of Not Fade Away at a small ledge just
above sea-level at the base of a big roof-capped groove,
gained usually by abseil. Climb the obvious steep groove to
reach the roof, then traverse right three metres to surmount
the roof via a crack. Continue up this to the top.

Sincerely El Cohen   30m   E3   5c   (1986)
This takes the left-hand exit from the groove, starting as for
the previous route. Climb the groove, over the first roof,
then move diagonally left up the golden-coloured wall to
reach the arête. Finish up the hidden groove.

End Game   30m   Very Severe   4c   (1982)
Interesting, but a little contrived. Gain the start by abseil.
From sea-level on the slab around the corner, follow the
left- hand arête of the North Stack Wall as closely as
possible, past one steepish section to the top.

Tsunami Zawn

This unfashionable and quiet area, situated between North
Stack and Holyhead Quarries, features various short walls
and zawns along the coastline, which provide good short
climbs and problems. Tsunami Zawn is the largest of these
and is reached by taking the approach path along the top of
the cliffs then scrambling down the hillside, just west of a
small stone building, then descending the east side of this
zawn to sea-level. Care should be taken as a heath fire has
rendered the top soil very unstable. Some of the older
routes may well have been affected by rockfall as a number
of parties have failed to locate them. To the left of the
entrance to the zawn a slab contains some cracks. These
have been climbed at Severe and Very Difficult.

A Groove   23m   Very Severe   4c   (1967)
Climb the left-hand of two grooves at the entrance to the
zawn. The groove is climbed to the top.

Another Groove   25m   Hard Very Severe   5b   (1967)
A bold pitch up the right-hand groove. Start beneath the
groove. Climb up, peg, to the overlap. Go left to a ledge on
the arête and surmount the overlap, continuing to the top.

Tsunami   102m   E2   (5 pts. aid)   (1971)
A big route taking a left-to-right line from slabby grooves
right of Another Groove. Start at a rock pedestal beneath
the bulging wall right of Another Groove.

John Kingston on A Groove and Baz Ingle on Another Groove.
Photo: Ken Wilson

1 25m. 5a. Go right then up the groove, through overhangs, trending rightwards to the brown slabs. Ascend the slabs to a hanging belay left of an overhung corner.
2 18m. 4c. Enter the corner beneath the overhang and go up this to slabs on the right. Peg belay at a jumble of unstable blocks.
3 25m. 5a. Go rightwards towards the overhangs, step down under a sharp fang, then continue traversing, peg, to a hanging slab. Cross this then tension from a peg to reach a groove and peg belay.
4 34m. 5a. Use three pegs to climb the groove and move onto a ledge on the right. Use a peg to move right then make an ascending traverse and go up overhanging heather to belay higher up.

Charlie Don't Surf   30m   E2   5b   (1985)
Start right of Tsunami, below a crack. Climb up to and over the initial overhang, then take the obvious diagonal line across a groove to reach the edge of the slab, peg in pocket. Follow the edge/groove to good ledges and finish up rightwards.

Shell Shock   35m   Hard Very Severe   5b   (1978)
This takes the obvious crack at the left-hand side of the Amphibian slab, starting as for the previous route. Start just right of Tsunami, below a crack. Climb to the overhang at six metres, surmount this, and gain the upper crack. Climb this with less difficulty to the top of the slab and go up right to a block belay on the ridge.

Reptile   43m   Hard Very Severe   5a   (1978)
A direct route through overhangs right of The Amphibian Slab. Start below a thin crack, just left of The Amphibian. Climb the thin crack to the large roof then exit right around this to finish up the continuation crack in the slab.

The Amphibian   43m   Hard Very Severe   4c   (1968)
A serious climb up the brown slabs between grooves and roofs, in the back of the zawn. Start, at low tide, at blocks at the back of the zawn. Trend left across the slab to the overlap. Surmount this on the right then make moves back left and continue to the top.

Too Cold for Comfort   55m   Hard Very Severe (5 pts. aid)
                                                       (1971)
Start beneath a ledge at ten metres, in the back left-hand side of the zawn.
1 25m. 5b. Ascend the slabs for six metres then aid right on three pegs to a bottomless groove. Go up this with the aid of two more pegs to a hanging stance where the angle eases.

2 30m. 5a. Move up for a couple of moves, then go left under a fang of rock onto the slabs. Climb the thin central slab to easier ground and belay at some blocks.

Sue P. 82m E2 (1 pt. aid)   (1982)
A truly terrible route, loose and dirty, up the back of the zawn, included only as a warning to would-be explorers. Start at the back right-hand side of the zawn.
1 35m Climb the left-hand groove to the top, gain a ledge on the right, and climb a short wall to gain a grass field. Cross this diagonally rightwards to reach another field, and belay (poor) on a ridge at the top of this.
2 22m Climb up loose flakes, and use a peg (not in place) to gain a ramp which leads up right to a flake crack. Avoid this by a ledge traverse leftwards to the base of a groove.
3 25m Climb the groove a little way, then step onto the left arête and follow it to the top.

A number of routes have been climbed on the right-hand wall of the zawn, that is the wall opposite the entrance to the zawn on the left. This is gained either by traversing the zawn from the left, or by descending a broken area to the right of the climbs, and traversing back left. A low tide is recommended. A belay peg can be found on a boulder about ten metres back from the top of the routes.

Cracked Slab 28m Hard Very Severe 4c   (1987)
Start at a crack, left of the left-hand of three obvious clefts. This takes the crack, trending leftwards on a flaky crack, to finish onto poor rock at the top. The last section needs some care.

Chimney Climb 25m Very Severe 4c   (1987)
The left-hand of three obvious clefts.

Overlapped Groove 25m E1 5b   (1987)
This takes the crack directly on the right of the last route. Where the crack splits, high up, follow the right fork into a small groove, and finish up this.

Crackers 25m Very Severe 4c   (1987)
Left of the next cleft, a crack and groove system runs up the wall. Climb this trending rightwards to finish up vegetated blocks.

Sirplum 25m E2 5c   (1987)
Between the previous route, and the cleft, is an overhanging wall split by a crack. Climb this to finish near Crackers.

★ **Tidal Wave**   30m   E2   5b   (1987)
The chimney cleft is reminiscent of Ormuzd. Traverse out
from the back to finish up a steep groove. Scary but
atmospheric.

Cracked Up   25m   E1   5b   (1987)
Just right of the cleft, a crack runs up the wall to meet the
overhangs at the top of the chimney. Climb this to the
roofs, and move around right under the overlaps, until it is
possible to climb straight up.

The Crack   21m   Very Severe   (1987)
A crackline running up the wall some five metres left of the
right-hand cleft.

★ **The Groove**   21m   Very Severe   (1987)
This takes the slanting groove, just left of the right-hand
cleft.

The Chimney   21m   Severe   (1987)
The right-hand chimney cleft.

South Stack

This is the collective name given to a number of wonderful cliffs which overlook the South Stack Lighthouse. It must be said that some of the routes are a little friable, but this is amply compensated for by the majesty of these huge colourful walls. The protection is often not as good as on The Main Cliff, but the technical standard is often lower, and having possession of a good stomach is one's best ally.

The friable rock devotee is almost in paradise here, but for the less wild, Castell Helen provides solid, good quality, climbs. The positions are often the outstanding feature of these climbs: strange and magical, they are often 'space walking'. Access is in most cases by abseil. This is quick and has the advantage of finishing near the car and cafe: often a deciding factor when the weather is less clement in other areas.

South Stack Island is the most obvious landmark, with the lighthouse: feature of a thousand post-cards. Overlooked by the steps down to the bridge, is Mousetrap Zawn, a large deeply seamed wall, bounded on its right by a steep spur. Right of this lie the huge expanses of Left Hand Red Wall, and beyond the next spur, Red Wall itself. A broken wall bounds the zawn, and around it lies the connected crags of Castell Helen and Yellow Wall. Dropping straight into the sea, Castell Helen is well marked by Ellin's Tower, now an RSPB Visitors Centre. Yellow Wall is not easily viewed from anywhere but along the cliff top path, and above Penlas Rock, a prominent rocky island. Smurf Zawn is farther along the cliff towards Abraham's Bosom, the bay below the road junction leading to South Stack.

It should be noted that many of the cliffs here are subject to a voluntary access ban, as described in the Access notes. Please ensure that this ban is observed. All affected climbs are noted with an (R) symbol.

South Stack Island Area

An isolated climb exists in the huge gully that descends to the sea, just beyong the last radio station, on the way to The Upper Tier. About 60 metres above the sea is a huge cave in the gully wall. **FEU 123 ELF**, 50 metres XS (1987), takes the gully wall, via the cave, onto the hillside above, and has little merit, other than for the lover of vertical vegetation and scree.

SKULL ZAWN

This small zawn lies some 500 metres from the bridge onto South Stack Island, and from the island it can be seen some way beyond Thunderbird Zawn. The area is gained by descending the hillside to gain easy slabs, Skull Zawn being found at the left-hand side (facing out) of these.

Sea Witch   30m   E6   6a   (1989)
An intriguing, but scary, route on typical South Stack rock. Start at the left-hand side of the sea-cave, and below a corner. Climb the loose corner to a peg, and make moves rightwards to another peg. Hollow flakes then lead to a pair of pegs, before hard moves up and right gain a short slab. Leave this by following the obvious Red Wall-like corrugations to the top. A good range of Friends is advisable.

THUNDERBIRD ZAWN

The main feature of this zawn is a large slabby sea arch, which marks the descent to the routes. It lies about 200 metres from the bridge, and it can only be viewed from South Stack Island, and even then not that well. An abseil, from blocks, can be made down the outside of the arch, to sea-level. From here a leftwards traverse, of about 40 metres, gains the area of the two climbs.

Thunderbird   37m   E4   (1987)
Start on the long quartz ledge, at the left-hand end of the slab, under the overhangs.
1   14m. 6a. Climb the obvious groove and step across the void onto a wall. Move left, peg, under the roofs, then step down around the arête, and move across to the bottom of a short groove. Climb this, moving left to a block belay.
2   23m. 5c. Climb rightwards along a quartzy gangway, under a roof, peg, and move round into a groove. Follow this to a small roof, step right onto the overlap and finish up an arête.

Sting Ray   48m   E5   (1988)
Another difficult route in this esoteric spot. Start a little down and left of the previous route.
1   15m. 6a. Climb onto a downward pointing fin in the overhang, then climb a stiff crack, until it is possible to step left to a foothold, spike belay.
2   18m. 5c. Move left onto the good hold again, then go left again onto the undercut wall. Climb up the arête for five metres, move down right, then go around and up, to a block belay, as for Thunderbird.

3 15m. 6b. Move left and go up to a groove. Climb this with desperate moves. Much scrambling gains the top.

SOUTH STACK ISLAND (Right part of)

The first route lies on the South Face, and is reached by abseiling from eyebolts near the lighthouse.

Steerpike 46m Hard Very Severe (R)   (1973)
Steep and exciting. Start below the obvious groove, in the middle of the face.
1 23m. 5a. Climb the groove to the overlap, and traverse three metres right, then move up and go back left into the groove. Climb the wall on the right to a stance.
2 23m. 5a. Go back left, and then ascend a steep groove on worsening rock.

Another route, **Arnold Seafood** E2, 5c, 5c, (1987), lies on the other side of the island. Go over the bridge, and rightwards into a zawn. Go through the tunnel (5c), and into the squeeze chimney, to exit on the other side (north) of the island on a slab. The route takes a thin crack, past two overlaps. It may well be possible to approach the route by abseil from the top.

Take the same approach to gain **The Pipes, The Pipes** 28 metres XS (1987), a serious and unrecommendable item. Upon emerging from the tunnel, a pipe can be seen exiting from a concrete groove. Climb the wall, three metres to its right, and go diagonally up to a bracket, and finish on appalling rock.

Mousetrap Zawn   (R)

On some routes, the rock leaves a little to be desired, but the intricate shapes and convolutions lend something extra to the climbing, especially to the aptly-named Mousetrap.

The easiest way of getting to grips with the delights are via the Lighthouse Steps. A hole in the wall on the left-hand side is soon reached, and a scramble down ledges gains the bottom of the zawn. Alternatively, opposite the steps and reached easily from the road, is an abseil anchor shared with Left Hand Red Wall, on the arête overlooking the zawn. One abseil gains a muddy slope, so two rope lengths may be preferred to reach the bottom of the zawn. The latter descent is better, when the tide is high, for reaching routes on the right-hand side of the zawn.

Mousetrap Zawn
Photo: Geoff Milburn

The first climbs are reached by scrambling under a wall on the left, from the lighthouse steps. This has been climbed on, but is left for the connoisseur to rediscover. The central crack is Hard Very Severe.

To the right is a beautiful high golden wall.

★★ **Hysteresis**   89m   E3   (R)   (1973)
Two brilliant pitches, but the route is unfortunately prone to some seepage. Strenuous and sustained. Start in the middle of the wall, at a ledge about six metres above the sea.
1   37m. 5c. Climb easily up the wall for six metres and go over a slight bulge to a reddish band. Go through this to a horizontal break, then climb rightwards until the higher break can be gained. Move back left to a crack in the roof, poor peg. Fluster over the roof and quickly layback up to a good ledge and belay.
2   37m. 5c. Slightly harder climbing now gains the large obvious niche. First go up and right, then back left until a difficult move gains the sentry-box. If attacked farther left, even harder moves are involved, but the climbing is still worthwhile. Continue up the wall, and go slightly left to a peg belay in a chimney.
3   15m. 4c. Climb the unprotected arête to belays well back.

★★ **Primate**   96m   E2   (R)   (1967)
Steep climbing with not much protection, followed by easier climbing, but all in a fine position. Start as for Hysteresis, at the ledge in the middle of the wall.
1   34m. 5b. Climb to the arête, up a short wall to reach a ledge, then swing around the arête into an overhanging groove, and ascend this to a peg. Make some blind moves left around the arête, easing quickly once on the front face, and go up to a small ledge. Climb a groove for five metres to belay on a pinnacle.
2   25m. 4c. Go up the obvious weakness to the ledge on the right side of the arête, then climb the wall three metres right of the arête.
3   37m. 4c. Climb straight to the top on the left-hand side of the arête.

★★ **Rosebud**   21m   E5   6a   (R)   (1986)
A juggy wall, overhanging eight metres, provides good sport, and is useful as a direct start to Primate. Start at sea-level beneath a gigantic chockstone. Climb the left-hand side of the chockstone, and move onto the steep wall on the left, a peculiar move, bringing large holds and two peg runners within reach.

Primevil 92m Hard Very Severe (R)   (1966)
An exciting but unpopular route, due to poor rock. Start at
the right-hand end of the overhangs in the corner of the
zawn.
1 30m. 4c. Climb the slab at its easiest point to a groove
on the left of the huge Green Slab. Go up the broken
groove to belay below a small roof.
2 25m. 4c. Climb the groove, and go up easier rock until a
small stance is reached.
3 25m. 4c. Climb the groove until it eases, and curves
right.
4 12m. 4c. Go over the roof on the left, and finish easily up
a groove.

★★ **The Green Slab** 106m Very Severe (R)   (1966)
A poor man's Mousetrap which provides good open
climbing, but it should not be approached carelessly. Start
to the right of Primevil, below a large groove defining the
lower right-hand part of the slab.
1 23m. 4b. Climb the left wall of the groove, trending left
to an obvious break on the arête. Thread belay just left of
the arête.
2 23m. 4b. Climb the crack above diagonally left into the
corner, and go up to belay, as for Primevil, below a small
roof.
3 30m. 4b. Move onto the slab, and take the easiest line
up and right to a small stance.
4 30m. 4b. Climb the short wall above into the long
diagonal breach, then follow this leftwards to the top, with
an uncommon amount of exposure.

★ **Helmet Boiler** 100m E5 (R)   (1984)
An impressive hostile line with some good climbing. Start
six metres to the left of Mousetrap, at the foot of a groove
leading to an overhang at 12 metres.
1 25m. 4b. Ascend to a ledge level with an overhang on
the left, and climb under this to a groove. Follow this to a
poor belay where it steepens and becomes difficult.
2 30m. 5c. Climb the right-hand wall above, trending to
the arête which is followed to large overhangs, peg.
Traverse right for five metres to a welcome ledge. Climb the
wall above trending right, peg, until a traverse line beneath
overhangs leads leftwards via a flake edge to the right-hand
side of the Green Slab.
3 30m. 4b. Follow the edge of the slab.
4 15m. 5a. Surmount a bulge, and go up over another
bulge in a groove.

Joe Brown on the 1st ascent of Mousetrap.
Photo: Ken Wilson

Mousetrap Zawn –
South Stack

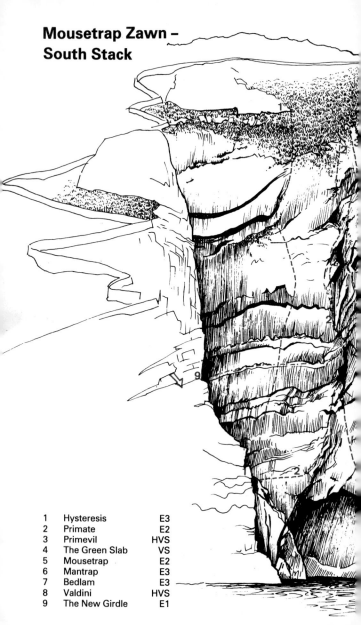

1	Hysteresis	E3
2	Primate	E2
3	Primevil	HVS
4	The Green Slab	VS
5	Mousetrap	E2
6	Mantrap	E3
7	Bedlam	E3
8	Valdini	HVS
9	The New Girdle	E1

GREG 87.

★★★ **Mousetrap**   128m   E2   (R)   (1966)
A definite must, easy for the grade and nowhere technical,
but very imposing. Care is needed to protect both leader
and second alike, on a climb where superlatives are
superfluous. Start just left of a large cave by a pillar, which
is left of a huge grey groove.
1 45m. 5b. Climb to the top of the pillar, by a groove on its
left, to the remains of a peg and a reasonable runner. Move
down and right to the start of the corrugated flutings. Enter
the chimney and pull out of it immediately, with a long
reach to a rib on the right. One can continue up the
chimney, but this is harder. Go up the rib and into the next
chimney. Move right into another chimney, which is
climbed to easier rocks and a slab. This easy slab is crossed
rightwards to belay on a good ledge.
2 46m. 5a. Climb up and right, a bit mystifying at first, to a
poor peg in a slanting groove. Go up a couple of metres
and around into a groove and gain a break. Climb the easy
slab on the left, peg, in a fine position, to a belay at the top
of the slab.
3 37m. 5a. Step right out of the niche above, to climb the
red wall, with a difficult move to gain a groove. Go more
easily now to the top.

Death Trap   78m   E5   (R)   (1982)
A poor and lethal start leads to an excellent, but dangerous,
slanting chimney. If started up Mousetrap the route gives a
good outing. Start at the right-hand side of the zawn,
almost level with the big stance on Mousetrap. Warthog
pegs are recommended equipment for pitch 1!
1 14m. 5b. Climb up leftwards for six metres to a grass
ledge, and from its left end move up left, until it is possible
to make a slightly descending traverse to belay, as for
Mousetrap.
2 12m. 4a. Move easily across the big slab, step round an
arête, and go up for five metres to a poor belay.
3 40m. 5b. Go out right to the left edge of the slanting
groove on the right, and bridge up this to a niche below
overhangs. Gain the chimney on the right, which leads to
the top of the slab on Mousetrap.
4 12m. 5a. Surmount the bulge above the stance, followed
by a groove with a bulge, to reach easy ground.

Variation
Death Trap Direct   E6   (R)   (1988)
2a 45m. 5c. A very strenuous and serious item. From the
stance of Mousetrap, climb directly up the obvious
overhanging faultline, to join the original groove/faultline on
pitch 3. Follow this.

★ **Mantrap** 103m E3 (R)   (1969)
A poor start leads to a good upper half. Again it is better to start up Mousetrap. Start on the right-hand side of the zawn at the base of the diagonal break, just right of the overhanging wall.
1 40m. 4c. Climb the right side of the break until it is possible to move left over a bulge. Go left past a peg, then up right to a poor ledge, below a steep section. Climb up, then go left to a ledge, and move up and right to a ledge and belays.
2 10m. Traverse left and go up to a belay on a sloping ledge.
3 28m. 5b. From the left-hand end of the ledge, climb diagonally left up the steep wall to an overhang. Pull over this, and climb up the overhanging chimney to reach the red wall above. Traverse right until it is possible to climb straight up, then move right to a stance.
4 25m. 5b. Traverse right for three metres, go left over an overhang, then diagonally right and straight up to finish.

★★ **Another Roadside Attraction** 58m E5 (R)   (1980)
A fine route with an excellent, but tiring, main pitch. Start up Mantrap, or more sensibly up Mousetrap. A downward traverse right for ten metres from Mantrap leads to a large ledge.
1 37m. 6b. Go rightwards and up to reach a rounded ledge below a shallow crack. Step left and climb up to a high peg below a slanting overlap. Move left to gain a left-facing corner, then ascend this, peg, to below a peg on the lip of an overhang. Pass this on a crumbly finger jam, to gain a smooth wall, where hard moves up another wall lead to a stance, on Mousetrap.
2 21m. 5b. Climb above the belay for three metres, then move left to a right-facing corner. Ascend this and the wall above.

Bedlam 83m E3 (R)   (1966)
The first pitch is very poor, but the last pitches are good and bold. The Mousetrap start is to be prefered on this aptly- named route. Start right of the cave, at a ledge in a wet groove, 15 metres above the sea.
1 37m. 4c. Make a descending traverse across an overhanging wall to a short groove. Traverse left into the break, which defines the right side of a tower, and make a long step left to a ledge. Move left into a groove which leads to block belays.
2 23m. 5b. Climb to the downward pointing overhang, then traverse right across the red wall to a shallow niche and peg. Go rightwards to grey rock on the edge of a pillar, and climb a shallow chimney, peg, to belays below a curving crack.

3   23m. 5a. Ascend the crack for a couple of metres, then step right and climb the steep broken groove.

Valdini   61m   Hard Very Severe   (R)   (1969)
A loose route up the obvious chimney in the corner to the right of Bedlam. Often wet, with poor protection. Start as for Bedlam, on the ledge in the wet groove.
1   40m. 5a. Climb the chimney to a grass ledge and peg belay.
2   21m. 4b. Take the continuation chimney to the top.

Locarno   34m   E1   (R)   (1969)
Serious, dirty and often wet, starting ten metres right of Valdini, by some blocks.
1   14m. 4c. Climb the wall on the right for three metres, then follow a slab leftwards to reach a large sloping ledge.
2   20m. 5b. Descend slightly right, and make a rising traverse rightwards under an overlap, into a groove. Climb this to exit left, with difficulty, by an overhang.

★ **The Original Girdle**   165m   E2   (R)   (1968)
An interesting bit of traversing, above big drops, and in fine territory. Start as for Hysteresis.
1   40m. 5a. Climb the grassy corner, to the left of the Hysteresis wall, to an obvious break about 15 metres up. Go along this to the right-hand arête, and then ascend a short groove to belay on a pinnacle.
2   43m. 4c. Traverse around the corner, and across to the Green Slab. Climb this diagonally rightwards to peg belays below a little wall.
3   8m. Traverse diagonally right to the top of the easy slab of Mousetrap, and descend a couple of metres to belay.
4   28m. 4a. Descend the slab to the top of a groove, peg, then traverse right, across the red wall, to the block stance of Bedlam, below a pointed overhang.
5   23m. 5b. As for Bedlam, pitch 2.
6   23m. 5a. As for Bedlam, pitch 3.

★ **The New Girdle**   155m   E1   (R)   (1971)
Easier than the old girdle, but just as good, starting as for Hysteresis.
1   45m. 4c. Climb the groove, but take a higher horizontal break across to a ledge, and continue across to the arête, to belay as for Primate.
2   37m. 4c. Climb the crack above for a couple of metres, then go around the arête to a break. Traverse this to a groove, which is climbed for 15 metres, then move across onto the edge of the Green Slab. Poor peg belay.
3   28m. 4a. Climb diagonally right across the slab to the belay of Mousetrap.

4   45m. 5b. Descend the slab for a little way, then climb up right to a ledge in a chimney. Move across the red wall, and traverse right to make a difficult move into Bedlam. Continue right for three metres, then climb up to a peg belay. Scramble up right to finish.

Left Hand Red Wall   (R)

This superb orange wall gives open climbing of a serious, and often precarious nature. None of the routes should be treated without respect, the situation contributing its fair share of intimidation.

To gain the first few routes, abseil down an arête at the left-hand end of Left Hand Red Wall, as for Mousetrap Zawn. An obvious grassy ramp can be descended to gain the routes.

Vena Cava   21m   Very Severe   4c   (R)
Really only an escape, but pleasant all the same. Start left of the arête. Follow the left-hand side of the arête, then step left to finish up a slight corner.

Auricle   109m   Hard Very Severe   (R)   (1967)
An ambling journey, begun by descending the grassy ramp under Left Hand Red Wall, until 12 metres above the sea.
1   43m. 4c. Descend a slab and mantelshelf across an overhang. Continue the traverse to belay in the corner.
2   21m. 4c. Climb the corner to a good ledge.
3   15m. 4c. Traverse right into an obvious break, and climb this to reach the grassy ramp.
4   30m. 4c. Climb the obvious break a couple of metres right of the arête to a bulge. Go over this and continue to the top.

Variation
Alternative Finish   E1   (R)   (1970)
4a   30m. 5a. Start as for the last pitch of Auricle, and climb up to the bulge. Move right to a slight and broken groove. Climb this, and the steep loose corner, to the top.

Ceefax   55m   Hard Very Severe   (R)   (1986)
Start near Auricle at an obvious rift.
1   25m. 4c. Step onto a ramp, go up this and a wall above to a corner. Traverse left into a groove to belay.
2   30m. 4c. Step left and go up a white stain, then ascend straight up on worsening rock to the ramp below the upper wall.

Left Hand Red Wall and Red Wall.
Photo: Geoff Milburn

Alligator 40m E1 5b (R)   (1978)
Fairly serious, and a good introduction to this type of
climbing, starting at the foot of a prominent crack, at the top
of the grassy ramp, about halfway between the top pitch of
Auricle, and Left Hand Red Wall. Climb the corner, poor
peg, to a ledge below an overlap. Move left, ascend a
shallow groove past a peg, and trend slightly right on large
loose holds to a deep break. Finish up the difficult crack,
three metres right of the Auricle Alternative Finish.

★★ **Cannibal** 43m E4 5c (R)   (1978)
Sparse protection on this good wall climb makes it a real
frightener. Start as for Alligator. From the corner, a low
traverse out right past a peg just above an overhang is
scary enough, but the loose groove which is climbed, and
exited leftwards, provides a real shock. A good peg
protects the solid wall to the deep slot. Above some big
crisp bubble pockets lead satisfyingly to a left-facing corner
to finish.

Variation
Cannibal Direct 10m E5 6a (R)   (1986)
Go over the roof to regain the parent route.

★★ **Schittlegruber** 56m E6 (R)   (1986)
A very fine top pitch. Start eight metres up left from
Left-Hand Red Wall, at a vegetated groove.
1 28m. 5c. Climb the vegetated groove to join Left-Hand
Red Wall at the small roof. Swing immediately left to a
hollow flake, climb this, and the wall above, until level with
the Left-Hand Red Wall belay. Traverse right to belay.
2 28m. 6b. Go diagonally up left to an overlap, and climb
strenuously on good rock to a ledge on the left, below a
huge groove. Ascend the groove, in a wild position, to
swing right at its end. Finish up the hairy wall.

★ **Left-Hand Red Wall** 62m E3 (R)   (1967)
Two good pitches, the first being loose, and perhaps harder
than the top one. Start about halfway down the ramp,
below a shallow groove.
1 25m. 5c. Ascend the groove on the left, to the roof, then
go right onto a slab, and move into a shallow rounded
groove. A hard section leads to a ledge and peg belays.
2 37m. 5c. Step right and climb a flake crack to a small
ledge. Traverse right, peg, into a shallow niche, climb a
diagonal crack above, then go straight up the wall to the
top.

Mein Kampf 46m E5 (R)   (1979)
A fierce and intimidating route. Start as for Left Hand Red
Wall.

1 23m. 5c. Climb up, as for Left Hand Red Wall, until a foot-traverse, on a flake about five metres up, leads rightwards into a depression of white rock. Move right into a groove, and climb it to a peg. Step left onto the belay of Left Hand Red Wall.
2 23m. 6a. Climb a flake crack, and move left onto a small ledge. Go up and over a small overlap, peg, then climb left and go up on layaways. A roller on the rock-over above the overhang is to be avoided.

Variation
Mein Kampf Direct   10m   E5   (R)   (1986)
2a 10m. 6a. Start pitch 2, and go directly up the wall to join the original route. Scary and on dangerous rock.

★★★ **Heart of Gold**   55m   E5   (R)   (1978)
An excellent wall climb taking the middle of the wall, by strenuous climbing on the first pitch, and elegant and varied climbing on the second. Start as for Left Hand Red Wall.
1 17m. 5c. Go up the groove for a couple of metres, and traverse right across the bulging wall to a good resting niche. Above a diagonal crack leads rightwards to a poor hanging belay.
2 38m. 6a. Climb up to the overlap, peg. Go up the wall above for three metres and make a precarious traverse right to a shallow groove. Ascend this until it disappears, necessitating a move left to a good spike. Follow a diagonal crack rightwards to a niche, where a steep move leads to Left Hand Red Wall at the steep crack on pitch 2. Finish up this route.

Variation
★★★ **Heart of Gold Direct**   10m   E6   (R)   (1986)
2a 10m. 6a. From the stance, ascend directly, missing out the traverse to the shallow groove.

★ **The Super Calabrese**   80m   E8   (R)   (1987)
A wild eliminate line, with very technical climbing, and minimal protection. A totally committing undertaking. Start as for Heart of Gold.
1 25m. 6b. Make a crumbly traverse right to a peg, and go up through the roof, before continuing to the belay, on Heart of Gold.
2 12m. 6b. An increasingly hard traverse right, along a seam, leads to the dreaded Enchanted Broccoli Garden belay.
3 43m. 6b. The Astro Turf Pitch. Move left from the belay, and go up a shallow groove. Exit from this, crux, and climb directly up the wall on tiny pockets. Take the hanging scoop on the right, and leave it leftwards to wander up rubble to the top.

★★★ **The Enchanted Broccoli Garden** 86m E7 (R) (1986)
Excellent wall climbing, but possible death for both members of the party should the leader muff pitch 2. Only survivors will confirm the star quality of the route. Start from a block belay, about ten metres above Pagan.
1 43m. 6b. Step onto the wall, and make a hard traverse right onto a pinnacle. Climb up on bubbly rock to a hinged block, and pull round the roof onto a porcelain-like slab. Delicate moves lead right to a slanting crack, which is climbed for five metres, before going up to an extremely inadequate belay on one poor peg.
2 43m. 6b. Climb rightwards to a foot-ledge, then go up to a thin crack. Ascend straight up to a ledge and spike. Carefully climb up the bouldery wall to a lichenous section, which is followed by a relatively relaxed groove to the top.

★★★ **Pagan** 92m E4 (R) (1973)
A series of serious pitches make this one of the best wall climbs at Gogarth. Start about 25 metres above the sea.
1 21m. 5b. Move right along the obvious traverse line, and go up to an obvious dusty chimney. Ascend to an overhang, RURP, and escape by faith up the steep wall on the right to an excellent hanging belay on decaying bolts.
2 28m. 5c. Climb up for three metres on dubious holds, until moves can be made leftwards along a break. Arrange good gear here, before moving up the wall strenuously, slightly right then slightly left, to reach another worrying hanging belay on a block, by a swing left.
3 43m. 5c. Move right along the flake until it stops. Climb a depression rightwards to a sloping ledge, which leads back left for a little way, before another depression leads up the smooth wall to a deep slot. A step left, then right, gains a vague groove leading to safety.

★★ **Deygo** 102m E3 (R) (1968/1973)
As good an outing as any on the cliff, but it is fairly serious, and has its share of strenuous climbing. Start as for Pagan.
1 21m. 5b. As for Pagan, pitch 1.
2 21m. 5c. Ascend for five metres, then go up and left to a peg. Go up the crack to a square-cut ledge, then traverse right to a peg in a groove. Climb a groove on the right to a small stance on the left.
3 30m. 5b. Climb up steeply for three metres to a peg, where the angle eases slightly. A further peg arrives five metres higher, then go up the crack again for five metres to another peg. Move right across the wall to a small ledge. Cowboys may be able to protect this by lassoing a metal horn above. From the ledge, peg, climb diagonally to a crack which is followed to a belay on a sloping ramp, Red Wall Escape Route.

Left-Hand Red Wall

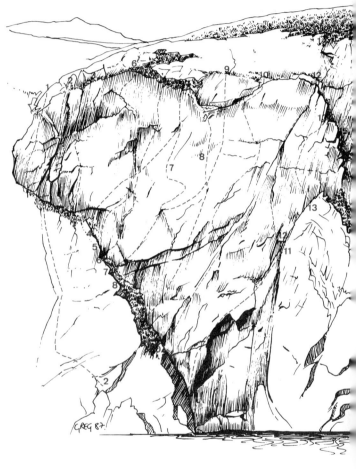

1	Alligator	E1	8	The Super Calabrese	E8
2	Auricle	HVS	9	The Enchanted	
3	Cannibal	E4		Broccoli Garden	E7
4	Schittlegruber	E6	10	Pagan	E4
5	Left-Hand Red Wall	E3	11	Come to Mother	E7
6	Mein Kampf	E5	12	Infidel	E3
7	Heart of Gold	E5	13	Anarchist	E1

Red Wall

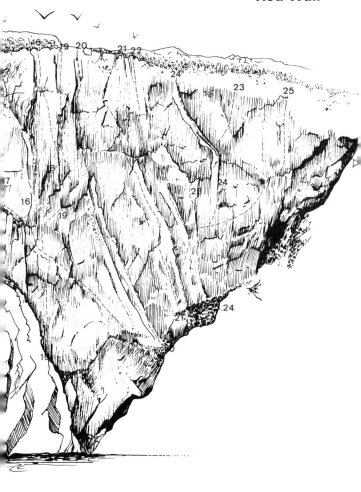

14	Red Wall Escape Rt.	VS	20	Wendigo	E3
15	The Cree	E3	21	Red Haze	E4
16	Television Route	E4	22	Red Wall	E2
17	The Electrification of the Soviet Union	E4	23	A Brown Study	E3
18	Khmer Rouge	E5	24	Communication Breakdown	E3
19	Redshift	E3	25	Dopplegangen	E3

4 30m. 4c. Climb the ramp and slab to the top, as for Red Wall Escape Route.

Salem 83m E5 (R)   (1987)
A nice eliminate, filling a gap on the wall, starting as for Deygo.
1 21m. 5b. As for Deygo, pitch 1.
2 28m. 5c. Follow Deygo for ten metres to a niche, and break out left on a handrail. Go up a pleasant wall to a short left-facing groove. Ascend this, then step left to belay on spikes, on Pagan.
3 34m. 6b. Go right and up Pagan for five metres, then climb direct, on good rock, until a move right, and a hard move up gains a ledge, hidden peg. Make a difficult move into the short hanging groove above, and follow it to finish.

Come to Mother 55m E7 (R)   (1986)
Something of a horror, in fact the large block forming the crack and belay now resides at the bottom of the zawn. This is the original description, and the route has not had a re-ascent at the time of writing. Start at the bottom of the zawn, (approach as for Heathen etc.) at the gigantic groove, left of the newly arrived large block.
1 30m. 6a. Work out left to the arête, and a big block, then climb up on quartz to a dirty roof. Go over this to a hand crack, and belay some way up this on large nuts.
2 25m. 6a. Traverse right on pockets, then continue less securely on a slightly descending traverse to the grassy promontory, and safety.

The following routes are gained by abseiling from stacked blocks, above a short slab, to gain the grassy promontory between Left Hand Red Wall and Red Wall. If a spare rope is not used, care should be taken to ensure that the ropes pull through.

★ **Infidel** 80m E3 (R)   (1978)
A steep route, on large holds, with a good feel about it. Start from the bottom of the abseil, and descend grass to where it gets frightening, ten metres above where the ramp drops away.
1 25m. 5b. Climb diagonally right, on poor rock, and move up to two pegs. Go up and left to large holds, and follow them to the obvious groove slightly on the right. Follow this to a belay at its top.
2 40m. 5c. Step left onto Deygo, peg, and follow it to the metal horn. A traverse leads right, and then back left at a higher level, to regain the diagonal crackline. A steep groove is climbed to belay on Red Wall Escape route.
3 15m. 4c. Finish up Red Wall Escape Route.

Variation
★★ Infidel Direct 30m E4 (R) (1978)
2a 30m. 5c. As for pitch 2, but avoid the traverses by climbing straight up. More strenuous, and with a bit more bite.

Outside the Asylum 40m E5 6a (R) (1988)
Another hard eliminate with at least some protection, starting at a pinnacle on the ramp, between Infidel and Anarchist. Climb carefully onto the pinnacle, and step left to a ledge. Move up and left around a steep rib, past a slot, and go up to a peg. Climb the wall direct for ten metres to a small ledge. Go rightwards to join Anarchist at the detached flake. Follow this to finish.

★ Anarchist 58m E1 (R) (1978)
Slight, but worth doing for the situation and views. Start from the promontory, at the base of the abseil.
1 37m. 5b. Traverse left to a series of grooves, and go up to a detached flake, peg. Climb the diagonal line, past a second peg, to join Deygo. Go up right, peg, to a crack, and climb it to belay on the ramp of Red Wall Escape Route.
2 21m. 4c. Finish up Red Wall Escape Route.

Variation Finish 50m E2 5c (R) (1987)
Follow Anarchist until it is possible to traverse across to the lasso peg on Deygo. Climb Deygo for five metres, then follow a traverse line left to ledges farther left. Climb the pillar to belay as the rope runs out!

★★ The Missionary 92m E4 (R) (1978)
A pilgrimage well worth the tribulations of crossing all of Left Hand Red Wall. Start as for Anarchist.
1 34m. 5c. Follow Anarchist to a horizontal crack, which leads to the stance of Pagan.
2 28m. 5c. Descend the layback flake on Pagan, then go right to a protruding ledge, level with the stance. A diagonal descent leftwards leads to a shallow groove on Heart of Gold. Climb this to a spike, step down left, and continue traversing to gain the stance of Left Hand Red Wall.
3 30m. 5b. Step down from the stance, and move left onto poor rock. Continue leftwards descending slightly until it is possible to cross a rib, and move up to a ledge line. Follow this, then step down and continue the traverse, passing large spikes, to finish on the arête.

The Girdle Traverse 130m E3 (2 pts. aid) (R) (1969)
An exciting rope move, and some hard climbing, make this a good outing. Start as for Vena Cava.

1 25m. 4c. Climb up the left-hand side of the arête to a block, and traverse right to a belay in a horizontal slot, at its left-hand end.
2 25m. 4c. Move along the slot, and continue traversing, until an abseil, from a small ledge, leads, with some manoeuvering, to the ledge belay of Left Hand Red Wall.
3 43m. 5c. Follow Left Hand Red Wall to the foot of the final broken wall. Traverse right for three metres and drop into a slot, and traverse across this to a large spike at its end.
4 37m. 5b. Descend the right side of the flakes, and traverse down rightwards to a small ledge. Move right for a couple of metres, and from a peg at foot level abseil down to a small ledge, peg, below the lasso peg on Deygo. Finish up this.

The next few climbs lie on the left wall of the sea-level buttress, beneath the promontory dividing Left Hand Red Wall from Red Wall. At low tide, the descent to Red Wall may be used, or an abseil can be made from blocks on the promontory down into the zawn beneath Left Hand Red Wall.

Puritan 51m Very Severe (R)   (1977)
Start at the foot of the chimney, opposite Come to Mother, and beneath Deygo.
1 30m. 4c. Climb the chimney, which is both dark and wet.
2 21m. Scramble up grass to the ridge.

Atheist 55m E4 (R)   (1977)
A good pitch, technical and strenuous, marred only by some poor rock at the overhang, taking the groove, left of Heathen.
1 37m. 6a. Climb the difficult groove to the overhang, cross this, and step right around the next overhang. Go up easier ground to belay on the slab.
2 18m. Scramble up grass to finish.

Three Men and a Cake 48m E4 (R)   (1988)
1 18m. 5b. The arête right of the previous route is climbed to a nut belay.
2 30m. 5c. Carry on up the arête, then move right to an area of grey rock, and go up this to a roof. Go back left onto the arête, on poor rock, and finish up a grassy slab, to poor belays.

Heathen 67m E1 (R)   (1977)
The obvious main groove gives a fairly good climb.
1 12m. Climb the groove to a ledge.
2 37m. 5b. The groove is climbed to a belay on the slab.
3 18m. Scramble off up the slab.

★ **The Cruel Seam**   43m   E5   6b   (R)   (1988)
The crack/seam left of This is The Sea provides a sustained struggle.

★ **This is The Sea**   45m   E5   (R)   (1987)
Start below the obvious central crackline, right of Heathen.
1   37m. 6a. Start the crack via the bulging wall, and continue in the same line to the first overlap. Go over this leftwards to a good foothold. Continue up the cracked wall, two pegs, to beneath the top overhang, poor peg. Go over the overhang, taking care with the rock, to better holds, and a belay in the crack.
2   8m. Traverse out on grass to the arête, and go up to belay on top of the promontory.

★ **The Featherstone**   45m   E5   6b   (R)   (1988)
Start six metres right of the previous route, and climb the obvious leftward slanting crack, on good locks, to a prominent projection in the roof. Pull over the roof, and move up left to join, and finish up, This is The Sea.

Another couple of routes lie around on the front face of the promontory.

Into the Light   36m · E2   (R)   (1987)
Start at the toe of the buttress, around on the front face.
1   21m. 5c. Climb up into a niche, move trickily out left, and climb a scabby groove to a belay ledge.
2   15m. 4b. Go up the arête behind the belay, to the top of the promontory.

Snatch in the Storm   30m   E3   6a   (R)   (1988)
Start right of the previous route, and climb the obvious V-groove. Swing out right, when it closes, and finish up the arête.

Red Wall   (R)

Right of Left Hand Red Wall is the huge sweep of Red Wall proper, an intimidating proposition, seamed by the pale lines of weaknesses revealing the underlying softer rock. All the routes are committing, and have great character. An incredulous audience is often available for the vain.

The easiest way to approach these routes is by abseiling down to the promontory, between Left Hand Red Wall and Red Wall, on a spare rope. Using a krab on this rope, abseil down again to a grassy corner, about 20 metres above the sea. From here it is possible to make a roped scramble

across to reach Red Wall Escape Route, and so to ledges at
the base of the wall. Here there is a block belay.

A poorer alternative is to abseil down the slabby ridge
around right of the wall, from the signs near Ellin's Tower.
Scramble down to sea-level, and then go back up to the
ledges at the bottom of the wall. This requires a low tide,
and the ropes often refuse to pull down. It is also possible,
but extremely frightening, to make an 80 metres abseil
down the wall, directly onto the base ledges. This should
make absolutely sure that the party beats a retreat up the
escape route!

There has been some confusion about the following two
routes as from the ledge to the break much of the climbing
is common to both, interchangeable, or at best, very close.
Certainly The Electrification's crux is the same as for The
Cree. The Cree takes more of a line whilst Electrification
provides more of an expedition and is a test in rope
management.

★ **The Cree** 34m E3 6a (R)   (1978)
A good route, with one move which seems much harder
than it should be. Start at a point where the grassy ramp of
Red Wall Escape Route steepens, in a corner on the line of
the abseil. A move up the corner leads to a traverse right to
an obvious ledge on the golden wall. Steep moves in a
diagonal rightwards line prove strenuous, until after a hard
move a vague crack can be reached on the left, before
climbing a bulging wall on large holds to reach a horizontal
break. Traverse right a few metric feet, peg in a wide
crack/fault line and finish just to the left of this through
choss.

★ **The Electrification of the Soviet Union** 43m E4 6a (R)
                                                        (1986)
Complex route finding keeps the leader occupied on a
lonely lead. Start along the obvious ledge, right of the
abseil, on two loose spikes. Ascend to a peg, go up and left
into an alcove and traverse six metres to the ledge on The
Cree, which is horribly close to the ground. Follow The Cree
right for six metres to a very good finger-slot, move back
left, and go up on diminishing pockets to a small overlap,
with a crack at its left-hand end. Climb this and a short wall
to a horizontal break. Go up right and undercut a big ear
leftwards to a rubble finish.

Safer Start! 45m E3 5c (R)   (1978)
This avoids the loose and scary start to Television Route.
Start as for the previous route, on the ledge with two
spikes. Go up to the peg, pass it on the left, until it is

possible to move right to a sandy area below an overlap. Traverse right below the overlap to join, and finish, as for Television Route.

★ **Television Route**   40m   E4   5c   (R)   (1966/1978)
Once a sacrilege, but now a fine free route. Start at the spike belay mentioned for previous routes and climb leftwards to gain the main groove line which contains much rusting scrap metal. Go up and over the bulge on loose rock, and trend left to many pegs where the rock improves. Traverse right into a groove under an overhang. Follow this groove, via two overlaps, to a small ledge on the right. Climb the short wall, and finish up a groove, past the last of the scrap iron.

The left-hand groove above the traverse, with tempting pegs etc., has been climbed at the same grade.

★★ **Khmer Rouge**   43m   E5   6a   (R)   (1978)
A nasty little number, but more civilised after its initial purge. Start from the belay of Television Route. Climb up past a peg runner into a bottomless groove. A peg at its top does not, unfortunately, seem to protect the moves up right to a ledge on the arête. Go back left into grooves and ascend a little wall to join Television Route at two pegs. Finish as for Television Route.

★★ **Redshift**   86m   E3   (R)   (1976)
A demanding route, especially on pitch 2, which has a sustained urgency about it. Start from the end of the second abseil, on the lowest ledge, in the corner on the right.
1   37m. 5b. Climb up slabby rock to leftward-trending cracks. Follow these, then bear right and go up to ledges and a huge block belay.
2   37m. 5c. Climb up above the belay, until moves right and then back left gain a groove directly above the belay. This leads to a ledge on the left. Go back up right onto the larger ledge, and belay, as for Wendigo.
3   12m. 4c. Move left into the continuation groove, which leads to the top.

Variation
Dangerous Liaison   20m   E3   6a
The obvious line three metres right of Redshift pitch 2. Start from the block belay at the top of pitch 1 of Redshift. Climb up and right passing a peg where a difficult sequence right allows better holds to be reached. Continue in a fine position overlooking the fault line of Wendigo to join it midway up pitch 3 (possible hanging belay on right). Finish up Wendigo or Redshift.

Red Wall Escape Route   116m   Very Severe   (R)   (1966)
A poor route, but very useful as it is well used as an escape.
Start from the end of the second abseil, and take the roped
scramble across right, and up to block belays, at the foot of
Red Wall.
1   20m. 4c. As for Wendigo, pitch 1.
2   30m. 4b. Start as for Wendigo, then climb the diagonal
break leftwards to the crevasse stance, as for the start of
Television Route. Block belays exist, a couple of metres
farther along.
3   6m. Walk left to a belay on the ramp.
4   45m. 4b. Climb the slabby, and grassy, ramp to the foot
of a slab.
5   15m. 4a. The slab leads easily to the top.

★★★ **Wendigo**   80m   E3   (R)   (1966)
A very fine route, stylishly taking perhaps the best 'easy'
line on Red Wall. There are no real hard moves, but the
route is fairly sustained. Start at the block belay, as for Red
Wall Escape Route.
1   20m. 4c. Move left into a shallow groove, and follow it
easily to a small ledge, below a steeper part of the wall.
Climb down to the left for five metres to a stance and belay.
2   17m. 5a. Climb the obvious leftward-trending break
above, to a shallow depression.
3   32m. 5b. Climb the obvious break to the bulge. Step up
and left to a steep wall, move slightly right and climb up, on
good holds, to a sloping ledge. Follow the big corner to a
large spike, and move left to a belay, peg.
4   11m. 4b. Climb the wall for three metres, bearing right
to a groove, and finish up this.

★★ **Blue Remembered Hills**   73m   E3   (R)   (1980)
A good route, taking the wall between the obvious
weaknesses. Start from the ledge five metres up pitch 1 of
Red Wall.
1   45m. 5c. Go up for a little way before gaining a groove
on the left. From the top of this groove, move left and climb
the wall to a large flake, peg. Continue until forced to join
Wendigo, then follow this to the sloping ledge. Poor belay
(Friend 3 useful).
2   28m. 5c. Climb rightwards passing a downward pointing
flake, and swing into a hanging groove which is taken to join
Red Haze at a sloping ledge, peg on the right. Using
hanging flakes, gain the groove above (or climb the wall as
for Red Haze). From the top of the groove (loose rock
abundant) continue dangerously more or less directly to the
top of the crag.

★ **Red Haze**   70m   E4   (R)   (1969)
The protection seems a long way away on pitch 2, but it is a
good climb, provided enough courage can be mustered.
Start from the block belay, described previously.
1   25m. 5a. From the left-hand end of the stance, move left
into a shallow right-facing corner. Move right across the
steep wall, and gain, then follow, a diagonal quartz break
over two small bulges, to a recess. Here a bolt belay can be
backed up by a loose spike.
2   45m. 5c. From the loose spike move left, then ascend
the steep wall, peg, until insecure moves lead left to a
groove. Go up this to a sloping ledge, peg, then ascend the
wall above direct to gain a groove, peg. After a few metres
move rightwards to gain and finish up a shallow chimney.

★★ **Rapture of the Deep**   70m   E4   (R)   (1978)
A very fine main pitch, but only for the loose rock addict, or
those seeking a cure for hiccups. Start at the block belay,
previously described.
1   25m. 5a. As for Red Haze, pitch 1.
2   45m. 5b. Follow the obvious sandy break, slightly to the
right of the belay, passing two pegs.

★★★ **Red Wall**   77m   E2   (R)   (1966)
A great route, fairly straightforward for the most part, on
huge holds, but with one technical section; always steep, it
remains a classic. Start at the block belay.
1   34m. 4c. Move left and climb the shallow chimney which
leads without effort to a ledge. Climb the steep groove on
the right; at the top on the right is a peg belay.
2   23m. 5b. Follow the diagonal line leftwards, climb up to
a peg, then cross the steep wall leftwards with some
temerity to a shallow chimney. Peg belays.
3   20m. 4c. Climb the overhanging chimney on monster
holds, past a peg, and follow the groove above moving
right to finish.

★★★ **Fantasia**   79m   E3   (R)   (1979)
Excellent wall climbing, on solid rock once out of Red Wall.
The route has reasonably good protection, and is sustained
at an interesting level. Start at the block belay.
1   34m. 4c. As for Red Wall, pitch 1.
2   45m. 5c. Follow Red Wall to a move right. Continue
rightwards to a sandy cave, and from its right-hand side,
move around onto the wall. Go straight up, then slightly left,
passing a peg, before gaining a small hanging groove.
From the top of this, bold and technical moves left lead to
larger holds.

Castell Helen and Yellow Wall.
Photo: Geoff Milburn

(N.B. This 79 metre route is left in its final form, just to prove to guidewriters that Editors do have their uses!)

A Brown Study 88m E3 (R) (1970)
Hard to follow, with serious climbing, especially on the first pitch. Start at the block belay.
1 18m. 5c. Climb the steep groove, right of Red Wall, to a ledge and peg. Continue up the groove to a good ledge.
2 40m. 5c. Climb rightwards and go up a corner, peg, before moving leftwards through shattered rock to a sandy ledge on the left (This is the sandy cave of Fantasia). A horizontal traverse rightwards leads to a solid area of rock. Head up into and through an inverted V-overhang to a good ledge just left of a curving fault-line. Poor belays.
3 30m. 5a. Climb up for a couple of metres, then traverse six metres right to a groove. Ascend this, and the corner above to a slab, which leads to the top.

★ **Communication Breakdown** 75m E3 (R) (1978)
This is exciting stuff, making the best of the rock hereabouts. Some interesting rock features are negotiated, but unfortunately the protection is inadequate. Start as for A Brown Study.
1 30m. 5c. Follow A Brown Study to the peg on pitch 2, then exit from the corner rightwards. Cross a compact wall and gain a vegetated ledge below a chimney fault-line.
2 45m. 5b. Climb the chimney-cum-crack, with embarrassingly little gear, to the top.

Doppelgangen 104m E3 (R) (1966/1978)
A hard and scruffy climb, taking a wandering line out of Red Wall. Start at the block belay, as previously described.
1 34m. 4c. As for Red Wall, pitch 1.
2 18m. 5b. Traverse up right and cross a steep wall, past a peg. Continue right to another peg on the right of a chimney. Descend to a grassy ledge.
3 15m. 5b. Move right, then go up to a peg, and move up again to traverse right into a corner, and a stance.
4 37m. 5b. Climb the fault-line, peg, keeping to the left, until the continuation chimney can be reached and followed to a slab, and the top.

★★★ **The Maze** 147m E4 (R) (1970)
Superb climbing in continually interesting situations, but it is tiring and difficult right to the end. Start five metres below the top of the ramp of The Escape Route, reached by a short abseil.
1 30m. 5c. Climb the short crack for five metres to the horizontal break, then move right, and go up to a ledge in the middle of the steep wall. Move up right to the arête, then continue right for six metres to good cracks, and a

peg. Climb down for three metres, peg, and climb straight across the wall to join Television Route at a sharp overhang. Move right to a good ledge.

2 12m. 5c. Climb down to good small ledges, then continue down for two metres, and step left to a corner. Climb this, and move out right onto a sloping ledge. Wendigo, pitch 3 belay, peg.

3 30m. 5c. Traverse right to a small ledge. Move round the corner and onto Red Haze. Go down the obvious broken ramp for six metres, until it is possible to gain the fault-line. At the same level move across, and go up to join Red Wall, then move down onto its belay.

4 30m. 5c. Climb across the wall until it is possible, at three metres, to pass a small nose. Climb up slightly to a little roof, then cross rightwards to a fault. Climb down this for six metres to a good ledge, on A Brown Study.

5 45m. 5b. Follow the most obvious line for 37 metres without gaining any height, and when the ledges end, climb the final impending loose wall and a slab, to belay on grassy rocks. Scramble to the top.

Castell Helen

Below Ellin's Tower lies the most solid of the South Stack cliffs. The routes are of good quality, with reasonable protection, and are often in fine positions. The routes are a good proposition on days when the weather is threatening, although they are exceedingly worthwhile anyway. To a certain extent, the routes on the left of the wall are rather 'climb anywhere' lines, and are on occasion a little vague in definition.

Access to the routes is by abseil, and it should be noted that the easiest route out is Very Severe. In front of Ellin's Tower, vague paths lead quickly down to a ledge and a short section of wall, with a large stainless steel stake at its top. Old pegs, and a good nut placement, exist on the short wall. An abseil of 35 metres gains a long ledge in the centre of the wall. A further abseil of 30 metres gains the base of the wall. Useful, at most states of the tide, are three good starting points.

Lighthouse Arête can be best started from a large niche, eight metres above the low tide platform, and gained by moving leftwards (facing in) whilst abseiling down. A perch beyond most seas, with good belays, provides a good starting point.

Rap can be started from a ledge, just left of the right-hand arête of the lower face, where a belay can be found in sloping cracks. It is also possible to traverse around to the foot of Atlantis from here. Both these abseils are best made by using a spare rope to get to the halfway ledge, and clipping a krab into this rope then abseiling again, from this, to sea-level. This avoids using the decaying pegs, or leaving behind gear, on the halfway ledge

To gain Atlantis, go to the right-hand end of the halfway ledge, and abseil down the corner to ledges, or the sloping platform, from a peg and runner belay. Great care should be taken with all these approaches as rope-eating rocks lie just below water level!

The first two routes are found beyond Lighthouse Arête, and should be considered to lie within the Red Wall area, and subject to the same restriction on access.

Captain Nemo   65m   E3   (R)   (1986)
A bit esoteric, but with interesting climbing. The route is best approached by a direct double abseil, via a ledge and peg, from the arête on the right (looking out) of the usual abseil point. It is just across the narrow zawn on the left of Black Light. Start on the ledge, below a short corner, at sea-level.
1   20m. 5b. Climb the short steep corner to easier ground. Continue right then left, around an overhang, and go up to a sloping ledge on the left, peg in the corner.
2   45m. 5c. Go up right around the corner, and make a scary traverse right, on interesting ground, to gain, via a dirty move, the upper reaches of Lighthouse Arête. Finish up this.

Black Light   82m   Hard Very Severe   (R)   (1969)
A good route, with a long approach, which takes a big slab at the left-hand side of Castell Helen. It is only possible at low tide. Starting at the niche, as for Lighthouse Arête, traverse left and around the big arête, and continue to reach ledges at the base of the big slab. It is best to rope up, as the last section of the approach is as hard as the route. Belay at the bottom of the slab at a large niche.
1   45m. 4c. Ascend the blunt rib on the left to a crack, which is taken for three metres. Step up and right onto an overhang, then go up for three metres and follow a rising traverse rightwards to a large flake. Get onto this, and go up for three metres to a peg. Continue up to belay just right of the top of the slab.
2   37m. 4b. Move up right, getting easier, to the abseil point.

★ **Lighthouse Arête**   80m   Very Severe   (1966)
The easiest route here gives very pleasant climbing. Start in the niche, as described previously.
1   20m. 4a. Step out left, and follow the easy line diagonally left to a ledge on the arête.
2   15m. 4b. Climb the wall on the right to a short crack. Ascend this, then move around the arête to a small ledge. Go up to belay below a small overhang on the arête.
3   15m. 4c. Step right, and pull up over the bulge to gain better holds into the groove above. Go up the groove to belay on the ledge above. Good nut in the corner.
4   30m. 4a. Climb up and right to easier ground, then follow a broken ramp diagonally rightwards to the abseil point.

Variation
★★ **Lighthouse Arête Direct**   75m   Very Severe
A better, more sustained way of doing this fine route.
1   45m. 4c. From the niche, step right, and climb diagonally left to gain a ledge below a straight crack. Move up and climb the crack, with a couple of interesting moves, to arrive at the base of the groove, guarded by an overhang. Pull into the groove, and go up to belay on the ledge, as for the original way.
2   30m. 4a. As for the original way, pitch 4.

★★ **Blanco**   71m   Hard Very Severe   (1966)
A good route which is mild for its grade. Start from the niche, as previously described.
1   28m. 4c. Climb up rightwards, then trend leftwards up the wall to a good stance by the first white patch.
2   18m. 5a. Move left and climb the steep wall to a niche. Go up the short groove on the left, and go over the overhang on the right. Climb straight up to a stance on the arête.
3   25m. 4a. Ascend the arête, trending right to the top.

A State of Saturation   73m   Hard Very Severe   (1984)
A well-protected eliminate which makes the best of the rock between Blanco and Poseidon. Start in the niche, as previously described.
1   28m. 5a. From the left-hand side of the niche, go up to the top of a small pinnacle, and climb the wall trending slightly left to a shallow groove. Ascend this to a belay in a black niche.
2   45m. 5a. Traverse right and onto a red slab. Move up right to a corner in the overhang, go over this and up to a block. Climb the thin groove and crack to finish on the arête.

Castell Helen

1	Red Wall	E2	6	Poseidon	VS
2	Captain Nemo	E3	7	Blanco	HVS
3	Black Light	HVS	8	Pel	VS
4	Lighthouse Arête	VS	9	North West Passage	E1
5	Lighthouse Arête Direct	VS	10	Rap	VS
			11	Atlantis	E1

GREG 87

★**Poseidon**   68m   Very Severe   (1970)
A good route with varied climbing. Start from the niche, as described previously.
1   28m. 4b. Climb the crack, and continue up stepping left to a small overhang. Go over this and continue up a groove to the second large ledge.
2   25m. 4c. Step left and climb the wall to overhangs. Move right to climb the deep crack, until forced out onto the wall. Step back left, and traverse left onto Lighthouse Arête.
3   15m. 4a. Climb the broken slab rightwards to the top.

Variation
Direct Finish   15m   Hard Very Severe   (1976)
3a   15m. 5a. Instead of traversing left, gain and boldly climb a shallow groove to the abseil point.

★★ **Pel**   65m   Very Severe   (1966)
A good route, strenuous and interesting. Start in the niche, as previously described.
1   28m. 4c. Climb rightwards to the crack, and go up this, and the wall on the right. Move left to a groove, and ascend this to gain the left end of the halfway ledge.
2   37m. 4b. Climb slightly left up the short wall to reach an obvious break. Follow this leftwards, and finish back right up broken ground.

★ **North West Passage**   71m   E1   (1978)
A good wall pitch, followed by an airy top pitch, makes this good value at its grade. Start as for Rap, on the small ledge, left of the arête.
1   28m. 5a. Move across the wall, trending slightly left at first, to a crack system in the middle of the wall. Go straight up the wall to a vague groove, and ascend this to reach the left-hand end of the ledge.
2   43m. 5b. From the right-hand end of the ledge climb up to a traverse line after six metres. Follow this rightwards to a peg, and gain the next break up. Climb left into and go up a short open groove, with difficulty, to make a step around leftwards onto the face. Climb a ledge and crack system, to finish in a fine position.

★ **Rap**   65m   Very Severe   (1966)
A direct route, steep throughout, with good climbing. Start at the small ledge, as previously described.
1   28m. 4c. Climb the wall on good holds, finishing up a steep groove to the middle of the platform.
2   37m. 4b. From the centre of the platform climb the wall to a ledge, thread. Step left and gain a line of holds, moving slightly back right, to gain a crack and shallow groove, which is followed back to the abseil point.

Limping Lisa 37m E2 5b (1982)
A varied wall climb starting from the halfway ledge. From the platform, climb the wall to gain a break, just left of the groove of Atlantis. Go up the ramp/groove, move up to a small overlap, surmount this and move right to a peg, then go left to a larger overlap. Traverse left along this to a break, and make a layaway move up. Traverse right to a groove and finish up this.

★★ **True Moments** 86m E1 (1978)
A bit of everything, including an exposed hand-traverse, with pleasant climbing throughout. Start as for Rap, as previously described.
1 28m. 4c. Ascend the wall, arête, and wall to the platform.
2 30m. 5b. Descend the corner, from the right-hand end of the platform, for three metres to an obvious traverse line. Follow this right, passing a peg, to a rest at 12 metres. Go straight up the wall to quickly gain better holds, and follow these slightly rightwards, to belay below the roof, on the slab.
3 28m. 5b. Move back left to where the overhang becomes an overlap, and go over this into a groove. Follow this to the top.

Variation
Caress of Steel 28m E2 (1978)
Good climbing, but really only a variation.
3a 28m. 5c. Climb straight up to the roof, peg, and move over this to gain the wall above. Finish straight up the wall, past a peg.

★ **Atlantis** 68m E1 (1966)
Fine climbing, with one very hard section, up a well-defined line. Start at the bottom of the big corner, as described previously.
1 28m. 5a. Climb the corner, sustained, to gain the left-hand end of the ledge.
2 40m. 5c. Go up the wall, from just right of centre, to the base of a groove sporting a peg. Make hard moves to pass this, then traverse diagonally right three metres to the foot of a long groove. Climb this, with interest, to the top.

★★ **Freebird** 104m E1 (1978)
A girdle of sorts, which starts on the left-hand side of Castell Helen, and finally takes a sweeping line across the steep walls above the big roofs. Start at the niche, as for Lighthouse Arête.
1 40m. 4c. Move up to the ledge on Lighthouse Arête, then traverse diagonally right past Blanco, and continue to gain the groove of Pel. Follow this to the platform.

2 30m. 5b. From the right-hand hand end of the platform, climb up to the lower traverse line, and follow this rightwards, peg, to belay below the roof line, on the slab.
3 34m. 5b. Step up left, to where the roof becomes an overlap, and pull into the groove above. Move right, then climb diagonally rightwards, across the exposed wall, peg, to eventually finish up an easy groove. A very fine pitch.

★★★ True Moments/Freebird   92m   E1
A popular hybrid, that provides the finest climbing on this part of the crag, on continually interesting ground in brilliant positions. Follow pitches 1 and 2 of True Moments, and finish up pitch 3 of Freebird.

The right side of Castell Helen is a foreboding area, guarded by huge overhangs, which some of the routes here avoid by beetling around either end. Others meet the challenge head-on. All the routes can be reached by traversing right from the bottom of the corner of Atlantis.

Atlantic Wall   70m   E3   (1969)
A fairly scary proposition, with some serious climbing. Start a little to the right of Atlantis.
1 40m. 5c. Go boldly straight up, directly beneath the left-hand end of the big overhang. Just below the roof, move left around the rib and overhang, and onto the wall. Take the little overhang above, trend right, and go up to reach the large break. Move right along this, then climb the wall and go up to a poor belay ten metres below the roof.
2 30m. 5b. Move diagonally leftwards to join a horizontal traverse line, directly above the first pitch. Take a groove, and a crack to its right, to a dirty finish. This groove is just right of the crux of North West Passage.

Variation
Caught 'twixt the Devil and the Deep Blue Sea   43m   E3
A much better finish to Atlantic Wall, squeezed onto the wall between Atlantis and North West Passage, having traversed left to gain the halfway ledge to finish the first pitch. This may share some ground with the latter route above.
2a 43m. 5c. Go straight up to the top break, old peg on the left, then mantel onto a small ledge on the right. Move across to the right, then go diagonally right to a spike. Traverse left to a shallow groove, and go up this to a ledge. Climb the wall above, left of centre, to the top.

★★ Obelisk   79m   E5   (1969/1981)
Taking a dizzy groove through the roofs, this route is both technical and strenuous on its second pitch. The protection pegs are a joke. Start eight metres right of Atlantis.

Geoff Milburn during the 1st ascent of Freebird.
Photo: Al Evans

Exploration of Castell Helen, March 1978
Photo: Al Evans

1 15m. 4c. Climb a large groove on big holds, and go up an easy slab to a good ledge, but poor belay.
2 34m. 6b. Ascend straight up to the big roof at its left-hand end, peg. (Use a long sling on the peg to prevent the rope from jamming.) Traverse left from the peg across the overhanging wall until it is possible to jump into the groove. Unfortunately this does not offer any respite until its end at the roof. Avoid this by traversing left to the arête, and go up to belay in the middle of the slab.
3 30m. 5b. Climb the rest of the slab, and traverse right to a steep groove. Continue up this to a little roof, which is avoided on the right.

★★ **Free Stone Henge** 73m E7 (1986)
The band of roofs, to the right of Obelisk, is breached by delightful and powerful climbing. Start as for Obelisk.
1 15m. 4c. As for Obelisk, but belay directly below the huge roof.
2 10m. 6c. Approach the roof from the left, attack by a crack and belay at its end.
3 18m. 5c. Traverse right to a huge hanging block. Go round this and undercut outwards across the roof on the diminishing slab. Belay five metres farther up.
4 30m. 5b. Trend right and go up to a cave, then finish up a crack.

★★ **Kalahari** 73m E3 (1966/1967)
This takes a diagonal line to round the roof band at its right-hand end. The pegs mentioned are particularly bad, and serve only as waymarks for the route. Start to the right of Free Stone Henge.
1 10m. 4b. Climb a gangway up right, then a short overhang to the left, to gain a small ledge, peg, at the foot of a large slab.
2 45m. 5c. Move right onto the overhanging nose, peg, and climb up over a bulge to a crack, splitting the steep slab. Follow the crack diagonally up right to an arête, and gain the groove above, peg. Pass this, and trend right to easy slabs. Belay below the final wall.
3 18m. 5b. Climb up onto the large block, take the thin crack above, and finish up the wall.

Gobi 76m Hard Very Severe (1967)
A disappointing route, considering the ground it passes over. Start on a slab which runs into the sea, 30 metres right of Atlantis, to the right of a very steep groove. It is possibly easier to approach from the base of the Yellow Wall abseil.
1 18m. 4c. Climb the shallow groove in the arête above the big slab, then broken rocks lead to the base of an obvious crack.

Yellow Wall

1	Lighthouse Arête	VS		6	Atlantis	E1
2	Where Puffins			7	Atlantic Wall	E3
	Daren't	HVS		8	Obelisk	E5
3	Freebird	E1		9	Kalahari	E3
4	Rap	VS		10	Gobi	HVS
5	True Moments	E1				

11	The Savage	E1	17	The Sind	E3
12	Perygl	E3	18	Isis is Angry	E7
13	The Moon	E3	19	Creeping Lemma	E2
14	The Cow	E5	20	Paddington	E3
15	Ludwig	E6	21	Pterodactyl	E3
16	Dogs of War	E3			

2   25m. 4c. Climb the crack, and continue to the right-hand edge of the slab.
3   15m. 4a. Climb straight up the slabs, and belay below a groove in the steep wall.
4   18m. 5a. Climb the groove to the top.

★ **Where Puffins Daren't**   195m   Hard Very Severe   (1978)
A new girdle of Castell Helen, with fine climbing, and some very exposed situations. It passes through intimidating territory at a reasonable grade, but still requires care. Start as for Lighthouse Arête.
1   45m. 4c. Lighthouse Arête Direct, pitch 1.
2   25m. 4a. Climb up for ten metres to gain the start of the big break, which leads down right, past a thread, to reach the corner of Atlantis. Belay on nuts in this.
3   30m. 5a. Move out right, onto the steep wall, to gain and follow the juggy break rightwards. Move down to the peg on Castell Helen Girdle, then go back up rightwards, until an awkward move downwards leads to better holds. Move up right to belay on the slab, beneath the roof, as for Freebird etc.
4   37m. Meander out rightwards across the slabby area, on a vague ramp, up to a corner. Drop down this to a nut belay.
5   37m. 4c. Carry on rightwards up the ramp, with great exposure, and traverse right above huge overhangs to a corner, and peg belay.
6   21m. 4c. Traverse three metres right to a foothold on the arête. Move steeply back up left, and climb the corner on good holds to the top.

★ **Castell Helen Girdle**   165m   E1   (1966)
Another good outing, giving mostly reasonable climbing, with one harder section, and an exposed finish. Start as for Lighthouse Arête.
1   40m. 4c. Freebird, pitch 1.
2   30m. 5b. From the right-hand end of the ledge, climb up rightwards to gain the traverse line, and follow this rightwards to gain the slab under the roof, and belay, as for Freebird etc.
3   37m. Go easily up rightwards across slabs to belay below a corner.
4   37m. 4c. Carry on rightwards up the ramp, with great exposure, and traverse right above huge overhangs to a corner, and peg belay.
5   21m. 4c. Traverse three metres right to a foothold on the arête. Move steeply back up left, and climb the corner on good holds to the top.

Yellow Wall

The red-splashed amphitheatre, to the right of Castell Helen, is a home to the addict of steepness and severity. The climbs normally take weaknesses through the roofs, or shuffle along them, with a full complement of exposure and intimidating situations. The left-hand side of the crag features overlapping bands of rock, alternating steep slabs, with strips of roof. The right-hand side of the crag, above the huge cave, is less featured, but is of poorer rock.

The approach is by abseil, from a spike belay, some 30 metres along the edge of the crag from Ellin's Tower. Abseil a rope length down onto a vegetated slabby area, which bounds the bottom left-hand side of the wall. Traverse across to the start of the climbs, trying not to look up!

It is also possible to approach from the Penlas Rock area (R), through a low tide tunnel, or from the bottom of Castell Helen, also at low tide.

The Savage 48m E1   (1969)
Only just on Yellow Wall, but with some interest, and a fine view of the other routes for inspiration. Start below a groove, right of the broken slab at the base of the abseil.
1 15m. Scramble up slabby broken rocks to the base of the groove.
2 15m. 5a. Climb to the top of a pinnacle, and continue up the groove for five metres, then step right and climb the wall to an overhang. Traverse right to the end of this, and pull onto the slab, moving right to belays below a short groove.
3 18m. 5a. Climb the groove for a couple of moves, then go diagonally left and continue straight up, trending slightly right to finish.

★ **Perygl** 48m E3   (1969)
The excitement is concentrated into a short section on pitch 2, where a bottomless groove is tackled. Start just to the right of The Savage, at a groove.
1 18m. 4c. Shuffle up the groove, and belay beside an obvious wide crack.
2 25m. 5c. Follow the crack around an arête to a bomb-bay groove. Difficult moves up and then back left under an overlap, lead onto a slab and a belay.
3 25m. 5b. Move up and into a groove, then cross the hanging slab to a stiff little wall. Climb diagonally right, and move around a steep arête, peg, to reach a steep groove, and finish up this.

★★ **The Drunk**   67m   E6   (1986)
A route of admirable character, with a second pitch full of
contrasts. Start between Perygl and The Moon.
1   21m. 4c. Sandy climbing to a step around the arête, by a
crack, is followed to an easy slab, and a belay on the ledge
of The Moon.
2   21m. 6b. Briskly stagger up the overhanging crack, then
technical moves (or a jump) lead athletically to a big ledge,
and an old peg. Go straight up the golden 'slab' above on
finger pockets.
3   25m. 5b. Finish up Perygl, pitch 3.

★★★ **The Moon**   79m   E3   (1971/1974)
'Only the best route in the world'. This magnificent route
weaves through the overhangs, finding reasonable
climbing, but in spacewalking situations. Nowadays solid, it
is low in its grade. Start by traversing along some ledges to
belay below a short, steep, broken corner.
1   15m. 4c. Climb the corner on large holds to a good
ledge and belays.
2   34m. 5c. Go rightwards six metres from the belay and
up to a noticeable peg. Climb the steep wall rightwards,
peg, around an arête, and onto a narrow slab, in a superb
situation. Go along the slab and around into a groove, peg.
Descend this until it is possible to move right to an excellent
stance and peg belays.
3   30m. 5b. Climb up rightwards, then go left, over
overhanging blocks. Move up, peg, and continue up the
groove, peg, to the top. Iron spike belay on the right.

★★ **Me**   103m   E6   (1986)
A meandering route, searching out steep areas, and finding
a barbaric top pitch. Start as for The Moon.
1   15m. 4c. As for The Moon, pitch 1.
2   35m. 5c. Before the first peg on The Moon go right,
along ledges, taking care to avoid rope drag. Hard moves in
a crouched position gain The Cow, large holds
compensating for the steepness. Follow The Cow to the
belay shared with The Moon.
3   10m. 5c. Go down, and then right under a roof, to a
belay in the middle of the wall.
4   43m. 6a. Climb up, easy but dangerous, to an overlap
six metres left of Dogs of War. Move left and go round the
overlap. Move up an insecure groove on flakes and small
fins, to two very poor pegs on the right. Carry on, on
sloping holds, until a long reach back right, on good rock, to
an inverted groove. This leads gingerly over a block to the
top. Regaining the rock in the event of a fall might be
difficult, because of the overhanging nature of this pitch.

★★ **The Cow**   67m   E5   (1976/1980)
Overhanging all the way, this spectacular and strenuous
route truly jumps over The Moon. Not so much hard as just
terribly impressive. Start as for The Moon.
1   37m. 6a. Climb up to an obvious overhanging crack. A
tricky layback move (often wet) leads, up the continuation
groove, to a traverse line leading to a corner. Go around the
right arête, and climb up to the stance, and peg belay, as for
The Moon.
2   30m. 5c. Climb the overhang directly above the stance
to another roof. Go over this and enter the groove,
continuing up this to reach a slab and the top.

★★ **Ludwig**   58m   E6   (1978)
A tough route, being both serious and uncompromising,
providing a thoroughly good scare. Start just right of The
Moon.
1   15m. 5a. Move up to the roofs and traverse right on the
highest ramp under these to below, but just right of a small
cave in the bulging wall above.
2   25m. 5c. Move back left across the groove,and go up to
the right-hand side of the cave, poor peg. Grovel leftwards,
and escape up the overhanging rock to the belay of The
Moon.
3   18m. 6b. Go left from the belay, and ascend to below a
big groove. Gain the groove and continue to a move right.
Throw yourself back into the groove, and pass a lonely peg,
on the way to the top.

★★ **Dogs of War**   71m   E3   (1976)
A good route, the main pitch is something of a struggle up
uncompromising territory. Start right of The Cow.
1   28m. 5b. Climb to the right on a diagonal break (not the
highest one), moving up a little when this proves too
difficult. Continue up, still diagonally, but more easily to a
belay in the middle of a traverse.
2   43m. 5b. Ascend more steeply on large, but uncertain
holds, to an anxious moment near a bendy peg. Move right
to a bottomless recess with two pegs, (possible hanging
stance). Step right around the arête onto the steep upper
wall, climb up to gain ledges, and then finish direct.

★★ **The Sind**   74m   E3   (1966)
This takes a parallel line to the right of Dogs of War, with an
anxious, but fine, second pitch. Start as for Dogs of War, at
the foot of the diagonal break leading up to the obvious
buttress.
1   37m. 5a. A diagonal line, below that of Dogs of War, up
a thin crack, leads first to a slanting groove, then to a ring
peg on the apex of the ridge on the right.

Ed Hart on The Cow.
Photo: Phil Robson

Alec Sharp on the 1st ascent of Creeping Lemma.
Photo: Dave Roe

2 37m. 5b. Step left and climb the diagonal slab, mostly with one's hands in the break, but sometimes on the wall. There is protection if it can be found. The slab runs out right at the top without easing.

★★★ **Isis is Angry**   112m   E7   (1986)
Looking for trouble? This route takes no prisoners! Start from the beach.
1 28m. 5c. Cross a wet slab to its left-hand end, to gain a slight groove, just right of an overhanging cement garden. Climb the collapsing groove, until able to make a traverse right across the top of the roof. Climb up on protruding quartz, until a traverse left can be made to a boulder belay. A serious pitch.
2 45m. 5b. Go back right for three metres over a detached flake, and make a move up to a long diagonal break, leading right. Finish on the ramp, and scramble the last few metres to some blocks.
3 21m. 6a. Traverse right for three metres and go slightly up under a roof. Move over this, ascend a short distance, then go sideways over a little roof, and flounder on to the slab of The Sind.
4 18m. 6c. With no high runners, climb sideways over the next roof, and go up to the alcove of Dogs of War, two pegs. Crouch over the roof in the middle, and commence battle with the contrary groove.

★★ **Creeping Lemma**   108m   E2   (1974)
Surprisingly straightforward for the most part, and the two hard sections are adequately protected. Traversing across all of Yellow Wall, the route has fine views and situations. Start by scrambling up a ridge right of Isis is Angry, to just above the cave, poor belays.
1 50m. 4c. Traverse left across the grey wall, in a very exposed position, mainly on ledges for 35 metres, until a groove is reached with relief. Climb up this to belay at the crest, as for The Sind.
2 18m. 5b. Move easily across leftwards to the end of the ramp, go onto the slab, then make wild moves across the corner, peg, and move up to a good stance, on The Moon.
3 40m. 5c. Move left, and go up a groove, peg. Traverse left on a slab to its end (The Moon in reverse), then move up and go leftwards beneath overhangs, with difficulty, to a groove (possible belay). Climb the groove to the top.

Paddington   45m   E3   5c   (1978)
Worrying rock, and doubtful protection, make this an unpopular route. Start at the top of the ridge, up from the start of Creeping Lemma. From the apex of the ridge traverse right, and climb the groove, with a horizontal traverse right to the base of another groove, (possible poor

belay). Climb the groove until it curves right, then pull out left onto the wall. Climb over a bulge and trend right to finish.

Pterodactyl   49m   E3   5c   (1966)
Similar to Paddington, starting as for that route. Climb up rightwards to the foot of a groove, (possible poor belay). Climb the groove, following it to where it bends right. Move right, then climb straight up to the top.

Penlas Rock   (R)

This is a grass-topped hillock that lies some 500 metres south-east of Ellin's Tower, and here there are a number of routes on the rock itself, and on the adjacent walls. There are no outstanding climbs, but the area is quiet and fascinating.

Access is a little tricky, but there are two ways. A high col joins the rock to the mainland. The summit of the rock can be gained by descending a grassy slope, on the north side of the promontory, until it is possible to move around to the col. Ascend a line of weakness to the top. A second way down starts 200 metres from Ellin's Tower, and follows a path steeply down to the left (facing out) to reach sea level. Traverse rightwards towards the rock, lowish tide only.

The first route is approached by the latter method, and follows the centre of the wall just before the narrow tunnel, at sea-level.

Mirage   76m   Very Severe   (R)   (1971)
1 40m. Climb straight up, moving right below the overhang. Traverse left for a little way between two overhangs, then continue to broken rock, and a belay below a sharp arête.
2 21m. Climb the short steep wall on the right, move back left to the arête, then climb it and belay a few metres along the ridge.
3   15m. Go along the ridge, and climb the short wall to the top.

In the middle of the bay is an attractive pinnacle which can be climbed at Very Severe standard.

On the south side of Penlas Rock is an obvious groove capped by an overhang. At low tides traverse round the foot of the arch to below the groove, or from the top of the rock descend down over the grassy dome of the arch and scramble down to the foot of the route.

Stochastic Groove 37m Very Severe (R)   (1966)
Start at the foot of the groove, which leads up to the left-hand side of the overhangs.
1 14m. Climb the curving chimney corner, on the left of the main groove, to join it at a small stance.
2 23m. Follow the groove direct, avoiding the big overhang to the left.

Serendipity 56m Very Severe (R)   (1967)
Start as for the previous route.
1 14m. Climb the main groove to a stance.
2 25m. Climb the groove to the roof, and traverse right, on a line of quartz, to the arête.
3 17m. Climb the arête, trending left through the overhangs, to easy ground.

Plimsoll Line 40m Very Severe (R)   (1967)
Start 15 metres to the right of Stochastic Groove, best reached from the other side of the rock, from the highest leftward ledge, at the southern end of the channel between the rock and the promontory.
1 10m. Step round to the left of the ledge, and climb the chimney groove to a platform.
2 18m. Follow the rightward slanting gangway, and move left to a stance under an overhang.
3 12m. Traverse left to the second little chimney. Ascend this and avoid the final bulge on the right.

The next routes lie on the mainland cliff, south of Penlas Rock.

Nonentity 50m Very Severe (R)   (1967)
Start halfway down the steep gully that descends to the south from the boulder bridge of Penlas Rock, just below its top block.
1 11m. Step across to an easy ramp, and follow this to the right to a poor block belay.
2 11m. Move left around the arête, and climb up to a shallow groove. Climb this direct to a large ledge, pegs.
3 28m. Go left to a diagonal chimney, and go up this to easy rocks. Climb up the back wall to a thread belay.

Moonshine 54m Very Severe (R)   (1967)
1 11m. As for Nonentity, pitch 1.
2 15m. Move left around the arête, continue for ten metres to a short wall, and climb this to a ledge and block belay.

3 28m. From the top of the block climb the chimney, and wall above, continuing up to a large overhang. Thread belay on the right.

Triffid Groove 60m Very Severe (R) (1968)
Go down the steep gully to the south, from the boulder bridge on Penlas Rock, to the zawn. The route follows the obvious corner in the slabby wall, on the other side of the zawn.
1 45m. Climb the groove, past a peg, then step left to a good ledge and belay.
2 15m. Step left into another groove, and go over a broken overhang to finish.

A little way farther on, a hidden zawn contains a sea cave. The next route follows a bomb-bay chimney, at the left-hand side of the cave.

Natalie 45m XS (R) (1988)
Start below the chimney, and climb it on generous jams and large quartz holds, to a continuation groove. Step right and follow a delightful traverse line, in a great position, over the top of the cave. After passing a large boss, step right and climb a groove to belay amongst the plant life at the top.

Smurf Zawn Area (R)

This pleasant little zawn lies around 900 metres south of Ellin's Tower, and is bounded on its far side by a large red wall, easily visible on the cliff top path. This path lies on land owned by a violent farmer, and coils of barbed wire etc. are likely to be encountered. This zawn now sports a good number of lines, and makes a pleasant change from the other crags.

There are three ways to approach this area. As the red wall comes in sight, turn towards the sea, and go down a slope and scramble down to sea-level over the end of a broad promontory. Then traverse around right to gain the left wall of the zawn, at low tide. Traversing right gains Blacksmith's Zawn.

At other states of the tide especially, a grassy gully can be descended to a boulder beach, below the red wall, and a traverse made (Very Severe at high water) around to the right-hand wall of the zawn. It may not be possible to gain the left-hand wall at high water.

It is also possible to make a very long approach from Abraham's Bosom, at sea-level, to gain this area.

BLACKSMITH'S ZAWN   (R)

The Compass   30m   E1   (R)   (1988)
Start under the obvious overhanging quartz flake.
1   18m. 5b. Climb the groove to the quartz flake, and continue on overhanging flakes, stepping left to a rest. Move back right and go up more flakes, then a pleasant groove to a big block belay.
2   12m. 5b. Climb the crack and wall, in a good position, to a loose finish. Belay well back.

Angel Dust   36m   E6   (R)   (1989)
This excellent route starts six metres right of The Compass, and follows an obvious diagonal line rightwards through some very steep rock. Strenuous and sustained. Large hexes and Friends are necessary for protection.
1   30m. 6a. Climb along a diagonal handrail for eight metres to a small resting niche. A hard move gains the continuation of the handrail. Moving right again enables cracks to be climbed to a bottomless niche. Swing right to a projection, then go up and left on huge holds, in an impressive position, to land upon an easy slab, belay here.
2   6m. Go easily up the slab to finish.

Farther back rightwards is a deep cleft, with a cave in its interior.

The Light That Didn't Shine   45m   XS   (R)   (1988)
A strange trip through a tunnel. Belay where it forks. Either sea-level traverse, or back-and-foot under the roof, then wriggle through a tight squeeze to emerge onto Green Light. Finish up this.

SMURF ZAWN   (R)

Funky Gibbon   33m   E3   (R)   (1981)
Start ten metres left of King of the Swingers below a short groove.
1   18m. 5b. Climb the groove to a sloping ledge. Traverse five metres left to a line of flakes going up and right to a large ledge.
2   15m. 5b. Follow the scary leftward traverse to an easy ramp.

★★ **King of the Swingers** 30m E3 (R) (1978)
A little climb, with a big punch. Don't lose contact with the rock! Start below the obvious overhanging groove, before the traverse becomes too difficult.
1 18m. 5c. Climb the bulge and the groove above to a ledge. Move left and go up another groove to a large ledge.
2 12m. 5c. Traverse out right, but don't fall off! Gain good holds on the arête, move around it and climb directly up to finish.

★ **Free Nelson Mandela Now** 30m E5 6a (R) (1988)
An appallingly overhanging area of rock is pierced by this strenuous pitch. Start three metres right of the previous route, and climb up a crack, then go up right, reaching frantically for each hold. A rest ledge is left for a better one higher up. Finish straight up to the top.

★★★ **Green Light** 57m Very Severe (R) (1969)
A unique route of considerable character, up the cleft in the back of the zawn. The chimney is taken on the inside, until it is possible to squeeze through a 'hole to the outside. Finish straight up, belaying at intervals.

★★ **Smurf** 51m E2 (R) (1978)
An excellent climb, sustained at the standard. Start about 12 metres right of Green Light, just right of a small hole on the traverse.
1 30m. 5b. Climb diagonally left under a slanting overhang to its end, and climb up the bulging wall to a ledge. Go right along this to a steep ramp, and follow it to the overhang. Traverse left under the overhang for six metres to a small stance.
2 21m. 5b. Climb directly above the stance to the next break. Traverse right for three metres and climb the wall above to a break. Go left two metres then climb diagonally right to the top.

★ **Gnome** 43m E2 (R) (1978)
This route is perhaps harder than its neighbour, but is similar in quality. Start six metres right of Smurf.
1 25m. 5b. Follow the diagonal ramp rightwards round an overhanging nose, then climb straight over an overhang, on large holds, to easier ground. Climb up to a good ledge on the right.
2 18m. 5c. From the left-hand side of the ledge climb up to a break, and continue to the next break. Step left to an overhanging pod and crack, and follow this, with difficulty, to the next break. Traverse left to the corner, and follow this to the top.

★ **Elf**   30m   E1   5b   (R)   (1978)
Worthwhile with some interesting climbing. Start below and
right of a fin of rock, in the centre of the wall. Climb up to
the right side of the fin, traverse left under it, and climb the
left side of it. From its top pull into an overhanging slot, and
follow this rightwards until it is possible to pull out onto the
wall. Climb the wall past two breaks to the top.

Balu   30m   Hard Very Severe   5a   (R)   (1978)
Start between Elf and the edge of the wall. Climb up to the
overhang at six metres. Traverse left, then go up the wall
trending right at the final overhang.

★★ **The Smurf Girdle**   79m   Hard Very Severe   (R)   (1978)
A good little trip around this exciting zawn, starting at a big
platform on the right side of the zawn.
1   30m. 5a. Follow the obvious break curving under the
overhang until the angle eases. Continue in the same line to
belay on Gnome.
2   15m. 4c. Climb up to the next break, and traverse under
the overhang to a junction with Smurf. Follow this to its
stance.
3   34m. 4a. Traverse horizontally into the corner, and
descend this for three metres to an obvious line. Follow this
to the easy-angled ramp and belay here. Scramble off to
finish.

Across the boulder beach from the previous routes is a 60
metres wall of red rock. In the centre is a prominent
chimney, with cracks on its left-hand side.

Red Cracks   60m   Very Severe   (R)   (1968)
1   45m. Start up the wall just left of the chimney, and go up
to a niche. Leave this steeply out left, then go back over the
arch of the middle groove. Climb steeply up a wall to a
good ledge and belay.
2   15m. Climb slabs and scramble up to finish.

Holyhead Mountain

The Holyhead Mountain crags are totally divorced from the atmosphere of the nearby sea-level cliffs, but nevertheless provide some good, albeit relatively short, routes. It is an ideal place for the novice, or a hard climber who wishes a respite from the intimidation and seriousness normally associated with Gogarth. The Mountain has a relaxed aura, although the climbs should not be underestimated. In contrast, the climbs in Breakwater Quarry are either very serious, or are modern desperates. It is certainly not worth a visit to the area in itself, but may provide some amusement on a rain-curtailed day.

Holyhead Mountain

The crags are situated on the South West side of the summit, and are well seen from South Stack. They comprise, from left to right, a series of six ramps (A to F), two compact walls, (the Yellow and Quartz Walls), some slabs, and finally some short steep crags well over to the right. The best climbs are undoubtedly on the walls, but the ramps also provide some excellent routes.

The rock varies from flakier, more friable rock on the ramps, to the solid, glass-hard, faces of the walls. Some of the rock has a coating of grey lichen, which makes it very greasy if damp. However, the crag receives much sunshine and the rock soon dries.

The best approach is to park at South Stack, and follow the Upper Tier approach until the path divides, just before dropping down towards Gogarth Bay. The crags are easily seen from here, and the right-hand path can be followed around to gain the numerous heathery tracks cutting up to the rocks.

RAMP A

The smallest of the ramps is just off the South to North Stack path, and has a reddish base-wall and a central V-groove.

Corkscrew 6m   Very Severe   5a
The central V-groove. A bit of a pig.

Thumbscrew 6m   Very Severe   5a
The cracked arête right of Corkscrew.

RAMP B

Higher up and to the right of the first scree slope is the first prominent buttress.

Vegetable Garden   22m   Very Difficult
A poor route up the vegetated ramp on the left-hand side of the buttress.

M Wall   18m   Hard Very Severe   5b
Good but short, this follows the white wall right of the ramp, through an M feature. Climb a thin crack up the left side of the 'M', past an old peg.

★ **Candlestick**   22m   Hard Severe   4b
A fine groove up the left edge of the buttress. Start at a pair of short cracks, below the groove. Climb the cracks to gain the groove, and follow it to exit right from the top.

The meandering route Suntrap has been rationalized to give the following two climbs.

Romulus   25m   Very Severe   5a
In the front of the buttress are two wide cracks and this takes the left-hand crack. Start below a square pedestal. Climb up onto the wide crack, and follow it to finish up a shallow groove in the arête above.

Remus   25m   Hard Severe   4c
The right-hand crack, starting just right of Romulus. Climb the crack, then gain a shallow corner on the left, and finish up an open groove in the slab above.

RAMP C

This ramp consists of a wide slab, a grotty corner, and an extensive but inconsistent area of rock.

Wally's Folly   30m   Very Difficult
The left-hand wall of the ramp, starting a few metres left of the edge of the slab. Climb the broken ramp to a niche, pull out left by a crack to gain a slab, before moving left and finishing up a crack on the right.

Pigeon Hole Crack   28m   Severe   4a
The left-hand edge of the crack is pleasant. Start at the base of the edge, and climb up to a wide crack. Follow this to a ledge, then go up the groove above to the top, exiting right to finish easily up the slab.

Primrose Hill Variation   30m   Very Difficult
From the ledge on Pigeon Hole Crack, step right onto the slab, and follow a slight groove to the top.

The Wandering Primrose   30m   Severe   4a
A poorly protected route across the main slab. Start on the right-hand side of the slab, and climb diagonally left to the top edge of the slab to finish as for Pigeon Hole Crack.

Primrose Hill Gutter   25m   Moderate
The abysmal dirty corner.

To the right of the gutter is a broad area of rock which has been climbed at various points, but only by poor and inconsistent routes. Connecting this to Ramp D is a shorter section, with two wide cracks in its front face.

Goin' Down Slow   20m   Severe   4a   (1986)
The left-hand crack.

Ain't Goin' Down   15m   Hard Severe   4b   (1986)
The right-hand crack.

RAMP D

Stairs   37m   Severe
A pleasant route, although a little vegetated. It goes in and out of the obvious inverted staircase up the left-hand side of the ramp.
1   25m. 3c. Climb diagonally right to a short corner, and go up this then back left above the overhang to the edge. Ascend this to the next roof, then traverse right to a stance on the arête.
2   12m. 3c. Go left to the edge and up to a square block. Finish up an exposed groove on the left side of this.

Teenage Kicks   30m   Severe   4a   (1981)
The arête right of Stairs. Start in the gully right of that route, and climb up leftwards to the arête. Follow it to join Stairs at its stance, then move left and finish directly up a cracked slab.

The Grip   36m   Very Severe
Start at the base of a reddish wall, in a short broken corner, left of the big horizontal projection.
1   18m. 4c. Climb the corner, trending left to a dirty gully. Ascend a shallow groove on the right, and go across the slab to a corner and belay here.
2   18m. 4b. Climb the corner above, or the slab on the right.

Holyhead Mountain – Left-Hand Section

Spreadeagle Crack 36m Hard Very Severe
The broken crack, just left of the big projection.
1 18m. 5a. Climb the crack, exiting right to a small stance.
2 18m. 4c. Go left to a crack in the left arête, and follow this to the top.

Ramps E and F are joined together by a slabby back wall. With this, the two ramps form a squarish amphitheatre.

RAMP E

The left-hand ramp is split by a boulder-choked chimney. The right-hand side of this is actually a huge pinnacle.

Curtains 30m Very Severe
A serious climb up the narrow rib just left of Plimsole. Start at the foot of the rib, behind a large block.
1 18m. 4c. Climb from the centre of the rib to a short shallow corner. Ascend this to an earthy ledge.
2 12m. 3c. Go up the groove behind the stance, step left into a deeper groove, then finish directly on the left arête.

★ **Plimsole** 27m Difficult
The obvious boulder-choked chimney. Pleasant but a little bitty. Start at the foot of the chimney.
1 18m. Climb the right-hand side of the chimney to a cave. Go left to a groove, then back up right to a block platform.
2 9m. Finish up the wide crack in the back wall.

Nuts 30m Hard Very Severe 5a
Follow Plimsole before entering the hanging groove on the right wall. Climb the thin crack above to the top of the pinnacle. Step down and take the jamming crack, three metres left of the finish of Plimsole.

★ **Grendel** 22m E1 5c   (1980)
A monster! This follows the overhanging crack in the centre of the pinnacle, starting just right of Plimsole. Step up right onto a large flake, and go up the groove in the centre of the buttress to the overhang. Rest on the right. Step left into the brutal fist-crack, and follow it to the top of the pinnacle.

★★ **Cursing** 22m Very Severe 4c
A well-situated route with good climbing, starting as for Grendel. Follow Grendel for a few metres, then layback up a flake on the right wall and gain the overhang. Swing boldly right around the arête, to finish, via a finger crack, on the top of the pinnacle. Little Women, pitch 2, provides a good finish.

Variation
Direct Start   12m   Hard Very Severe   5a
Climb the crack in the arête, just right of the parent route, to
join it at the overhang.

Around to the right is a steep wall, bounded on the right by
an obvious tall cave mouth.

★ **Skinned Up**   20m   E4   6b   (1986)
A fine strenuous pitch with good protection, taking the thin
crack in the wall, around to the right from Cursing. Start up
in the left-hand side of the amphitheatre, below a tall cave.
Pull into the crack and go up to the first bulge. Pass this
with difficulty, pegs, and pull over the second bulge, crux.
This gains a dubious spike, and easier ground then leads to
the top of the pinnacle.

Little Women   24m   Hard Very Severe   (1982)
Interesting, with two contrasting pitches, starting in the tall
cave.
1   15m. 5a. Bridge up the cave and pull into the steep
shallow corner above. Ascend this, and another shorter
corner, to a block platform.
2   9m. 4c. Climb the centre of the blank-looking wall
behind the stance, just right of Plimsole, pitch 2. Serious.

★ **Teaser**   22m   Very Severe   4c
A good pitch up the obvious white corner in the back
left-hand side of the amphitheatre. Start at the broken rocks
below the corner and climb up easily to the foot of the
corner. Climb the corner, with interest, to the top.

Laceration   22m   Very Severe   5a   (1983)
The slightly dirty crack, two metres right of Teaser. Good,
but difficult. Follow Teaser to the back wall, then step right
and climb the crack, past an overlap, to the top.

Pleasant Suprise   23m   Hard Severe   4b   (1983)
Varied climbing up the wall right of Laceration. Start three
metres right of that route. Climb a short white wall to a
broken slab. Go up to the back wall, and follow a shallow
corner to a small ledge on the right. Step left and finish on
good holds.

New Boots and Panties   22m   Severe   4a   (1982)
A scrappy start leads to a fine finish up the diagonal crack
ten metres right of Teaser. Start three metres right of
Pleasant Surprise, below a short wide crack, and climb up
just left of the crack then go right to the top of a large
pinnacle. Step off the top of this onto the crack, which is
followed to the top.

Variation
Rhiannon   23m   Hard Severe   4b   (1983)
From the top of the pinnacle, traverse left to twin cracks, and go up these to the top.

Old Boots and Cut-Offs   20m   Hard Severe   4b   (1984)
A filler-in twixt New Boots and Mrs Murdock. Start as for New Boots, and climb the wide crack above. Continue to a point just right of the pinnacle, then step right and climb thin cracks in the white wall to the top.

Mrs Murdock   18m   Severe   4a
Climb the shallow white corner crack on the right-hand side of the amphitheatre.

RAMP F

Duffel   30m   Hard Severe
This climbs the blank-looking wall on the left side of the ramp. Start on the left side of the ramp. below a half-hidden cave.
1   12m. 4b. Follow a vague line of flakes diagonally right to the arête, then go diagonally back left to a big broken ledge.
2   18m. 4b. Traverse left, above a broken gully, to climb the left-hand crack of three.

Mental Block   12m   Very Severe   5a
Climb the short steep corner, immediately left of Duffel, finishing up the slab on the right.

C'est la Vie   18m   Hard Very Severe   5b
Climb the right side of the arête, right of Duffel.

The Abbey   36m   Very Severe
A poor climb between C'est la Vie and The Sump, starting two metres right of the arête.
1   18m. 4c. Climb a thin crack to a chimney, and ascend this to a big broken ledge.
2   18m. 4b. Walk left to finish up Duffel, pitch 2.

Variation
Direct Finish   8m   Hard Very Severe   5b
From the big broken ledge, climb the central groove in the short back wall, with no little difficulty.

The Sump   27m   Difficult
This takes the 'V' feature in the centre of the ramp. Start just right of The Abbey.

1 15m. Step right steeply and go up into the slabby 'V' groove. Ascend this to the back wall, then go up the slab on the right to a cosy nook above a cave (The Sump).
2 12m. Stride across 'The Sump' to the right, and cross the slab to finish up a shallow groove near the right-hand edge. (Either descend carefully down the back of the ramp, or go up to the top of the ramp to gain the descent gully).

★ **Sump Direct** 25m Hard Severe
A good route. Five metres lower down to the right is an obvious corner. Start at broken rocks a little to the right of the corner.
1 15m. 4a. Move into the corner, and follow it on good, but sometimes friable, holds. Move into the continuation groove and go up to belay on The Sump.
2 10m. 4b. Climb the steep corner above the stance.

The Elephant's Arse 24m Severe
An entertaining, though escapable, struggle up a system of rocky through caves. Start three metres up and right of Sump Direct, three metres below a hole.
1 8m. 4a. Climb directly up to the hole and squirm up the slot directly above this to land in an 'alley'.
2 16m. 4b. Go up directly into the roof of the cave before escaping through a side exit onto a big, block-covered, ledge. Either go left to finish up Duffel, or go right to descend a short tricky chimney.

To the right of Sump Direct is a series of Steep Cracks and corners. These are short, but have been climbed.

Kit Kat 8m Very Severe 4c
Gain and climb the short steep corner, the right-hand of two.

Farther right is a short steep white wall.

Pisa 10m E1 5b
The leaning crack in the centre of the wall.

Right again are The Walls, which boast the highest concentration of quality routes on these crags.

YELLOW WALL

A fine facet. Steep, solid and impressive, this is the main feature of the crags. It has a slabby grey left side, and a steep yellow right side. A central crack cleaves the cliff from top to bottom, providing King Bee Crack, which is a useful

Holyhead Mountain – Right-Hand Section

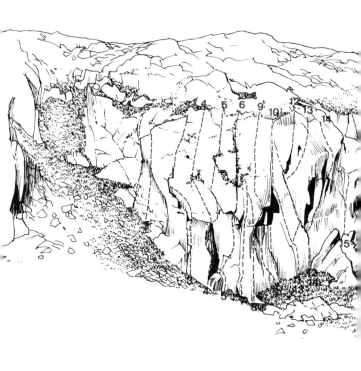

1	The Raver	S	7	Croissant	E3
2	Bloody Fingers	HS	8	Mirrored in the Cleft	E4
3	Thread	S	9	Big Jim	E3
4	Wind	E1	10	King Bee Crack	HVS
5	Uhuru	VS	11	Katana	E4
6	Bran Flake	E2	12	Penny	E3

landmark. Descents may be achieved down gullies on either side of the cliff.

The first rock, a slab up and left of the wall, is poor, but its right wall has two short problems.

The Raver   10m   Severe   4a
This takes the slabby left groove, high up.

Bloody Fingers   11m   Hard Severe   4b
Ascend the steep green corner.

On the left-hand side of Yellow Wall is a slabby grey buttress, with a broken chimney in its centre.

Thread   34m   Severe
Start on the path, five metres up and left of the broken chimney.
1   12m.   4a. Climb a slanting break rightwards to near the chimney. Make a hard move over the bulge on the left, and go up to belay near the back wall.
2   22m. Go left to a huge flake, and from halfway up this, step right around the arête to gain a ledge. Follow heathery steps rightwards to a corner. Ascend this and the cracks above to finish.

Wind   37m   E1
Round to the right of Thread is a big deep corner, with a clean chimney, and a slabby edge above. Start at the foot of the arête.
1   15m.   5b. Climb the right-hand side of the arête, with difficulty, then follow a quartz band around to the left. Follow the arête directly and exit up a shallow groove to gain block belays at the back wall.
2   22m.   4c. Climb a short steep crack, just right of the huge flake on Thread, to gain that route. Step up and left to follow the slabby left edge, thin and poorly protected.

Uhuru   40m   Very Severe
Pleasant, especially with the Direct Start, although it is quite hard for its grade. Start in the corner chimney.
1   18m.   4c. Climb the chimney for about ten metres, then swing left on good holds to reach a narrow ledge. Traverse left until it is possible to step up right to the centre of the wall, and boldly climb this to gain the big ledge.
2   22m.   4b. Step up to a horizontal break, and follow this rightwards to an open groove. Climb up this for 3 metres before stepping right onto a slab. Finish directly up this.

Variation
Direct Start 17m E1 5c
A better start, but much harder. Start two metres left of the
chimney, and climb the small bulging wall, crux, via an
undercut flake, to gain the narrow ledge on the parent
route. Finish up this.

Jones' Crack 18m Very Difficult
The chimney corner direct, starting at the foot of the
chimney. Climb up the outside for three metres then enter
the chimney. Climb up the inside, a struggle, to finish on
the big ledge. Finish up Thread, pitch 2.

★ **Bran Flake** 30m E2 5b   (1981)
This is the fine flake crack immediately right of Jones'
Crack, starting as for that route. Climb up the outside of the
chimney for three metres, then step right to a shattered
scoop. Climb this to a bulge and pull over this leftwards to
gain the crack. Follow this steeply to gain the upper slab,
and easy ground.

Croissant 30m E3 6a   (1981)
A very difficult and steep route taking the crack just left of
the arête, six metres right of Jones' Crack, starting just left
of the arête. A hard start leads to the foot of the main crack,
which is followed, steep and sustained, to a cave. Finish
easily up the slab above.

★ **Mirrored in the Cleft** 30m E4 6b   (1984)
Obviously desperate, this follows the shallow groove high
in the arête, right of Croissant. Start at the foot of the arête.
Climb the arête for three metres, then trend rightwards to a
vague crack. Follow this up and left, to a long horizontal
pocket, left of the groove. Climb the groove, move left to
the cave, and finish up Croissant.

Big Jim 30m E3 6b   (1982)
The system of steep cracks between Mirrored in the Cleft
and King Bee Crack proceed to a difficult finish. Start two
metres left of King Bee Crack and climb up to a left-sloping
ramp. Follow this to it's top, gain a steep flake crack, and
climb this to a horizontal break. Exit onto the easy slab
above.

★★ **King Bee Crack** 37m Hard Very Severe 5a
A very good route, the classic of the crag. Well protected.
Start just right of the crack, and climb the crack just right of
the main cleft to a small ledge at about five metres. Step left
to the main crack and climb it, past a bulge near the top,
crux, to gain the slab. Finish up the crack in the slab.

★ **Snakebite Wall** 37m E5 6a   (1986)
An eliminate, but with excellent climbing. Quite bold, it takes the smooth wall between King Bee Crack and Katana, starting a couple of metres right of the former. Climb a short diagonal crack up left to a ledge at three metres, then move right into the centre of the wall at an obvious handhold. Climb directly up to a peg and continue to join Katana at some quartz. Follow this to the top.

★★ **Katana** 37m E4 6a   (1986)
Sharp and to the point! The painfully obvious lower diagonal crack, right of King Bee Crack. Start just left of the crack, climb the wall to the overlap, and pull up to the crack, crux. Follow the crack, steep and sustained, into King Bee Crack, and finish up this. Shouts of 'Banzai' obligatory!

★★ **Sai Dancing** 37m E3 6a   (1988)
An excellent direct line through the highest point of Yellow Wall, starting as for the previous route. Climb straight up the wall to the halfway ledge on Penny. Follow this to its second peg then go diagonally right on technical ground to reach a thin crack. From good holds at the top of this, peg, go diagonally left to an overhanging groove and climb this, baffling, to finish on an easy slab.

★ **Penny** 37m E3 5c   (1982)
Another good climb, this time taking the upper of the two diagonal cracks, right of King Bee Crack. Start five metres right of the crack, behind a huge leaning flake. Climb the steep wall, and swing left to a groove formed by the crack. Ascend this to a small ledge on the left, then continue up the crack, past two old pegs, to make a hard exit into the finishing slabby corner above.

★ **Twilight Zone** 35m E4 6b (1 pt. aid)   (1986)
A sustained pitch up the ramp and overhanging groove directly above the start of Penny. Follow Penny for about six mtres, then step right to a small heather ledge. Climb the steep ramp, poor peg, to the foot of the overhanging groove, and ascend this with great difficulty, to a fine flake crack at its top. Finish up this, and the wall above, trending left. (A rest point was used in the difficult groove.)

★ **The Electric Spanking of War Babies** 25m E3 5c (1986)
Good steep climbing, with dubious rock and protection, up the flaky scoop right of Twilight Zone. Start six metres left of Patience. Climb a thin crack to gain a big tottering spike, wedged in a horizontal break. From the top of the spike, step leftwards onto the wall then go up trending rightwards to a thin crack formed by the left-hand side of a flake. Climb the crack, move right past a pencil of fragile rock, and gain

the leftward slanting groove. Ascend this exiting slightly right on flaky holds. Perverse!

Patience 25m Very Severe 4c
The shattered overhanging corner at the right-hand end of the crag has a spectacular move at its climax. Start at the foot of the corner, and climb it to a sloping ledge. Move right to a jagged crack and go up to the overhang. Go left to the chimney, climb up a couple of metres, then swing right across the overhanging wall to the arête. Finish up the slab above.

Drying Out 22m E3 6a (1985)
The very steep curving crack in the wall to the right of Patience. Start two metres right of the sharp arête, by a large boulder. Climb easily up rightwards to the start of the main crack. Follow this round a bulge, crux, old peg, to the upper part of the slab, and finish up the continuation crack in this.

QUARTZ WALL

To the right of Yellow Wall is another greyer wall, streaked with horizontal quartz veins at two-thirds height. This wall is actually the left flank of a steep buttress. In its centre is an open corner which runs up to a big sloping roof. This corner is the first section of Tension/ Black and Tan. Descent is by walking back from the crag top rightwards to descend a short wall, and double back down a gully, past Tempest, to the foot of the crag.

The Unblue Crack 25m E1 5b (1983)
This takes the slanting pink crack at the left of the wall, but is not as good as it appears. Start in the broken corner, ten metres left of the corner of Tension. Go easily up the corner to a heathery ledge, step right and climb the slanting crack, diagonally rightwards, crux. Finish up an easier wider crack

Andover 25m Very Severe 5a (1980)
A scrappy climb up the straight crackline six metres left of Tension. Climb the crack, passing a bulge at half-height, crux, before moving left to finish up The Unblue Crack. Some loose rock.

★★ **Tension** 25m Very Severe 4b
An excellent climb with good holds, protection and situation. Start below the central corner, and climb up to the big roof. Step left, around a block, to a groove and climb it to a bulge. Swing left on huge holds, to finish up a crack in the wall above.

★ **See Emily Play** 28m Hard Very Severe 5a (1983)
Although essentially variations on Tension, this provides
good exciting climbing. Start just left of Tension, at the foot
of an arête. Climb the left side of the arête, serious, to join
Tension at the roof. Go left and follow Tension for five
metres, before moving right across an undercut flake, to
finish up a vague groove.

★ **Black and Tan** 28m Very Severe 4c
A good route going up under the big sloping roof. Start as
for Tension and follow that route to the roof. Take the
diagonal crack up rightwards, peg, to an intimidating exit up
the top corner.

★★★ **Breaking The Barrier** 26m E1 5b (1980)
A superb climb that breaches the centre of the
quartz-streaked wall. Start a couple of metres right of
Tension. Climb up and right to gain a large triangular
foothold. Climb the thin crack above this, then step right to
another intermittent crack. Go up this to a good hold, then
finish up a steep shallow corner. An excellent pitch.

★★ **The Echoes** 28m E3 6a (1983)
Another very good route, taking the shallow groove right of
the previous route, with a mean start. Start six metres right
of Breaking the Barrier, at the toe of the buttress. Climb
steeply up the overhanging wall, then swing left into the
bottomless shallow groove. Ascend this to its top, and
continue up the wall above, to finish up a short shallow
corner.

Relief 26m E2 5c (1986)
A contrived, but enjoyable, eliminate. It follows the arête
just right of Echoes. Start at the foot of an impressive
straight crack, right of the arête. Move up the crack for two
metres, then go diagonally left to the arête. Step around
this, and follow its slabby left-hand side to a flake in the
arête. Ascend this and the wall above.

★★ **Bruvers** 25m Hard Very Severe 5a
The impressive straight crack. Climb the crack direct,
strenuous and well protected.

Apostrophe 28m Hard Very Severe 5a (1981)
A wandering line up the wall right of Bruvers, starting just
right of that route. Climb a disjointed layaway crack to gain
the left end of a rightwards sloping gangway, and follow it
to near the right end. Take a short steep crack back up left
to finish.

Variation
Direct Finish E2 6a
From the left-hand end of the gangway, step up left and climb the hairline crack, with difficulty, to the top. A poor blade peg protects the crux.

Right of Bruvers, the crag becomes more broken, consisting of a recessed quartzy slab and steep walls.

Contestant 30m Very Difficult
Start three metres right of Bruvers, at the foot of the slab, and climb it to a steep open groove. Go up this to the slab above and take the steep green corner direct to finish, or the chimney on the left.

Dreaming of Home 28m E3 5c (1986)
This takes the front of the steep tower at the back of the recess, and right of the top corner of Contestant, starting as for that route. Follow Contestant to the back wall, then move right to a steep crack splitting the centre of the overhanging wall. Climb this, past an alarmingly detached flake, to the top.

Blackfoot 22m Hard Severe 4b (1982)
Scrappy and contrived, starting about five metres right of Contestant. Climb a smooth slab up a short heathery corner. Ascend this to the slabby corner above, and follow it to climb a wide chimney on the right.

Time to Reflect 15m E1 5c (1983)
This follows the short capped groove, just left of Tempest, starting as for that route. Climb up to the groove, pull leftwards over the roof, and continue up a vague crack and pockets to a pinnacle stance.

★ **Tempest** 15m Severe 4a
The obvious cracked groove in the right-hand edge of the buttress. Start at the foot of the groove, and climb it to finish up an awkward wide crack.

Momser 12m Severe 4a
A poor route up a groove and crack just right of Tempest.

★ **Tinseltown Rebellion** 50m E2 (1982)
An interesting girdle of the Quartz Wall, fairly serious with good technical climbing. Start at the foot of The Unblue Crack, by an undercut horizontal break running rightwards.
1 20m. 4b. Step up and right to gain the break, and follow it rightwards to a belay on Tension, at the top of the corner.
2 30m. 5c. Step down onto the wall and follow the quartz bands rightwards to a good hold, on Breaking the Barrier.

Move right around the arête to gain the crack of Bruvers, and finish up this.

Variation
Pointless 25m E1 5b
Easier, but missing the point. Follow Black and Tan to the peg, then traverse right below the steeper headwall, to finish up a crack just right of Breaking the Barrier.

THE SLABS

These commence immediately right of the Quartz Wall descent gully, and finish just before the steep red rocks. They are divided into three sections by two gullies. The left-hand slab has two vegetated Moderate routes, but they are not worth describing. Right of this is a steepish gully, marking the left edge of the Central Slab, a broad expanse with the dirty corner line of Route 66 up the centre.

Black Owen 38m Very Difficult
A wandering line with pleasant climbing, starting at the foot of the left edge of the slab, just right of the gully. Climb the arête to the back wall, then traverse right to the foot of a shallow chimney, and climb it to finish up the wall above.

★ **Slab Direct** 30m Very Difficult
Good climbing, but not very direct! Start five metres right of Black Owen, on a small blunt pinnacle. Quite hard for its grade. Step off the pinnacle and trend leftwards to the top edge of the slab, spike. Move up to gain a steep slabby groove in the left edge of the back wall, and ascend this to the top.

Lost Hope 28m Hard Severe 4b (1984)
Pleasant, but contrived with a serious start. Start on a large block leaning against the slab, up and right of Slab Direct. Climb straight up the centre of the clean slab to the large overlap. Traverse left under this, then pull up rightwards to gain the base of a crack, just right of the Black Owen chimney. Climb the crack and finish up the wall above.

Route 66 28m Difficult
A poor climb up the vegetated corner right of Lost Hope, in the middle of Central Slab, finishing diagonally rightwards up a shallow groove in the back wall.

Slippers 34m Very Difficult
A nice route up the arête right of Route 66, starting in a grassy bay down and right of Route 66.

1   23m. Climb the slab directly to a horizontal break, pull left over the bulge and continue up the left edge to a heathery stance, below a white pillar.
2   11m. Climb the front of the pillar, then step right across the gap to a heathery ramp, and finish up short twin cracks. Alternatively, from the top of the pillar, step left and climb the pleasant slabby wall.

D'Elephant   34m   Very Difficult
This follows the vegetation just right of Slippers, to finish up a fine hand crack in the headwall. This can also be used as a finish to Slippers by traversing right from the stance.

Snowfall   34m   Very Difficult
The right-hand edge of the main slab, starting at the foot of the slabby edge six metres right of Slippers. Climb the edge of the slab to a broken stepped ledge, and go up the short corner above. Make a steep pull right into a broken groove, and climb this, passing a ledge on the right, to finish up the wall above. Peg belay.

Right of Snowfall is a smaller slab, bounded on the right by a gully that provides a useful descent.

Rock and Ice   22m   Hard Severe   4a
Pleasant, with one hard move, starting at the foot of the slab. Climb the centre of the slab to the headwall, and pull up leftwards with difficulty to gain a deep crack. Finish up this, or the left arête.

Comfortably Numb   22m   Very Severe   4c   (1983)
A pleasant eliminate up the slab and wall, starting just right of Rock and Ice. Take the hardest line up the slab to reach the back wall, where difficult moves gain a faint crack and a precarious exit.

Right of the descent gully is another broken wall, and right again is another large sweep of slab, the Sub Slab. The broken wall has a few routes which are short and not distinct enough for description. The slab itself has a number of lines, but the following two are the most worthwhile.

Delicate   22m   Difficult
Ascend a series of broken corners on the left side of the slab through much vegetation.

Hat   25m   Very Difficult
This takes the break in the centre of the slab, starting under an overlap at its foot. Pull up and left to the crack, and follow this to the back wall. Finish up steep twin cracks. The

original finish made off along a horizontal break rightwards at 20 metres.

On the right are the Red Rocks, a short but extensive section. Never more than 15 metres in height, but 100 metres long, there is ample scope for those with a penchant for 'Diddy Desperates'. All the obvious lines have been climbed, in some manner at least!

The Pillar is a small grey buttress, across the path and to the right of Red Rocks. The problems are short, but pleasant.

Hammer   10m   Severe   4a
The obvious central crack.

Gelli   10m   Very Severe   4b
The wall and layaway crack one metre right.

Surprise   10m   E1   5b
The fingery wall and rounded flake two metres right.

Breakwater Quarry

These quarries are to be found behind the old brickworks (big chimney) at the end of the pot-holed track where one parks to approach the North Stack Climbs. The site of the brickworks has recently been developed into a Country Park, and all the routes have been affected to some degree by earth-moving operations. It is understood that no attempt will be made to stop climbing in the quarry.

The older routes were never really recommended and have since lost significant portions of their starts under an earth bank recently piled up, consequently their descriptions are included as a mainly historical record. The more recent lines, especially those in the centre of the steep red wall, are of much better quality and are unusual in that they boast almost total fixed protection.

The first four routes take the slabs and walls some way to the left of the steep red wall.

The Mad Hatter   81m   E2   (1 pt. aid)   (1974)
Takes a line up the central buttress, via its right-hand edge with some loose rock at the top.
1   31m. 5a. Climb directly up the right edge of the grey slabby buttress to a loose-looking block. Gain the ramp

above, then go over the next ramp using a peg. Grassy ledge stance above.

2   25m. 5b. Move up onto the short rib above then go left for three metres. Go up right to a gorse ledge then climb the wall on the left, past a spike, and go right to a loose ledge with peg belays higher up.

3   25m. 5a. Gain a yellow pillar on the left, then a scoop on the right which is just left of a hanging flake. Pull over a bulge then climb the loose corner and easier ground to the top.

Gerontion   68m   Very Severe   (1969)
At the left-hand side of the main (right-hand) wall is an obvious rib of light-coloured rock, also a small tunnel entrance possibly now buried.

1   25m. 4c. Ascend the rib then after 12 metres head up right to the edge of the buttress. Climb this to a block on a ledge.

2   43m. 4b. Go easily up the rib to an obvious crack in the upper buttress. Move right and climb this crack moving right at its top to finish up short walls and grassy ledges.

Dementia   73m   E3   (1969)
Loose and dangerous especially on the last pitch. Start 15 metres right of the previous route, beneath a light-coloured buttress.

1   45m. 5b. Go up to a ledge on the left at 12 metres then go left to the pale rib. Traverse left onto its front and ascend this to a ledge. Gain a big detached block below the overhang then traverse right and move up onto a slab. This leads up leftwards to a big grassy ledge with a peg belay five metres to the left.

2   28m. 5c. Step right a couple of moves then move up to an obvious crack forming the left-hand side of a pedestal. Climb this to a peg on top of the pedestal then ascend the short green corner on the right to a sloping ledge. Go three metres to the right and move up to an overlap. Carry on a few metres to finish up a short rib on the left.

Progeria   70m   E1   (1969)
Again unpleasant and dangerous especially at the top. Start three metres right of the previous route, and at the blunt right edge of the buttress.

1   45m. 5a. Follow the rib to a small recess on the right at 12 metres. Go left to grass then move up right to a detached block. Pass this, and once above, go up left to more grass in a small recess. Ascend the grass to a ledge. On the right is a short corner crack which leads to a ledge.

2   25m. 5a. Gain the top of the shattered pillar on the left – peg. Step left then go up a steep rib to another ledge. Ascend right, past a peg, to a spike then carry on, over loose rock to another recess. Finish up this to a high belay on the right.

The Twilight Zone   25m   E4   6a   (1988)
Start some 30 metres left of the steep red wall, below a steep wall with an overhanging crack in its centre. Climb the crack then traverse right to the arête. Climb this to a ledge then climb the upper wall past a bolt, first left then back right to finish. Abseil descent.

THE PHYSICAL FACE

This is the obvious steep red wall containing the best routes, and rock, in the quarries. Staying dry in pouring rain is an advantage, however the next route now starts five metres from the ground, due to recent landscaping.

★ **The Terrible Thing**   20m   E6   6c   (1988)
This takes a line up the left of the wall, past a number of bolts, with a desperate start and only slightly easier climbing above. Abseil from fixed gear. Superb climbing.

★ **The Crimson Crimp**   20m   E5   6b   (1988)
Another sustained line of high-quality climbing taking the right-hand side of the wall, passing five bolts to a lower-off point, with a tricky move to stand up on the ledge at six metres. This route was unaffected by the earthmoving at the time of writing.

The corner at the left-hand side of the face has also been climbed at E4.

Lord Snooty   23m   E3   5c   (1988)
This takes the slab right of the last route from the apex of the heather mound. Climb directly then slightly left to below an overlap. Pass this rightwards to reach a sloping ledge, traverse right then with difficulty climb a right-facing ramp to its end. Belay stakes a long way back.

Rhoscolyn

These delightful little cliffs lie tucked away on the south-west side of Holy Island on a section of coast littered with secluded coves, small dark zawns and open headlands. It is an area of outstanding geological interest, and has been declared an SSSI. The rugged coastline comprises a variety of rock types; mudstone and shales with quartz intrusions, plus quartzite of a similar nature to Gogarth.

Rhoscolyn is reached by following the A5 across Anglesey as far as the traffic-lights at Valley. Turn left here and follow the road to reach Four Mile Bridge. Take the first turning on the left beyond the bridge (signposted), and follow the narrow road for about 2.5 km to park outside Rhoscolyn Church (Grid ref. 268 757). Care should be taken not to block or in any way restrict the passage of vehicles. Walk back about 20 metres to a gate on the left of the church and follow a farm track (cars NOT allowed) across a field and between some buildings before a closed gate and slight rise lead to a Coastguard Lookout post. The Lookout Crags lie directly behind the building, whilst about 500 metres away on the right, the top of Llawder and the main climbing area are clearly visible, with The White Arches beyond.

South-facing, the cliff receives more than its fair share of sunshine and there are routes to cater for all tastes from 'Delightful Diffs' to 'Dynamic Desperates'. Despite the fact that the cliffs are only around 35 metres at their highest point, the harder routes have a 'Gogarth feel' without the attendant grip factor normally experienced on that crag, and are well worth doing, while many of the easier climbs are no less worthy. There are also many enjoyable sea-level traverses and picnic sites when one gets tired of roped climbing.

THE LOOKOUT CRAGS   (Grid ref. 263 750)

Below and to the south-east of the Coastguard Lookout is an area broken with small but steep-sided zawns. Numerous lines have been climbed in the easier grades – up to Very Severe – but are usually escapable or lack a definition and so have been left unrecorded. The routes seldom reach 30 metres in height although several traverse lines give around 200 metres of scrambling and climbing. One route traverses the area and is a little more continuous and worth recording:-

Sunset Slab   130m   Very Difficult   (1968)
Follow the path to the south from the Coastguard Lookout
and scramble down to a small pinnacle about 15 metres
above high tide mark. A rather broken and very rambling
route which gives enjoyable climbing in a fine situation.
1   35m. From the pinnacle follow the obvious line across
the slab to belay in the small halfway break.
2   35m. Make a delicate rising traverse following the
obvious line to belay at the far top right-hand edge.
3   30m. Traverse back left, descending slightly, along the
top of the slab.
4   30m. Continue leftwards to the edge and climb this
trending left to the top: or gain the steep wall on the left
and traverse to its far left-hand side. Climb the cracked
groove to finish – Severe.

The right-hand area of the slab provides many short, but
worthwhile pitches, gained by traversing along from the
left, just above the water.

The two prominent coves on the north-west side have been
explored and found to be repulsively loose. Nothing has
been climbed...yet.

LLAWDER   (Grid ref. 258 754)

These consist of a central overhanging red wall bounded on
the left by a steep orange slab, taken by Little Queenie, and
separate from a narrow red buttress on the right by the
huge corner, taken by Icarus. From the large perched flake
at the foot of that route, the overhanging bottomless
groove of The Sun rises the full height of the crag. Great
care is needed as belays at the tops of routes are generally
only just adequate and difficult to arrange, unless pegs are
carried. The descent is to the right of the crag where a
saddle halfway down is a convenient place to dump gear.

The routes on this wall are described from right to left, the
direction from which they are approached. A useful
landmark on the wall is the obvious flake stuck onto the
centre of the wall at the foot of Icarus and The Sun.

Adrenalin   15m   E3   5c   (1970)
A serious and slightly friable pitch up the corner at the
right-hand side of the wall. Climb the slight corner to the
small overhang, and gain the main groove to finish via the
crack on the left.

The Cocktail Trip   37m   E4   5c   (1984)
A deceptively steep and scary pitch. Start below the groove
in the arête of the narrow red buttress. Climb the short
groove moving right to a bulge at eight metres. Pull over
this onto a sloping shelf, then go steeply up the groove on
the right, to reach a perched block. Step left to climb a short
corner, crux, and continue in the same line to the top.

★ **The Savage Sunbird**   37m   E2   5b   (1984)
An excellent and popular pitch which takes the leaning
groove just right of Icarus. Quite serious for its grade. Start
below the pocketed wall two metres left of The Cocktail Trip
starting groove. Climb boldly up the wall to a ledge at six
metres. Gain jugs on the sloping shelf three metres higher.
Balance left and pull up onto a ledge using large friable
holds. Climb directly up the corner into the superb groove
which has an awkward exit. Finish up left.

Medicine Man   35m   E4   6a   (1984)
A sustained and technical eliminate linking The Savage
Sunbird start with The Cocktail Trip, finish via a shallow
weakness – a tonic for the technical! Follow The Savage
Sunbird to the sloping shelf at nine metres. Move right and
go up to a good hold. Climb the groove, passing two peg
runners, then ascend the wall above, until moves right lead
to a small ledge and finish up the final six metres of The
Cocktail Trip.

★ **Icarus**   40m   Hard Very Severe   (1969)
The huge open corner at the right-hand end of the
overhanging wall is a must for aspirant high fliers. It gives
reasonable climbing with a steep and awkward finishing
corner. The original way up the face.
1   28m. 4c. From a belay on the slab, move left and
layback up the right-hand side of the large flake to a ledge
(possible belay). Move right to gain the slab/ramp which is
climbed delicately up its centre to gain the right edge (or
climb the corner direct). Continue more easily to a nut belay
at the foot of the leaning corner.
2   12m. 5a. Tackle the strenuous corner crack, which
becomes decidedly antisocial at the top – the strong have
nothing to fear... Belays well back.

Big Boys   30m   E5   6a   (1984)
A bold and impressive climb which takes the curving arch
and groove up the impending wall above the start of Icarus.
Ascend the short flake-crack as for Icarus then step right to
another flake. Follow the arching crack/shallow corner to
difficult moves left below the bulge. Pull over this, using a
flake – this section is strenuous and poorly protected. Move
awkwardly up the corner on the right to reach good holds

below a bottomless chimney. Step left into this and wriggle up in an exposed position to exit left onto the last moves of The Sun.

★★★ **The Sun**   44m   E3   (1984)
The huge red hanging groove left of Big Boys gives an impressive outing. Superb climbing, both thuggish and technical, with 'bomb-proof' protection and airy situations combining to make this a classic of the crag! There is some seepage at the foot of the crack. Start as for Icarus.
1   8m. 4b. Climb the flake crack as for Icarus to a large tape belay.
2   36m. 5c. From the left-hand end of the belay ledge, peg, traverse left into the bottomless groove on good holds. Make a couple of difficult moves up to a peg runner in the seepage area, which is bilious green in certain conditions. Just above the crack dries out and yields to laybacking and jamming, all very strenuous, before a ledge at 18 metres gives a welcome respite. Continue more easily up good rock in an exposed position before moving right about three metres below the top of the crag. Finish direct.

Icarus Variation Start   15m   Very Severe   4c   (1970)
This takes the left-side of the large flake at the foot of The Sun. Climb the broken rock and mud to the start of the wide curving crack which proves tricky. Move right at the top to a flake belay (as for The Sun). Finish up Icarus.

Left of The Sun is a blunt arête, around which lies two smoothish facets separated by a broad open groove. The following routes all start from a sloping grassy terrace which runs along the foot of these facets about 12 metres up the crag. The approach requires care, the ledge being gained by climbing up just right of a small pointed block. The left- hand facet is taken by The Wild Rover, whilst the right-hand wall provides The Mask of the Red Death, the separating groove being El Dorado.

★★★ **Warpath**   38m   E5   6a   (1984)
Those who tread bravely will find that the compelling arête gives a tremendous pitch. The positions are sensational with a degree of exposure that is rarely encountered on small cliffs. Very photogenic. Start near the right-hand end of the ledge, at a peg and block belay about eight metres left of the arête. From the right-hand end of the ledge, move up and traverse right to the base of the orange hourglass slab, peg. Climb the slab to its apex. Wild jamming over the roof leads to good holds, above they get smaller. Continue with difficulty up the strenuous and technical wall past a peg to reach the haven of a ledge on the arête. Finish easily and airily leftwards – a memorable outing.

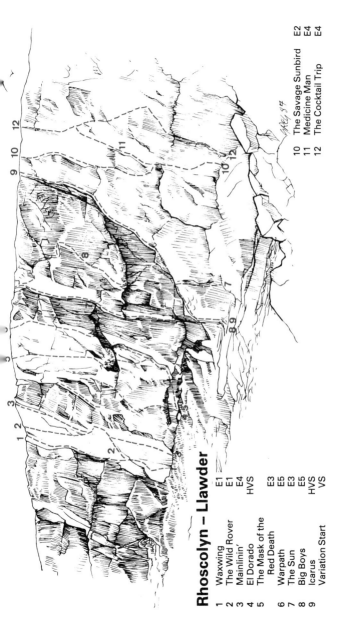

Rhoscolyn – Llawder

1	Waxwing	E1
2	The Wild Rover	E1
3	Mainlinin'	E4
4	El Dorado	HVS
5	The Mask of the	
	Red Death	E3
6	Warpath	E5
7	The Sun	E3
8	Big Boys	E5
9	Icarus	HVS
	Variation Start	VS
10	The Savage Sunbird	E2
11	Medicine Man	E4
12	The Cocktail Trip	E4

★ **The Mask of the Red Death**   42m   E3   (1984)
A very good climb with a steep and exposed finale up the thin crack splitting the headwall just left of the arête. Start as for Warpath, at the peg and block belay.
1   25m. 5c. From the right-hand end of the ledge, move up and traverse right to the base of the orange hourglass-shaped slab, peg (as for Warpath). Climb the slab for five metres to gain good footholds. Step down (hands on the square ledge) and swing left into a small groove. Climb this and continue to a large horizontal crack. Pull directly over the bulge to a small belay ledge. Peg belay.
2   17m. 5c. Stride right, then climb the crack which is sustained and exposed with a hard move near the top. Good value for the grade!

El Dorado   33m   Hard Very Severe   (1970)
A varied route with pleasant climbing. Start as for Warpath, at the peg and block belay about eight metres left of the arête.
1   15m. 5a. Step up onto the powdered rock flakes. A steep slab leads left and is climbed on jugs to a loose pinnacle. Step down onto a small ledge, then move up to belay on the next ledge. Pegs may be needed.
2   18m. 5a. Step across the corner onto the left wall to reach a finger crack. Move left to the edge of this wall then go up and gain the groove that leads back right. From the top of this slender groove go left and gain the wide crack under the top left wall. This leads around the exposed left edge to finish up a groove on the right-hand side of the Wild Rover Wall.

Mainlinin'   30m   E4   6a   (1984)
A serious start leads to a more amenable finish in a fine position. Climb directly up a shallow groove just right of the start of The Wild Rover, to arrive at the diagonal crack leading out to the arête. Go up left to the groove and climb it directly to finish on the last few metres of El Dorado.

★ **The Wild Rover**   34m   E1   5b   (1984)
Good exposed climbing up the right-hand edge of the wall. From the block below the centre of the wall, climb up to the ledge at ten metres, and take the obvious horizontal crack rightwards to a flake on the arête. Move up and then left to the ledge at the base of a groove. Step left and finish up the centre wall past an obvious flake.

Little Queenie   30m   E1   5b   (1984)
Fine delicate climbing with spaced protection up the centre of the wall. From the block below the centre of the wall, climb up to the ledge at ten metres (as for The Wild Rover). Continue up just right of the pointed flake with a tricky

move to gain a ledge on the right. Move onto the ledge, at the base of a groove, above. Step back left and finish up the centre of the wall past an obvious flake.

Cocaine 28m E1 5b   (1970)
This takes the left-hand corner of the wall direct, starting in the bottom of the corner, at the left-hand side of the slabby orange wall. Climb the corner, difficult and dirty for the first ten metres, with the upper section being much cleaner and in a good position.

Combining the first ten metres of The Wild Rover with a short leftward traverse to gain the corner, before finishing up the top section of Cocaine, provides a much better way of climbing this feature; **Waxwing** E1 5b.

Helios 28m E5 6b (1989)
This strenuous route takes the discontinuous crack in the overhanging wall left of Cocaine.

FALLEN BLOCK ZAWN

This compact zawn contains the highest concentration of hard routes at Rhoscolyn and lies just beyond (NW) and at right angles to The Sun Walls. On the left is the slabby corner of Truant with the impressive central hanging blade of rock, The Fin, jutting out before the crag steepens at the concave and undercut orange wall on the right hand side. At the top of The Fin ·is a narrow saddle from which it is possible to view the massive fallen blocks which reside on the zawn bottom. The approach is either down a steep gully on the right (looking out to sea) which should be treated with caution and sympathy during the nesting season, or by an easy sea level traverse around from The Sun Walls.

Access to the routes on the back wall is probably impossible for about two hours either side of high tide, and belays at the top are difficult to arrange. Despite slight drawbacks, the zawn should be on the itinerary of any competent team seeking relief from the multi-pitch horrors on Gogarth.

On the right of the descent gully, facing out, is an obvious wide crack.

Baggers Crack 22m Severe   (1970)
A short, but well worthwhile, route. Start below the crack, and climb it mainly on the outside. An awkward section, past a closing of the crack, soon gives way to easy ground and the top.

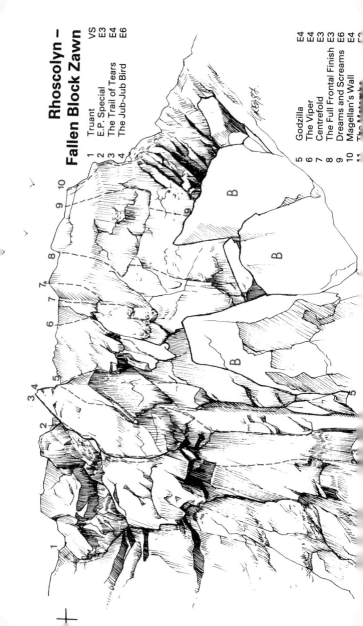

Rhoscolyn –
Fallen Block Zawn

1	Truant	VS
2	E.P. Special	E3
3	The Trail of Tears	E4
4	The Jub-Jub Bird	E6

5	Godzilla	E4
6	The Viper	E4
7	Centrefold	E3
8	The Full Frontal Finish	E3
9	Dreams and Screams	E6
10	Magellan's Wall	E4
11	The Mangho	E3

Human Camel   22m   Very Severe   5a   (1984)
Start three metres right of Baggers Crack. Climb up the
right-sloping slab and move boldly leftwards and pull onto
a small ledge. Go right again, up the ramp, then finish
leftwards up good flakes.

The Trip   30m   Very Severe   4c   (1970)
A poor climb when viewed from below, yet the climbing is
reasonable. Start up a crack in the slab leading slightly right.
At the bulge, climb the chimney to some tottering flakes
(possible belay). Step down and move left, easier than it
looks, to a thin curving crack. Climb this with care, to finish.

Left of the descent gully, and at right angles to the back
wall, is the large red Truant Slab.

S.... Hawk Alley   36m   Difficult   (1970)
A worthwhile, though broken pitch. Start at the bottom
left-hand of the red slab. Climb the slab trending diagonally
left to its edge. Continue pleasantly up this on good holds,
passing a large perched section with care.

Sea Shanty   37m   Very Severe   4c   (1970)
An arbitrary central line up the slab with pitiful protection in
the upper part. Poor in as much as the line is lost once
started and the difficulties may be bypassed. Gain and
climb cracks up the centre of the slab. At 35 metres
surmount the difficult bulge onto reddish rock and move up
boldly before finishing more easily near the arête.

★ **Truant**   35m   Very Severe   4b   (1970)
A pleasant route taking the corner formed where the
right-hand edge of the slab abutts the steep back wall. It
may be approached at any state of the tide along ledges,
but the corner weeps a little after rain. Climb the corner
direct to a ledge. Move into the recess and step left onto
good footholds. Continue up the corner to a second ledge.
Climb the bulge onto reddish rock, awkward, and continue
more easily to finish up the short groove.

Right of Truant, the impending back wall of the zawn
bristles with high-quality routes; none of them is easy, but
all give adventure!

★ **Drunk on Arrival**   30m   E3   6a   (1988)
A good steep and varied climb. Start five metres left of
E.P.Special. Climb the crack for six metres, move up and
right, then go through the roof and follow the obvious
cracked groove on the left. Go straight up to spiky roofs,
then traverse left into a green groove to pass a niche on the
way to the top.

E.P.Special   36m   E3   6a   (1970/1984)
A good lower section deteriorates into a grotty finish. From
some blocks below The Fin, take the obvious line to the
sloping ledge just below and left of the overhanging
chimney/crack. Step right and climb this strenuously past a
peg runner to a good resting spot. Finish up the direct
slabby groove above, taking some care with the rock.

★★★ **The Trail of Tears**   36m   E4   6a   (1984)
This very fine route, both strenuous and delicate,
culminates in an elegant finish up the left arête of The Fin.
Follow E.P.Special to the ledge. Step right and fight up the
chimney/crack to a peg, then make committing moves right
onto the leaning wall of The Fin. Climb boldly up rightwards
on sidepulls to a peg. From this, an adrenalin surge gains a
small ledge on the arête. The difficulties then ease, and the
exposed arête may be enjoyed up to the 'saddle' at the top
of the crag.

★★★ **The Jub-Jub Bird**   40m   E6   6b   (1984)
A sensational and powerful undertaking which traces a
highly improbable path up the right-hand side of The Fin –
one of the most audacious climbs of the North Wales Coast.
In the words of Lewis Carroll, "Beware the Jub-Jub Bird"
(Prophetic and quite amazing, as Carroll had never done the
route!). Start below The Fin, then climb the groove and
crack up the right-hand side of the pillar. Step right onto the
arête for the last three metres to a resting place (junction
with Godzilla). Look left – yes, it does go across there!
Psyche up, chalk up, then go for it across the outrageously
overhanging wall in a position of ultimate exposure to
(hopefully) gain a poor peg on the wall's left extremity.
Layback strenuously up to a good slot on the front face of
The Fin. Continue, to land gasping on a welcome ledge.
Thin moves up the right-hand arête gain the sanctuary of
the saddle at the top of The Fin – a real pumper!

★★ **Godzilla**   45m   E4   5c   (1984)
This impressive route tackling the monstrous corner formed
by the right-hand wall of The Fin and the back wall of the
zawn has some exciting moments and proves to be a real
beast, especially on the large roof two-thirds of the way up,
negotiated on Damoclean fangs of rock, which have
withstood strenuous usage – so far! A large rack of gear is
needed. Start up the corner and groove to a short undercut
traverse left at ten metres. Continue to a rest, just below
The Fin (The Jub-Jub Bird comes in here). Follow the large
flake crack diagonally rightwards to a niche below the roof,
peg. Chimney and jam up past two more pegs until right
under the roof. Launch boldly out on creaking flakes to
attain a sensational bridging position on its lip. A couple of

steep pulls lead to easier climbing up the final groove. A very good pitch. Long slings under the roof are essential to avoid excessive rope drag!

★ **The Viper** 40m E4 5c (1970/1984)
A fine powerful route, now climbed direct, which snakes up through the overhangs just right of Godzilla, taking in some dramatic rock scenery en-route. Start in the centre of the wall below the prominent diagonal crack. Pull over the bulge and climb the wide crack until a move left leads to easier climbing, past a couple of ledges to below the prominent hanging rock fang (The Viper's Head). Go up to an ancient peg, make a long reach for a good hold, then climb directly up the crack/groove past another peg and rotting wire to a steeper section (the original finish went right). Continue up the ever steepening crack on good jams, exiting right via a large flake hold. Make a difficult and exposed step back left across a small corner to reach better holds. Finish precariously up the steep airy slab.

★★ **Centrefold** 40m E3 5c (1984)
Deceptively steep climbing which finishes up the prominent groove in the central headwall. Protection is good. Pull over the bulge (as for The Viper). Move three metres right and take the slight groove to a ledge. Continue up the steep flaky corner/crack, until a bold swing out right, then a short leaning wall, leads to good holds and runners below a small overhang split by a crack. Battle round this via the crack then undercut right into the interesting finishing groove. The worst is then over, the remainder is a breeze!

Variation.
The Full Frontal Finish takes the arête on the right, at the same grade, but is perhaps a little more sustained.

★★ **Dreams and Screams** 41m E6 (1984)
Fierce and electrifying climbing up the twin cracks splitting the concave wall right of Centrefold. A nightmarish problem that was previously A3.
1 11m. 5b. Follow Centrefold to the top of the slight groove. Move two metres right to a good belay near the foot of the impressive twin cracks.
2 30m. 6b. Muscle up the cracks for 15 metres then move left awkwardly into a slanting crack. Follow this rightwards for three metres to a painful jam. Make an improbable swing right onto a hanging flake which is rapidly laybacked to good holds over the bulge. Alternatively, gain the first crack and follow it direct to the top, much more logical. Finish easily up the slab. An exhausting pitch.

Variation

Wet Dreams Start   11m   E5   6c   (1986)
The brutal and perplexing roof directly below the leaning
twin cracks gives a sticky problem to which there is only
one solution! Combining this start with the top pitch of
'Dreams' gives the hardest route on the crag.

★★★ **Magellan's Wall**   48m   E4   (1984)
A magnificent route which navigates a course along the lip
of the concave wall before tackling its hanging right arête.
1   11m. 5b. Follow Dreams and Screams to the twin crack
belay
2   37m. 6a. Traverse right, then go up via the obvious
undercut to a small ledge. Move right into a groove and
climb to better holds by a peg. Follows jugs right to the
hanging rib and groove. Ascend boldly, all rather strenuous,
and finish up a slab. A quality pitch.

★ **The Motombo**   45m   E3   (1988)
A varied climb breaking out from the back of the cave under
the right-hand side of the concave wall. Technically it can
be said to be a 25 metres roof, but support is gained from
the side wall of the cave.
1   30m. 5c. From the very back of the cave, climb up the
side of the fallen block into the subterranean chamber, peg
runner. Wriggle out rightwards, then back-and-foot
outwards to the end of the hanging chimney. Reach across
for a jug then continue right for 15 metres, then reach out
backwards to gain a jug on the lip of the cave, and pull onto
this to gain a sitting rest. Stand up and layback out on large
flakes to reach the hillside.
2   15m. 5a. Climb the overhanging pod, and finish just
right of Magellan's Wall, up a crack in the slab.

SEA CAVE ZAWN

To the left of Fallen Block Zawn is a huge sea cave,
traversed by Electric Blue, which is best viewed from the
prominent white headland on its left-hand side. Right of the
cave is a small headland split down its centre by the crack
of Triffids, Baggers Crack being on the opposite side of this,
whilst above the cave an easy-angled slab, Solo Slab, slants
up from left to right. Next comes a jutting tower before the
overhanging face of the headland itself, taken by Fan Fare.

Access to the first few routes is either by a traverse round
from Baggers Crack, with an interesting section to reach
Tomorrow etc. or by abseil.

Tomorrow is Reinstated   28m   E1   5b   (1984)
Start below a diagonal crack splitting the headwall left of
Baggers Crack. Climb up to the cracks moving slightly right,
then pull over the roof on sloping holds. Finish up the wall
and groove above.

Aquaseal   25m   E1   5b   (1988)
This takes the right arête of the black wall that is split by the
crack of Triffids. Climb up to the overhang, runners, and
make a difficult pull to get established on its right-hand side,
before continuing delicately, on the left, to the top.

★ **Ciment Fondue**   25m   E2   5b   (1988)
A steep and intimidating route starting up the wall just right
of Triffids. Friends are useful for protection. Climb the slab
and pull up the wall to good footholds, bold. Move right to
an undercut pocket, Friend, before stepping back left to
continue up trending right, Friend, to an easing and the top.

Triffids   25m   Very Severe   4c   (1984)
This takes a crack up the centre of the black slabby wall, on
the headland right of the sea-cave. The crack is climbed
direct, using undercuts.

Tetrion   25m   E1   5a   (1988)
A neat pitch between Triffids and Tomorrow etc. Climb the
slab to the flaky break, and climb this steeply, runners, with
a long reach to gain the easier finishing slab.

★ **Tomorrow Has Been Cancelled (Due to Lack of Interest)**
      25m   Very Severe   4c   (1970)
The steep corner crack, where the black slabby area meets
a steeper wall, right of the sea-cave, gives a pleasant pitch.
Climb over easy rock to the start of the crack proper. Go
over the bulge on good holds and continue until it is
possible to reach a crack on the steep left wall. Finish up
this.

Wellectic   22m   E4   6a   (1988)
A steep and strenuous pitch taking the black streak up the
orange wall just left of Tomorrow etc. Climb steeply on
good holds for ten metres, then make long moves and
right, boldly, to steep pulls into a finishing niche.

Eric   28m   E1   5b   (1984)
Start just left of Tomorrow etc. at an overhung triangular
niche. Follow the thin crack leftwards to a groove guarded
by an overhang. Struggle over this, crux, then finish up the
right arête.

Into The Deep   22m   E2   5b   (1986)
A parallel curving line to the previous route, taking the wall just right of its left arête.

★ **Round the Horn**   37m   E5   (1988)
An impressive main pitch. Start right of the sea-cave, gained by traversing in from the right.
1   22m. 6a. Three metres left of a square groove is a roof and a vague groove, which leads to another roof. Above, a step left to gain the prominent hanging fin leads intimately around it and up the bottomless and thrutchy chimney with effort to the belay ledge.
2   15m. 4c. Finish up the corner.

The next routes start just left of the sea-cave.

★ **Solo Slab**   30m   Difficult   (1970)
This takes the slab in the wide break. It is used as a descent, but the top is often greasy and wet, and should be approached with care. Climb up the slab to the top, the grade being for the right edge, the left is easier.

★ **Kissing the Pink**   34m   E2   5b   (1984)
A hard pitch up the left-hand side of the cave. Start a little right of Solo Slab. Climb up for three metres and move left to a flake. Go directly up for five metres to a curving crack. Follow this, then traverse right for 12 metres, before finishing straight up.

★★★ **Electric Blue**   37m   E4   5c   (1983)
An excellent trip across the lip of the cave. Start as for Kissing the Pink, at the left-hand side of the cave. An obvious juggy line soars up to the right, across the apex of the arch. Follow this, finishing straight up at the far side.....a voyage to remember.

The sea-cave is traversed by **Galleon** 43 metres E3 5b which starts as for Electric Blue, and then crosses on a line of weakness just above the lip, belaying on a good small ledge. It finishes up the loose wide chimney to the left of Eric.

Moving leftwards from Solo Slab gains:

Solo Surprise   28m   Severe   (1970)
On the left of Solo Slab is a series of bulges running up a poor corner. Dirty, serious and not recommended. Climb the bulges on jugs to a wide rib. On the back wall and right of the rib, is a rightward-slanting groove, which is climbed to the top.

The quartz vein on the left-hand side of the next, wet, bay has been climbed, **Harvest Crunch** Very Difficult, but is serious and friable.

Flobalob 20m Hard Very Severe 4c (1984)
A serious little pitch which takes the left end of the overhanging wall about 30 metres to the left of the sea-cave. Step across the chasm and climb the wall to the ledge. Go left to a second ledge, then back right up the groove and arête, on large holds.

Left of Flobalob is an area of broken ribs and corners. **January Jaunts** Difficult, takes the corner formed where the headland abutts the back wall of the zawn, and provides the descent for the next few routes.

Hi, Jack! 15m Very Severe 4b (1988)
Start just above and right of Fan Fare and trend diagonally right up the gully wall to take a line of flakes up the wall to finish by two obvious protruding flakes.

★ **Fan Fare** 15m Hard Very Severe 4c (1984)
An exciting pitch, on good holds, which follows the black streaks up the impending wall to finish via a short crack on the left. Much better than it looks. Belay a few metres up the descent gully, beneath some large flakes. Climb past a large spike and continue up the flakes to a narrow ledge, by a suspect block. Traverse three metres left and climb direct to finish on good holds at the top of the short crack.

Daddy on Sight 14m E3 5c (1988)
A good open pitch following the thin crack and pockets, just left of the black streak on Fan Fare. Steep and sustained on small positive holds.

★ **Fear Test** 12m E3 5b (1984)
A short route with a mighty 'grip factor' which tackles the ludicrously steep groove between Daddy on Sight and Symphony Crack. Only the weak and unsure are spurned... Bold and committing moves up the groove lead to a strenuous section, gaining the upper headwall. Finish rapidly – a surprising pitch!

★★★ **Symphony Crack** 15m Difficult (1970)
A sea-cliff classic and hard to beat at the grade. At the left-hand end of the headland is a bottomless right-angled corner, which provides the substance of the route. Scramble down and left at the end of the headland and traverse back right to good belays just left of the corner. Traverse steeply across into the corner, and climb it on positive holds, escaping left just below the top. It is possible

to finish direct over some blocks, and also to start the corner from down on the right-hand side, below Fear Test.

The right arête of Symphony Crack, gained from part way up that route, gives **Serpent**, Hard Very Severe 5b.

BLACK ZAWN

On the opposite side of the headland is a cove with several lower-grade climbs, reached by involved and awkward scrambling. Traversing around rightwards (facing out) from the end of the headland gains some of the routes.

Toccata Crack   15m   Very Difficult   (1970)
Starting from sea level, climb steeply up and follow the curving crack rightwards to finish at the top of Symphony Crack.

Crack and Corner   15m   Very Difficult   (1970)
This takes the first groove reached on the sea-level traverse from the end of the headland.

Patella, Severe, breaks out left of the last route, to finish up the arête.

The second break after a steep wall gives:

Blackbits   20m   Hard Severe   (1984)
Take the steep black corners, then the corner of the slab to finish.

Twilight Passage   20m   Very Severe   (1984)
Start at the chimney five metres left of Blackbits. Climb the chimney and slab to finish via a short crack.

Farther left is a series of pleasant ribs and slabs where parties can wander at will.

THE WHITE ARCHES   (Grid ref. 258 760)

A most complex area. Many short pitches have been done here, but few have been recorded. From the previous areas, follow the path along above the broken cliffs towards Trearddur Bay, past a deep narrow zawn, to reach a stream running down into Porth Saint after about five minutes walk. Here there is a beach backed by an interesting multi-coloured wall of crumbling rock, and a prominent pinnacle which resembles a submerging submarine at certain states of the tide. From this point a walled footpath leads around a farm and back to the parking area. The cliff-top path continues over the top of colourful crag and onto the next section of headland immediately beyond.

A sloping terrace runs below good bouldering walls, and above interesting traversing rocks. Just beyond a deep gully in the terrace, the rocks below the terrace rise and steepen to provide some worthwhile pitches. The best line on this section is **Sea Spray Wall** 12 metres Severe, which takes a jug-covered wall between a V-groove and a steep slimy corner.

Farther along the terrace (rightwards looking out) is a steep-walled inlet, bounded on the left by a wall containing a prominent capped groove that gives The Cruel Sea. Access to all the routes depends on the tide, abseil or traverse in according to one's degree of hydrophobia.

★ **The Cruel Sea**   15m   Hard Very Severe   (1984)
A good climb taking the obvious central corner, turning the bulge on the right.

Generation Gap   15m   Hard Very Severe   5a   (1983)
Traverse out right to climb the arête right of the Cruel Sea.

The Sea Shall Not Have Them   15m   Hard Very Severe
    5a   (1984)
A nice pitch up the wall right of Generation Gap. From the foot of the corner, swing around the arête onto the overhanging wall. Ascend this rapidly to a ledge at six metres. Step up, then finish diagonally rightwards across the juggy wall.

★ **White Water Wall**   15m   E1   5a   (1984)
This takes the bulging wall left of the central corner. Start just left of The Cruel Sea (runners in this make the grade Hard Very Severe), and climb to gain jugs at four metres. Continue steeply up then leftwards to finish up the arête.

Some 35 metres left of the Generation Gap area is an obvious arête, taken by **Hanging Hippies**, Hard Very Severe 5a. 50 metres left again is another arête on the right-hand side of a crag, and just left of a gully. This is **Indiana Fudge and the Tuckshop of Doom**, Very Severe 4c.

Continuing 150 metres along the coastal path leads to a bay containing The White Arch. Walk onto the main bulk of the Arch.

December Days 15m Hard Severe   (1969)
Go down the north side of the rock and traverse back
towards the inside of the Arch. Belay about five metres left
of the edge. Climb the steep wall and bear right to climb a
shallow groove. Take this and climb the poor rock above in
a good situation. There are no runners after the first few
metres.

On the other side of the arch, gained by traversing around
the opposite way from the previous route, is a steep wall
and short groove. This is **A Friend in Need** Very Difficult,
and it is started where the traverse towards the arch
becomes more difficult. The complete traverse of the
'island' is both amusing and quite difficult!

Other routes have been done in this area, but the rock is
poor and offers few, if any, cogent possibilities.

The Range

This area of Holy Island offers a pleasant, non-serious alternative to the Gogarth crags, although there now exist a number of harder problems. The crags lie around the headland that separates the South Stack bay from Trearddur Bay, usually known as Penrhyn Mawr. It is both an SSSI, and an RSPB Bird Reserve.

The rock on Independence Slab is somewhat loose; however the low angle of the climbing compensates for this. The other routes are steeper, but the rock is at least as good as that on Red Wall. Belays at the top of all routes are usually poor.

From the car park at Grid reference 216 804, follow the track until overlooking the old Lifeboat station. The coast going left (looking out) then leads to Independence Slab.

INDEPENDENCE SLAB

Approach from the headland at the top of the slab descend rightwards (looking out), down an easy corner, to sea level. Scramble right (looking out) to the right-hand side of the slab. Traverse the base of the slab using a good line of holds, available at low to mid-tides only.

The routes are described from left to right.

The Corner   20m   Very Difficult
An obvious line on the left of the slab. Finish off leftwards.

Psych 'n Drown   20m   Hard Very Severe   5a
Right of the corner is a diagonal crack. Start at the foot of this. Climb the short corner until just below the roof. Move right using a flake, and follow this to a shallow corner. Trend slightly right to a crack running through a small overlap; follow this, then bear left to finish on steep grass.

Misty Days   25m   Very Difficult
From the foot of Psyche 'n Drown, climb the diagonal crack.

Tired of Toeing the Line   20m   Severe
The diagonal crack right of Misty Days.

High Stakes   20m   Hard Very Severe   4c
Right of Tired of Toeing the Line is a good jug about six metres up. Climb straight up to Tired of Toeing the Line,

then trend left, crossing Misty Days, to finish up a short corner.

Independable   20m   Very Severe   4b
Right of High Stakes is a short crack, about five metres left of the large corner. Climb the crack to its end, then continue up the slab to join Tired of Toeing the Line at a flake. Step left and finish by trending slightly left.

Roberts Eve   18m   Very Difficult
Ascend the straight crack right of Independable, finishing slightly left.

Walk on the Wild Side   15m   Very Severe   4b
Climb the corner for about ten metres, then move on to the arête on the left by a large block. Finish up the arête.

The Mover   12m   Severe
The shallow scoop and flake about five metres right of Walk on the Wild Side.

Plastic Pearl   12m   Difficult
The crack system three metres right of the Mover.

Without Further Ado   12m   Difficult
The shallow corner right of Plastic Pearl.

Girdle Traverse   35m   Hard Very Severe   5c
Mainly Very Severe standard climbing, with a short very hard section.
Start as for Psyche 'n Drown. Follow this route until it is possible to traverse right beneath a roof. Continue right to an obvious ledge after 12 metres then step up and traverse to the arête of Walk on the Wild Side. Move right for five metres (crux) then go diagonally right to finish up a scoop in the arête.

★ **The Ramp of Pink Emulsion**   31m   Very Severe   4c
A superb climb, traversing the next small zawn to Independence Slab to gain the hanging ramp above a cave at the back of the zawn. From the left tip of the headland at the top of Independence Slab, scramble down a slab (Moderate) to sea-level.
1   10m. 4c. At low to mid-tide, traverse left just above the sea, to belay in a corner, just before and below a horn of grey rock.
2   6m. 4c. Climb up and left, around the arête, to the horn. Make a descending traverse leftwards to a corner, and move left to belay on small ledges.

3 15m. 4b. Continue left under the overhang, and move out over the lip of the cave. Climb the ramp and finish up a short wall.

Variation
1a 15m. 4c. If the tide is too high for the first traverse, start higher up the descent slab, at a ledge just below and to the right of a large overhang. Make a descending traverse left to belay in the corner before the horn of grey rock. Slightly harder, and not as atmospheric as the original route.

Continuing leftwards (looking out) along the coast from the large zawn containing Independence Slab, another zawn is reached which contains a long, narrow island. It is separated from the mainland by a low water boulder choke.

Grimper 12m Very Severe 5a (1988)
At the west side of the boulder choke, climb a steep short wall onto a slab. Step left and finish up a groove.

The Prat in the Flat 12m Very Difficult
The friable slabby back corner, finishing rightwards, in the small zawn, with the deeply seamed steep wall.

The next small headland between the two has a prominent fin of rock at its end.

Icameosaurus 15m E4 6a (1988)
The obvious fin, taken direct up a crack, and holds on its right-hand side.

EMMENTHAL ZAWN

On the other side of this headland is a narrow gully descending beneath a steep wall of red rock. Right of that is a superb steep wall of 'Mousetrap' rock, with slabs bounding it on the right. A metal stake can be found in the grass, some way back from the edge.

Reasonable Wall 12m Very Severe 4c
Descend the gully to a triangular ledge about six metres above the bed of the zawn. Pull onto the wall and follow a line of quartz up to a small ledge. Continue up a series of corners to another small ledge, then move left and go up to a niche. Step right and finish direct.

Smooth Operator 12m Very Severe 4c
A slightly harder line up the wall. Start six metres higher than Reasonable Wall, at a diagonal crack. Follow the crack rightwards until beneath a triangular pocket, then go

straight up to the niche of Reasonable Wall. Traverse diagonally left to finish.

Waddy's Edge 12m Hard Very Severe 4c (1988)
The right-hand arête of the wall is taken direct.

Midsummer Madness 15m Very Severe 4c (1988)
The obvious groove line, on the left of the steep wall.

Kanga 15m Hard Very Severe 5b (1987)
the curving crack and groove line, immediately left of the steep wall.

Tigger 15m E2 5b (1987)
Straight up over the large roof at eight metres, on the left-hand side of the wall, passing left of its tip, to finish up an easy groove.

Flake Out 17m E2 5b (1988)
Over the roof three metres right of the last route, taking it at the widest point. Finish up the face of the arête above.

★ **Emmenthal** 18m E2 5b (1983)
This takes the central chimney line, trending right at the top.

Nempnett Thrubwell 18m E3 5b (1988)
The obvious overhanging line a few metres right of the previous route, joining it near the top.

Hieroglyphics 15m E3 5c (1988)
Pull over the roof at the right-hand side of the wall. Go straight over the next roof, then move left more easily along the obvious line, to finish direct.

Gorgonzola Slab 15m Hard Severe (1988)
The slab on the right is taken from bottom left to top right.

Variation
Direct Finish 15m Hard Very Severe 5a (1988)
Finish direct from the overlap at half-height.

POOH BAY

This zawn is another 200 metres on from the Emmenthal area, and has an obvious slab on the right-hand side on a steep bay. Belay stakes can be found in the grass on top of the promontory below which the slab lies. Approach by abseil, or from the opposite side of the zawn at low water.

Winnie The Pooh   30m   Hard Very Severe   5a   (1986)
This takes the right-hand side of the arête, taking in an
obvious line of flutings.

Teddy Bears Picnic   30m   E1   5b   (1987)
The obvious groove in the big slab. Climb the groove and
overhangs directly, with a swing right through the final roof.

The next route is best viewed from the top of the previous
routes. From the top of the promontory an overhanging
arete can be seen in the next zawn.

★★ **Dichotomous**   32m   E3   6a   (1989)
A powerful line up the overhanging arete, giving tentative
climbing on suspect rock with surprisingly good protection
(except the top slab). Enter a groove, swing left on to the
arête and climb through steep rock (two pegs) until below a
large roof. Move left and pull on to a hanging slab below a
steep wall, peg. Move right on undercuts (RURP) and gain
the hanging nose at the foot of the final slab. Climb the slab
carefully to the top. Belay on stakes well back.

Between Pooh Bay and Porth Dafarch there exist numerous
rocky walls and zawns where interesting short pitches may
be found.

Other Crags on Anglesey

There are many cliffs other than those mentioned in the main text, but none of them is of the same scale as Gogarth or even Rhoscolyn. This is not to say, however, that they are not worth a visit. Many provide interesting bouldering or traversing, or simply places to get away from the crowds and go exploring. The crags are described clockwise around the island from Gogarth Bay.

YNYS Y FYDLYN   (Grid ref. 291 917)

Various routes can be made from the pebble beach, and the cliffs running northwards provide larger crags. Most of the obvious lines have been climbed and there are some entertaining traverses.

CARMEL HEAD   (Grid ref. 29 92)

Similar to above, the main feature here is a large groove, which also has routes on both walls, situated on the south-west side of the headland. An SSSI on account of its geological interest.

Grass Tripper 60m Severe
The obvious V-groove, gained from the north, and climbed on the slab, via a ledge, to finish up a more broken slab.

PORTHLLECHOG (BULL BAY)   (Grid ref. 419 948)

From the west side of the bay, cliffs of varying height run west towards Porth Wen, the best of which lies some 900 metres along the cliff top path.

EQUESTRIAN WALLS

Either approach along the coast path from Porthllechog, or via a minor road leading to a riding school, from just along the Cemaes Bay road. Keep left at the first junction and continue until the road swings 90 degrees right in front of a house. A footpath leads past the left-hand side of the house, and into the riding school paddock. Cut down to join the coast path at a dip, by an old wall, and the crag is 100 metres to the west.

The crag consists of a slabby area, facing the sea, and a steep dark wall, just beyond, and at right angles to the sea.

A steep grassy ramp leads down below this wall, it is well above the water. The slabs are more liable to sea conditions, and may have to be gained by abseil on some days. Otherwise traverse in from an easy descent on the west of the little bay. A good belay, and in situ peg, can be found on the same rocky outcrop back from the edge of each facet.

In the slabby-backed bay, a wall at right angles to the slabs, and encountered at the base of the descent, provides an interesting pitch, **Derek and Clive**, 18 metres, E1 5b, taking a cleaned crack line on the slabby wall. The next routes described lie on the bigger slabs forming the back wall of the little bay.

Camel Crack   18m   Hard Very Severe   5a   (1988)
Climb the corner at the left-hand side of the crag direct.

A Sea Change   30m   E1   5a   (1987)
This takes a central line up the slab through the small, half-height, overlap. Follow a vague corner up the lower slabs boldly up to the overlap. Surmount this, using a flake on the right, and step left to a crack. Follow this for five metres, then move left to another crack, which leads to a tricky rightwards finishing move. Belay well back.

Free Bourn   30m   E1   5c   (1987)
A bold start leads to well-protected crack climbing. Start at the bottom right-hand side of the slab. Climb up to an overlap and small corner. Go over this, on the left, then move up and back right to the bottom of the left-hand of two cracks. Go up this until it is possible to pull into the right-hand crack, and finish up this with fingery moves. Belay well back.

The next three routes lie on the steep black wall.

Captain Mark Phillips   34m   E5   5c   (1986)
This follows the main feature of the wall, a repulsive hairy cleft. It is hard and serious.

★ **Three Day Event**   34m   E4   6a   (1986)
This route goes left from the start of the previous route and up the thin face crack three metres right of the arête. Sustained, with good protection, large Friends are handy. An awkward step gains the wall to the left of the big crack line. Go diagonally leftwards, via two overlaps, to gain the wall below the thin crack. Hard moves up and left lead to sustained climbing up the crack, peg, to the top.

A Limpet Trip   25m   E5   6b   (1988)
Good sustained climbing, starting to the right of Captain
Mark Phillips, below some pegs on a blankish wall. Climb
the wall for six metres, move left to a pod, Friend 3, then
make sustained moves past three pegs to a rest on the left.
The groove above leads, with a wild move, peg, to the top.
Belay well back.

BABY ZAWN

200 metres farther on from Equestrian Walls lies a small
bay, with a slabby base, which provides a few short routes.

The Dark Side of Growth   12m   E4   6a   (1988)
Start just right of the prow, and climb the overhanging spiky
wall for six metres, Friend 2, and make difficult moves over
the lip, to finish up an easy wall.

Fatty on Sight   12m   Very Severe   4c   (1988)
Five metres right of the previous route is a crackline. Make
an awkward move to gain the crack on the left, and climb to
the top.

Gumshoe   12m   Hard Very Severe   5a   (1988)
A good climb up the crack right of Fatty on Sight.

Babes in Consumer Land   12m   E1   5c   (1988)
The crack, right again.

In the next bay back towards Porth Llechog from Equestrian
Walls, an obvious ramp, gained by a bulge and finishing up
a steep cleaned corner, provides **Bye Bye Sunday Blues**
Very Severe 5a(1988).

On the way to Equestrian Walls, from Porth Llechog, a sea
arch can be seen down and right from a headland. From the
cliff top, scramble down left, then traverse towards the arch
over boulders. The first steep wall is split by a chimney at
the bottom.

Aliens Ate my Bewick   18m   E1   (1988)
Climb the chimney, then step right and go up the wall to a
break. Move left into disjointed grooves, and follow them to
the top, passing some loose rock, in a good position.

Big Wednesday   21m   E1   5b   (1988)
Start as for Aliens, and follow the rightward-curving crack,
with interest, to a step left at the top. Belay well back.

TRAETH LLIGWY   (Grid ref. 504 873)

At the south west end of the beach a low limestone cliff juts into the sea. It is not however as impressive as it appears from the car park. Slippery boulders run along the bottom giving access to some shortish problems. Fall off at your peril.

MOELFRE   (Grid ref. 517 869)

These long low cliffs stretch away north-west from the headland, and although similar to the previous crags, they do have some pleasant clean areas giving interesting problems and traverses.

MYNYDD BODAFON   (Grid ref. 464 849)

Nice spot...shame about the climbing. The best crag lies at the roadside near the church, but it is dirty and rather overgrown. Good views!

BENLLECH   (Grid ref. 52 82)

Some low rocks for traversing, with some higher cliffs farther north towards Borthwen.

RED WHARF BAY   (Grid ref. 532 816)

The main feature here is large rock island, Castell Mawr, the remains of an old quarry. It is obvious from the car park, and there are many lines, but beware of the top which is covered in man-eating gorse bushes. The top can be gained at the north-west corner. Unfortunately, a band typical of horizontally bedded limestone provides a nasty loose finish to most routes. It would be sensible for any visiting climbers to keep a low profile, especially in the holiday season. The rock castle is an SSSI, in respect of its geological interest.

CASTELL MAWR

The landmark feature is a small through cave, at the nearest corner to the car park. Here an overhung, and partially overgrown, bay provides a couple of interesting problems. **Old Wedge Route** 37 metres E3 6a takes the obvious left-hand crack, although retreat from below the overlap might be prudent. The right-hand start to the route is Hard Very Severe.

S W Arête   30m   Hard Severe
This starts as for the previous route, and takes a rising line to reach the arête on the right. Climb the wall around the arête to the top, loose. The direct starts have been aided.

Red Wharf Groove   28m   Very Severe
Around on the East Face is a faint groove, halfway along the wall. Climb the right-hand side to ledges, then move left on an easier wall, before moving back right, across the groove, to finish. It has been climbed direct with some aid.

Enchanter's Nightshade   25m   Hard Very Severe   (1967)
This is the greenish wall right of the previous route, and it is climbed via ledges and the arête.

Brown Split   18m   Very Severe   (1967)
The groove system, some way right of the previous route, is climbed on loose rock.

North Face Route   37m   Very Severe (2 pts. aid)   (1967)
Around on the North Face, a line over the obvious overhang, with two points of aid, and up to the top via a large ledge on the right.

Mobil   30m   Extremely Severe   (2 pts. aid)   (1964)
A little way right of the easy way up, on the West Face, is a groove. This is taken direct over bulges with some aid.

WHITE WALLS   (Grid ref. 58 82)

The cliffs in this area contain an old quarry and a long stretch of sea cliffs stretching eastwards for some distance. Both the quarry and the natural crags are dirty and loose in huge chunks, and although interesting have little or no climbing potential.

PENMON   (Grid ref. 628 806)

A few old quarry faces provide some interesting, but slightly loose, problems and can be found in the fields near the Priory. From Penmon Point (Grid ref. 641 815) sea cliffs run away westwards, providing some lines but mainly scrambling and some traverses. A large disused quarry, just inland from these cliffs, is another matter and consists of sub-Fowler tottering vertical death. At Trwyn Dinmor (Grid ref. 629 817) a route has been climbed in an old quarry, just above the sea. This can be gained by a track from Penmon Priory, or with more interest by traversing the coastline one kilometre from Penmon Point.

Elephant Talk   21m   E2   5b   (1988)
A reasonable route that lies on the seaward end of a large,
loose, quarried limestone wall. Climb friable rock to the
base of the obvious crack, and follow this to a niche at 14
metres, pegs. Traverse left onto the exposed upper wall,
peg, and finish straight up with a long reach, crux. Belay
well back at an iron stake.

LLANGEFNI ROCKS   (Grid ref. 465 758)

These now reside in a housing area, and are covered in the
usual detritus of barbed wire and snotty kids. The few
accessible bits of rock, not in the grounds of an Old
People's Home, are above a thick bed of nettles. Included
only to save the reader wasting time.

MENAI BRIDGE and BRITTANIA BRIDGE
                   (Grid ref. 558 713 and 542 710)

A number of traverses and problems can be found on the
bridges' pillars and retaining walls, which are made of large
limestone blocks. The recently popular Telford's Leap does
not impress the local police, so a high profile is unwise,
particularly following a recent fatality.

PORTH TRECASTELL (CABLE BAY)   (Grid ref. 333 707)

The low cliffs either side of the pleasant bay provide easy
traversing and a few short problems.

TREARDDUR BAY   (Grid ref. 25 79)

The cliffs on both sides of the beach area provide many
problems and entertaining traverses, although the cliffs
running north-west, past a number of small bays, have
most potential.

PORTH DAFARCH   (Grid ref. 233 799)

This small overhanging cliff, above a wave-washed
platform, is a gorilla's playground. Follow the coast road
from the South Stack towards Trearddur Bay, and at a
turn-off to Holyhead there lies a sandy cove, with some
public toilets, where there is a prominent dip in the road.
The crag lies about two minutes walk away, and is situated
on the left side of the left-hand headland when looking out
to sea. A narrow rock terrace runs down rightwards to the
platform below a wall which leans over at an angle of 50

degrees. Huge horizontal bands of mainly solid juggy flakes provide excellent sport and the routes have a 'big feel' despite their shortness. Popular with youth groups mainly for the giant swing awaiting any failure to reach the top.

The Flakes of Wrath 12m E1 5a   (1981)
The original way up the face has some exciting moments. Start where the terrace meets the wave-washed platform and follow the obvious diagonal line up rightwards to finish at the notch.

The Smog Monster 14m E1 5b   (1982)
The route of the crag gives a sizzling pitch. Start as for the last route and climb diagonally left to gain a ledge at six metres. Finish direct on some thin flakes – scary.

Fantastic Day 15m E1 5a   (1982)
The longest of the routes on this little crag. Start about three metres left of The Smog Monster and pull over the small roof. Move up leftwards to the edge of the wall. Go wildly up rightwards and traverse right just below the top of the wall to finish at the top of The Smog Monster.

The following two pitches take the wedge-shaped wall above the sloping terrace immediately right of The Flakes of Wrath.

Dog Poo 12m E2 5c   (1982)
An interesting pitch, more strenuous and not as well protected as the previous climbs. Gain the rightward-leaning ramp and follow it with difficulty, finishing direct.

Poo Dog 8m E2 5b   (1982)
The obvious short, creaking flaky overhang on the right-hand end of the crag above a perilous landing will be ignored by all, save the most ardent of tickers!

Other possibilities exist in the next but one bay, which has a similar, but somewhat larger wall. The groove near the seaward end is **Fisherman's Friend**, Hard Severe. The intervening bay contains a very friable wall, which is occasionally climbed in mistake for the Smog Monster; this is not recommended.

Climbing Walls

PLAS ARTHUR SPORTS CENTRE, LLANGEFNI
(Grid ref. 453 756)

A very large DR wall, taking the whole of one end of the sports hall. The staff are not overly co-operative, but the wall makes the effort worthwhile. Take a rope etc. if full use is to be made of the whole wall. (Phone 0248 72966)

ON THE MAINLAND

Well rated walls also exist at The Welsh National Watersport Centre, PLAS MENAI (Grid ref. 503 660), near Porth Dinorwic, (Phone 0248 670964), and at The National Centre for Mountain Activities, PLAS Y BRENIN, Capel Curig, (Phone 06904 214). The latter is overseen by real climbers and is open virtually 24 hours a day!

Sea-level Traverses

An attractive aspect of the Gogarth area is that on days when it is too cold (or hot even!) to climb routes, a great deal of enjoyment can be gained from sea-level traversing along the various sections of coastline. The constant movement, and problematical zawn crossings, provide continual interest. The larger the party, the more fun the activity is. Watching other people in extremis is good spectator entertainment, and tasks of rope work are spread amongst the group.

The best time to start traversing is on a falling Neap Tide, although it is possible to climb throughout a Neap Tide cycle. Spring Tides often submerge holds or expose large areas of sea-weed covered rock. Care should be taken to avoid being cut off by high Spring Tides. Because of the range of tides and weathers, it is possible to do the same traverse several times, and find the character completely different on each occasion.

The standard of the traverses can usually be varied by using a greater or lesser number of tyroleans to cross zawns, rather than climbing around them, although the tyroleans may be difficult to set up. This can normally be achieved by lassoing spikes or flakes, but it may be necessary for the holder of the short straw to swim across to fix the rope.

The traverses are normally soloed, but if the sea is rough, or the party contains non-swimmers, great caution should be exercised. There have been serious, sometimes fatal, accidents and the power of the sea should never be underestimated. In event of falling into the sea on a cold day, retreating for a change of clothes should be considered, as one's standard of climbing drops considerably when wet and cold, and hypothermia is a genuine possibility.

Generally, little gear is required beyond a rope to make the tyroleans. Extra gear can be added to make life a little more comfortable: slings, harnesses, nuts and extra ropes. Friends will be found very useful for making belays safe. It is worth remembering to thoroughly wash any climbing gear used in freshwater after the traverse, salt water has an extremely corrosive and damaging effect on both metals and fabrics.

There are many sea-level traverses on the Anglesey coastline, and some are noted in the previous section. Following is a brief description of the traverses on Holy Island. They have all been climbed in both directions, but the most common way of doing them is right to left, facing in. Each section can usually be completed in three to four hours, giving over 900 metres of climbing. It should be noted that some traverses are subject to a voluntary access ban.

THE RANGE TRAVERSE   (Grid ref. 225 795 to 217 798)

Park at the Bird Reserve car park on Penryn Mawr, and walk SSW to the zawn containing the old lifeboat station, Porth Ruffydd, this being a convenient finishing point. Walk in an easterly direction for one kilometre until a wall is reached. Cross this and descend to sea level. After three difficult zawns an island is reached, which can be avoided, but is worth doing. Beyond an island is a cave, impassable at high tide without swimming, and another cave near the end may require a pendulum. This traverse can also be started from Porth Daffarch, if a longer day is required.

PENRHYN MAWR   (Grid ref 217 798 to 215 815)

This starts at the aforementioned Porth Ruffydd, and provides some interest, including a nice through route in a huge cleft. A little farther on, an island can be traversed, but some way beyond this the coast turns north-west, and the strata of the rock causes the traversing to be less pleasant. Care should be taken on the very end of the headland, as the tide race off here makes the flow of water very fast.

ABRAHAM'S BOSOM TO YELLOW WALL   (R)
(Grid ref. 215 815)

A good traverse, starting at the road junction leading to South Stack. The first 200 metres are walking, then excellent climbing leads to a cave, most easily crossed by tyrolean. Good views of Smurf and Blacksmith's Zawns. The difficulties end just after Penlas Rock.

YELLOW WALL TO SOUTH STACK   (R)   (Grid ref. 207 817
to 204 823)

Excellent views and situations. A tyrolean is necessary just beyond Lighthouse Arête. Exit as for the Mousetrap Zawn approach.

SOUTH STACK ISLAND   (R)   (Grid ref. 203 823)

Short, but with some hard climbing, although the caves may halt progress.

SOUTH STACK TO THE MAIN CLIFF   Grid ref. 204 823
to 215 833)

The longest and most interesting traverse, requiring a full day, and starting in Mousetrap Zawn (R). Traverse towards the bridge. and descend a chain to sea level, first making sure there is something to land on! During the restricted period, this traverse can be started by abseiling from the bridge; Mousetrap Zawn must not be entered. Continue to The Main Cliff passing the mysterious Thunderbird Zawn. Several tyroleans may be required.

THE MAIN CLIFF TO NORTH STACK   Grid ref. 215 833
to 215 839)

A great traverse for a very hot day, but as several swims are required, it is not recommended for the winter! Great views of the crag, with some excellent climbing. Exit through Parliament House Cave and finish easily. At some tides, it is possible to traverse the base of North Stack Wall to the tip of North Stack (a very powerful flow of water here).

NORTH STACK TOWARDS HOLYHEAD HARBOUR
(Grid ref. 215 841 to 225 836)

Start from the tip of North Stack, or by abseiling into Parliament House Cave and exiting out of the through cave. The climbing is good and continuous, and two or three tyroleans may be required.

HOLYHEAD BREAKWATER
(Grid ref. 238 839)

It is possible to traverse on either side, difficulty variable, however a fall into the water may be serious as there are limited places to climb out! Potentially 4,500 metres of climbing.

Graded List of Climbs

This graded list, presented in order of difficulty, hardest to easiest, for routes of Very Severe and above, is included to a certain extent as entertainment for puerile tickers. It does, however, give an indication of the relative difficulty of leading a route within the given grade, although it should be noted that, on the day, this might depend upon reach, stamina, hangover, determination, and whether or not your partner is particularly keen on swimming/seconding overhanging diagonal traverses/having no belay! The grading is for an on-sight flashed ascent – this is of obvious importance when there is little protection. Thus the list reflects the difference between a bold lead and a merely difficult, but safe climb. It was put together by confirmed Gogarth devotees, but should on no account be taken as absolute truth.

Impossible
Parliament House Cave (Free)

Fairly Impossible
Spider's Web (Free)

Fairly Tedious
Any more routes on North Stack Wall

E8
The Super Calabrese (6b, 6b, 6b)

E7
The Bells! The Bells! (6b)
The Enchanted Broccoli Garden (6b, 6b)
Isis is Angry (5c, 5b, 6a, 6c)
The Hollow Man (6b)
Hardback Thesaurus (6b)
Free Stone Henge (4c, 6c, 5c, 5b)
Flower of Evil (6b)
Stroke of the Fiend (6b, 6b)
The Clown (6b)
The Demons of Bosch (6b)
The Angle Man (6b, 6b)
A Wreath of Deadly Nightshade (6b)
The Unridable Donkey (6b, 5c)
Conan the Librarian (6b, 6b, 5c)

E6
Hang Ten (6c)

The Cad (6a)
Skinhead Moonstomp (6a, 6b, 5a)
Barbarossa (6b, 4c)
Me (4c, 5c, 5c, 6a)
Psychocandy (6c)
Art Groupie (6b)
Birth Trauma (6a)
Blackleg (6b, 6a, 4c)
Ludwig (5a, 5c, 6b)
Schittlegruber (5c, 6b)
Strike Direct (6c)
Headbutt (6b)
Death Trap Direct (5c)
Dreams and Screams (5b, 6b)
The Drunk (4c, 6b, 5b)
The Jub-Jub Bird (6b)
Eraserhead (6a)
The Big Sleep (6a, 6b 5a)
Heart of Gold Direct (6a)
Wall of Fossils (6a, 6b)

E5
The Long Run (6a)
Obelisk (4c, 6b, 5b)
Mammoth (6b, 5c)
Alien (6b, 5c, 5c)
Rosebud (6a)
Stingray (6a, 5c, 6b)
The Horrorshow (6b, 5c, 4c)
Salem (5b, 5c, 6b)
The Red Sofa (6b)
Evidently Chickentown (6b)
Dinosaur (6a, 5b, 5c)

E5 (contd.)
Warpath (6a)
Khmer Rouge (6a)
Seal's Song (-, 5b)
The Cow (6a, 5c)
Energy Crisis (6a, 5c)
Hunger (6a, 5c, 5b)
Death Trap (5b, 4a, 5b, 5a)
Mein Kampf (5c, 6a)
Free Nelson Mandela Now (6a)
The Tet Offensive (6b, 5c, 5b, 5a)
Citadel (6b, 6a)
Another Roadside Attraction (6b, 5b)
Ordinary Route (6a, 6a, 5c, 5b)
Helmet Boiler (4b, 5c, 4b, 5a)
Positron (5c, 6a, 6a)
Heart of Gold (5c, 6a)
Games Climbers Play Original Start (6a)
The Cruise (6b, 4c)
The Ancient Mariner (5c, 6b)
Penelope Undercling (6b)
Big Boys (6a)
The Emotionary (6a, 5a)
Run Fast, Run Free (6a)

E4
Sebastapol (5c, 6a, 5a)
Graduation Ceremony (5c, 6a)
The Electrification of the Soviet Union (6a)
The Wastelands (5c, 6a, 5a)
Staying Alive (6a, 5a)
Rapture of the Deep (5a, 5b)
High Pressure (5c, 5b)
Afreet.Street (6a, 4c)
The Maze (5c, 5c, 5c, 5c, 5b)
Pagan (5b, 5c, 5c)
The Missionary (5c, 5c, 5b)
Manor Park (5c, 6a)
Television Route (5c)
Hyde Park (5b, 6b)
Cannibal (5c)
Not Fade Away (5c)
Red Haze (5a, 5c)
Medicine Man (6a)
The Trail of Tears (6a)
Fifteen Men etc. (6a, 5c, 4c)
The Camel (6a, 5b)
Thunderbird (6a, 5c)

Atheist (6a)
20,000 Leagues Under the Sea (6a)
Magellan's Wall (5b, 6a)
The Cocktail Trip (5c)
Arachnid (5c)
Puzzle Me Quick (5b, 5c)
Bubbly Situation Blues (6a, 5c)
Blue Peter (5c)
Godzilla (5c)
Electric Blue (5c)
The Viper (5c)
Ormuzd (5b, 5c)
Falls Road (4b, 5c, 5a)

E3
The Horizon (3 pts.)
Dogs of War (5b, 5b)
Blue Remembered Hills (5c, 5c)
Deygo (5b, 5c, 5b, 4c)
Hysteresis (5c, 5c, 4c)
A Brown Study (5c, 5b, 5a)
Infidel (5b, 5c, 4b)
Trunk Line (5b, 5a, 5c, 5b, 5c, 5c)
Mantrap (4c, -, 5b, 5b)
Redshift (5b, 5c, 4c)
Fantasia (4c, 5c)
The Cree (6a)
Strike (6a, 4c)
Tumbing Dice (6a)
Left Hand Red Wall (5c 5c)
Communication Breakdown (5c, 5b)
Paddington (5c)
Bedlam (4c, 5b, 5a)
Atlantic Wall (5c, 5b)
Dangerous Rhythm (4b, 5c)
Get the Stroll (5c, 5c)
Supercrack (5c)
T Rex (5c, 5b, 4c)
The Moon (4c, 5c, 5b)
Pequod (5c)
Wonderwall (6a)
Winking Crack (5a, 5c)
The Grim Reaper (5a, 6a)
Gobbler's Arête (6a, 5a)
Centrefold (5c)
The Mask of the Red Death (5c, 5c)
The Assassin (5b, 5c, 4c)
Captain Nemo (6a)
Blue Oyster Cult (5b, 5a, 5c)
The Needle (5b, 5c)
Big Groove Direct (5c)

E3 (contd.)

Perygl (4c, 5c, 5b)
Pterodactyl (5c)
Kalahari (4b, 5c, 5b)
The Sun (4b, 5c)
Syringe (5c, 5c)
The Rat Race (5a, 5c, 5b, 4c, 5a)
This Year's Model (5c, 5a)
King of the Swingers (5c, 5c)
E.P. Special (6a)
The Sind (5a, 5b)
The Big Groove (5a, 5c, 5b)
South Sea Bubble (5c)
Wendigo (4c, 5a, 5b, 4b)

E2

Spider's Web (5b, 5a, 4c)
Transatlantic Crossing (5a, 5c, 5b, 4b)
Blowout (5c, 5a)
Emmenthal (5b)
Wall of Horrors (5b)
The Quartz Icicle (5b, 5b)
Wrangler (5c)
Stimulator (5c, 5b)
The Strand (5b, 4b)
Street Survivor (5a, 5c)
Red Wall (4c, 5b, 4c)
The Original Girdle Mousetrap Zawn (5a, 4c, 4a, 5b, 5a)
Primate (5b, 4c, 4c)
Volcano (5a, 5c)
Dropout (5b, 4a)
Zeus (5a, 5b, 4b)
The Tail (5c)
Aardvark (6a, 4a)
Hypodermic (5b, 5c)
Kissing the Pink (5b)
Star of the Sea (5c, 5a)
The Bluebottle (5a, 5b)
Ceilidh (4a, 4c, 5c, 5a)
Genuflex (5b)
Flytrap (4a, 5a, 5b, 4b)
Talking Heads (5b)
The Eternal Optimist (5b, 4c)
Creeping Lemma (4c, 5b, 5c)
Belvedere (5c, 5b)
Gnome (5b, 5c)
Jaborandi (5b, 4c, 5b)
Blind Pew (4c, 5b, 5b, 5b, 4c)
Tequila Sunrise (5b, 5c)

Cartwheel (4c, 5b)
Smurf (5b, 5b)
Caress of Steel (5c)
Mousetrap (5b, 5a, 5a)
The Savage Sunbird (5b)
Archway (4a, 5b, 4c)
Charlie Don't Surf (5b)
U.F.O. (5b, 5b)
Toiler on the Sea (5b, 5b)
Hurricane (5c)
Fail Safe (5b, 5a)

E1

Alligator (5b)
Park Lane/Doomsville (5b, 5b, 4b)
True Moments/Freebird (4c, 5b, 5b)
Resolution (5a, 5b, 5b)
Mestizo (4c, 5b)
Slow Dancer (5a)
The New Girdle – Mousetrap Zawn (4c, 4c, 4a, 5b)
Gogarth (4b, 5a, 4c, 4b, 5b)
High Noon (5b, 5b)
True Moments (4c, 5b, 5b)
Atlantis (5a, 5c)
Grendel (5c)
North West Passage (5a, 5b)
Crowbar (4b, 5a, 5b)
Nightride (4c, 5b, 4c)
Swastika (5c, 5a, 5a, 5a)
Hombre (5b, 5b)
Waxwing (5b)
Fifth Avenue (5b, 5a)
Praetor (5c, 5a, 5a)
Breaking the Barrier (5b)
The Third Man (5b)
Green Gilbert (5a)
Dream Seller (5b)
Phaedra (5c, 4c)
The Savage (5a, 5a)
Bitter Days (5a, 5b)
Merchant Man (5b, 5a)
Freebird (4c, 5b, 5b)
Emulator (5b)
Anarchist (5b, 4c)
Castell Helen Girdle (4c, 5b, -, 4c, 4c)
Heathen (5b)
Gringo (5b, 5a)
Nice 'n Sleazy (5a)
The Wild Rover (5b)

Neutrino (5b)
Little Queenie (5b)
The Whip (5a, 5a)

Hard Very Severe
The Concrete Chimney (5a)
Spider Wall (5a, 4c)
Shag Rock (5a)
Black Spot (5a, 4c)
Fluke (4b, 5b, 4a)
Heroin (5b, 4c)
Phagocyte (5a, 5a)
Shagger's Start (5b)
Diogenes (5a, 4c)
Exit Groove (5a)
Sprung (5b, 5a)
Another Groove (5b)
A Dream of White Horses (5a, 5a,
    5a, 4c, 4c)
Amphitheatre Wall (4b, 4c)
Pentathol (5a, 4b, 4c, 4b)
Hud (5a)
Mulatto (4c, 5a)
Central Park (4c, 5a)
The Cracks (4c, 5a)
Times Square (5a, 5a)
Shell Shock (5b)
The Gauntlet (5a, 4b)
Cordon Bleu (4a, 4b, 5b, 4b)
Icarus (4c, 5a)
Belial (5a)
Black Light (4c, 4b)
The Ramp (5a, 5a)
The Girdle Traverse (Main Cliff)
    (4a, 4b, 4c, 4c, 4b, 4c, 4b)
Wen (5a, 4c, 5a)
Gazebo (5a)
Scavenger Direct (5a)
Britomartis (4c, 4c)
Rock Island Line (5a, 5a)
Ahriman (5a, 5a)
If (5a, 5a)
Tape Worm (4c, 4c)
Primevil (4c, 4c, 4c, 4c)
King Bee Crack (5a)
Scavenger (4c, 5a, 4a)
Where Puffins Daren't (4a, 4a, 5a,
    4c, 4c)
Dde (5a, 4c, 5a)

Generation Gap (5a)
Gobi (4c, 4a, 4a, 5a)
The Hustler (4c)
The Smurf Girdle (5a, 4c, 4a)
Fan Fare (4c)
Black Light (4c, 4b)
Balu (5a)
Hash (5a, 5a)
Bullitt (5a)
Blanco (4c, 5a, 4a)
The Trap (4c, 4a)

Very Severe
The Rift (4c, 4c)
The Green Slab (4b, 4b, 4b, 4b)
Bezel (4b, 5a, 4b)
Red Wall Escape Route (4c, 4b, 4b,
    4a)
Pantin (4b, 4c)
Poseidon (4b, 4c, 4a)
Bloody Chimney (4c, 4b, 4c)
Green Light (!)
Sulcus (5a)
Ipso Facto (4c)
Pel (4c, 4b)
Imitator (4c, 4b)
A Groove (4c)
Human Camel (5a)
Rap (4c, 4b)
Vena Cava (4c)
Teaser (4c)
Big Gut (4c, -, 4c)
Diagonal (4c)
Diatom (4c)
Patience (4c)
Tomorrow Has Been Cancelled (4c)
Thor (4c, 4b)
Mr Seal (4c)
End Game (4c)
The Ramp of Pink Emulsion (4c)
Lighthouse Arête Direct (4c, 4a)
Truant (4b)
Colditz (4c)
Miura (4c)
Maverick (4b, 4c)
Lighthouse Arête (4a, 4b, 4c, 4a)
Perpendicular (4b, 4b)
Exit Chimney (4c)

First Ascents

This list does not include many early routes on Holyhead Mountain, and other crags around Anglesey, as many had previous ascents prior to being recorded, or first ascent details were not available. The number in brackets after the climb indicates the number of aid points used in the first ascent, where known. AL and VL in brackets indicate alternate and varied leads respectively. On each first free ascent no height was gained by artificial means. The style of these ascents has varied, according to the accepted ethics of the period.

1950s	*Many climbs on Holyhead Mountain and some minor forays onto the other cliffs by C Fishwick, R.A.F. climber based at Valley, and K C Jones and D Durkan. Details mostly unrecorded.*
1964 Apr. 4	**Gogarth** (1 pt. aid) B Ingle, M A Boysen (AL)
	The first foray onto Anglesey's major sea cliff.
1964 Apr. 4	**Shag Rock** (1 pt. aid) M A Boysen, B Ingle
1964 Apr. 24	**Pentathol** P Crew, B Ingle
	'...I can remember going along that traverse, thinking, "God, we're going to die if we're not careful", and then struggling on that first pitch of Pentathol, watching the tide coming in and wondering if we were going to drown.' (The route name is now traditional, but should probably have been recorded as Pentothal. Ed.)
1964 Apr. 25	**Bezel** B Ingle, P Crew (AL)
1964 May 2	**The Gauntlet** P Crew, B Ingle (AL)
	Described as climbed by T Herley, J Baldock in 1967, as the original finish fell down in 1969.
1964 May 3	**Simulator** P Crew, B Ingle
1964 May 10	**Emulator** P Crew, B Ingle
1964 May 10	**Amphitheatre Wall** M A Boysen, C Rowlands
1964 May	**Pantin** A Williams, B Royal
	Of these first nine routes, five are still considered amongst the finest and most popular on these crags.
1964 Nov.	**Mobil** D Peers, G Milburn
	(No relation! Ed.)
1965 Jun. 5	**The Green Slab** S Wroe, D Crilly, P Braithwaite
	The first explorations on the South Stack cliffs. 'The Alpha club ceased to be a major force in climbing after 1964. Most of its members, who were to the man brilliant rock climbers, continued to climb hard rock, but the days of the big team were over. Crew and Ingle bought a cottage and spent much of their time altering it. Boysen disappeared to the Lakes as did Nunn, Woolcock, Rowlands, McHardy, Williams and all the others. Exploration on Craig Gogarth, as the cliff was now called was curtailed, and those left in Wales were largely

ignorant about its tremendous possibilities, and they concentrated their energies elsewhere. Although Crew never really forgot the possibilities of the cliff he was ready to shelve his ambitions with the opposition safely out of the way; but throughout 1965 the ambitious climbers who were finding new rock in Snowdonia posed a growing threat, and both Crew and Ingle knew that once those possibilities had dried up the new "Turks" would find their way to Gogarth.'

Ken Wilson, Mountain Craft, Summer 1967

1966 Mar. 12   **The Rift**   C E Davies, A Cowburn
The ascent opened some eyes to the possibilities of Gogarth.

1966 Mar. 19   **Heroin**   P Crew, Jancis Baldock

1966 Apr. 3   **Diogenes**   P Crew, I G MacNaught-Davies

1966 Easter   **Television Route** (A1)   J Brown, I G MacNaught-Davies
'Meanwhile Messrs. Baillie, Gray, Smith and Amatt were pegging up the Red Wall. As they twisted and thrashed at the end of their 150-foot life-lines, pitons and hammers pounding out a staccato bass, they invoked nostalgic memories of pre-war Munich Spider men... None of the principal actors participated in the early rehearsals. The producer explained that this was necessary to conserve an atmosphere of tension... I knew for a fact that Rusty was deliberately spacing the pegs and bolts so as to combine maximum economy with minimum security.'

Tom Patey

The complete climbing team was Joe Brown, Ian MacNaught-Davies, Tom Patey, Royal Robbins (legendary American climber to strengthen the likelihood of a replay on the American TV), Rusty Baillie, John Cleare, Dennis Gray, John Amatt and Roy Smith.
First free ascent: J Moran, B Wintringham, P Williams, 13 August 1978.
'Dave Durkan led Television Route using 5 points of aid. Pete Sandall seconded it with only 4. The ascent was done as a training clinb in preparation for the crack to the right of Winking Crack, which went at XS/A1 and was named **The Nod**.*'*

1966 Apr. 11   **Ceilidh** (1 pt. aid)   A R McHardy, P Crew (AL)

1966 Apr. 11   **Interpolator** (1 pt. aid)   B Ingle, P Crew

1966 Apr. 24   **Bloody Chimney**   D E Alcock, D Potts (AL)

1966 Apr. 24   **The Ramp**   P Crew, J Baldock
'I looked at The Ramp for week after week, trying to work out whether it was a slab, or an overhanging wall with jugs.'

1966 May 7   **Dirtigo**   M Yates, J Jordan

1966 May 7   **Fail Safe** (1 pt. aid)   D E Alcock, P Crew (AL)

1966 May 8   **Wen**   J Brown, M A Boysen

The first contribution from the most outstanding of Gogarth's many devotees, climbed using borrowed gear from a large sea-level traversing team. The carefully restrained cat was definitely out of the bag!

1966 May 13   **Dde**   J Brown, B Sharp

1966 May 14   **Scavenger** (1 pt. aid)   M A Boysen, J Jordan
Direct Finish by R Evans, D Cuthbertson, May 1974.

1966 May 14   **Central Park** (10 pts. aid)   P Crew, D E Alcock (AL)
'I though it was a hard route, but that's the problem with new routes: often the psychological and physical effort of pioneering is out of all proportion to the eventual route, and of course Central Park soon came to be regarded as a very reasonable climb.'

1966 May 14   **Fifth Avenue**   M A Boysen, M Yates
'At Whitsuntide Crew and Alcock, after several attempts, climbed the magnificent Central Park, rather like Great Wall on Cloggy. They were met at the top by Boysen who had just finished an adjoining and equally difficult route, aptly named 5th Avenue. This was Boysen's second new route of the day, the first being a delectable crack line, Scavenger, on the Main Cliff. The Lake District ace, Geoff Cram paying his first visit to the cliff the following day climbed Scavenger and enthusiastically claimed it as a new route but Boysen corrected him; the same thing happened a few weeks later when Brown tried to claim 5th Avenue as his own; such are the pitfalls of fast exploration.'

Ken Wilson, Mountain Craft

1966 May 21   **Cordon Bleu**   G Birtles, P Crew

1966 May 21   **Crow Bar** (7 pts. aid)   D Scott, W Cheverst

1966 May 22   **Puffin**   R Edwards, J Fletcher
Climbed Direct by R Edwards, J Hutchinson, 14 November 1967.

1966 May 24   **Strike** (5 pts. aid)   R Edwards, E Fry
First free ascent: P Gomersall, S Foster, 1976.
Direct Start by J M Redhead, 4 April 1982.

1966 May 27   **Imitator**   B Ingle, G Rogan (AL)

1966 May 28   **Main Cliff Girdle**   P Crew, G Birtles (AL)

1966 Jun. 5   **Winking Crack** (6 pts. aid)   J Brown, A Cowburn
The crack that winked at Brown every time he passed eventually winked once too often, but it did not give up without a considerable struggle.

1966 Jun. 11   **Hustler**   M Howells, B Whybrow

1966 Jun. 11   **Jaborandi** (4 pts. aid)   P Crew, D E Alcock (AL)

1966 Jun. 11   **Syringe** (7 pts. aid)   D Scott, R Gillies
'...when it was learned that no less than 9 pegs had been used on a nominally free route there were murmers of discontent from those who had tried to avoid this. One could hardly fail to notice that Scott's earlier route had

used 3 slings and 4 pegs for aid, which even for Craig Gogarth seemed extravagant.'

Ken Wilson, Mountain Craft, Summer 1967

1966 Jun. 14	**Hud** J Brown, H Drasdo
1966 Jun. 18	**Phaedra** M Howells, B Whybrow
1966 Jun. 18	**Big Groove** (1 pt. aid) P Crew, D E Alcock

The route proved to be highly technical and at the time was thought to be one of the hardest routes on the cliff. Direct Finish by E Drummond, B Campbell-Kelly, 27 September 1969.

Probably Crew's best line on the whole cliff.

1966 Jun. 19   **Dinosaur** (10 pts. aid)   P Crew, J Brown

Top Pitch added by P Crew, E Fry, 24 July 1966.
First free ascent: R Fawcett, 1980, although climbed by P Minks, B Molyneux with 1 point aid some time earlier.

'At that time the old man was definitely short of a good partner, but that was the only route on which I ever really burned him off, or climbed better than he...every time since, he's definitely been the boss - I don't mind admitting it.'

'On the 19th June, 1966, Joe Brown and Pete Crew climbed together for the first time and probably the strongest team ever to set foot on rock in this country made a bid to crack this "last great problem." They started early but they encountered such difficulty that both climbers were driven back several times. Late afternoon they were established on a stance in the middle of the wall. The cliff at this point was appallingly loose and it seemed as if they were hanging from tottering blocks all the time. All the lose material they pulled off was dropping into the sea 20 feet out from the base of the climb. They eventually finished at 9.30 p.m. The technical difficulty was high and the danger from loose rock was so considerable Dinosaur, as they called the climb, must stand out as one of the most formidable expeditions in Wales.'

Ken Wilson, Mountain Craft, Summer 1967

Brown said of Crew "Long neck and no brains."

1966 Jun. 23   **Blind Pew** (10 pts. aid)   J Brown, J Cheesmond
First free ascent: D Knighton, D Cronshaw, 12 September 1978.

1966 Jul. 23   **Rat Race** (1 pt. aid)   M Howells, B Whybrow
Pitch 1 initially done by G Birtles, C Jackson.
Pitch 2 first climbed by J Brown, 8 July.
Pitch 4 M Boysen, C J S Bonington, 1965.
Final Pitch J Brown, P Crew, 24 July 1966.

1966 Sep. 2   **Red Wall**   J Brown, P Crew
'Doing something like Red Wall you snapped some of the holds off. You could see that they weren't loose, they were just so thin and big that they snapped off like biscuits, and

you very quickly got the hang of just smashing them off, so that what was left was thicker and stronger'

1966 Sep.6	**Wendigo** J Brown, A J J Moulam

Two very fine routes marked the start of real explorations on this imposing wall.

1966 Sep.15	**Red Wall, Escape Route** and **Blanco** J Brown, D E Alcock
1966 Sep.16	**Atlantis** (1 pt. aid) J Brown, D E Alcock

Yet another crag opened up by the master, this one was again spotted during filming on Television Route.

1966 Sep.18	**Doppelgangen** (2 pts. aid) J Brown, D E Alcock

First free ascent: S Haston, 1978.

'By July (1966) Crew had prepared the draft for an interim guide and the amazing total of 39 routes appeared in it...a pace of exploration unparalleled in the history of the sport.'

Ken Wilson, Mountain Craft, Summer, 1967

1966 Oct. 2	**Kalahari** (3 pts. aid) J Brown, P Crew.

Top Pitch added by G Birtles, J Brown, B Ingle, 1967.
Top Pitch Direct by R Edwards, 1967.

1966 Oct. 8	**Pel** and **Rap** P Crew, D Alcock (AL)
1966 Oct. 8	**Lighthouse Arête** and **Castell Helen Girdle** A G Cram, M Yates.

A Smith and party had previously climbed the final section of the latter.

1966 Oct. 9	**Mousetrap** (2 pts. aid) J Brown, P Crew (AL)

An instant classic.

1966 Oct. 14	**Bedlam** J Brown, P Crew (AL)
1966 Oct. 16	**Pterodactyl** A G Cram, M Yates

As serious a route as any at the time.

1966 Oct. 16	**Stochastic Groove** I G MacNaught-Davies, A Alvarez, G Clarke
1966 Oct. 22	**Primevil** P Crew, G Birtles (AL)
1966 Oct. 28	**The Sind** J Brown, P Crew (AL)

An impressive direct attack on the defences of Yellow Wall.
'...The whole of the wide crack on the left of the slab was full of yellow dust, and we both had bad guts for months afterwards because of all the dust we'd taken in.'

1966 Dec. 31	**Resolution** (1 pt. aid) P Crew, G Rogan

Climbed direct by A Pollitt, H Clover, 13 March 1982.

1967 Jan. 1	**Gobi** P Crew, J Brown

Much of this had been climbed previously.

1967 Jan. 6	**Thor** J Brown, P Crew (AL)
1967 Jan. 8	**Big Gut, Small Gut** and **Diagonal** J Brown, D Alcock

Another area again, and so many lines to go at.

1967 Jan. 15	**Tape Worm** and **Volcano** (3 pts. aid) J Brown, P Crew

First free ascent of Volcano: A Sharp, S Humphries.

1967 Jan. 22	**Crossover, Exit Groove** and **Ahriman** J Brown, P Crew (AL)

The original start of Ahriman fell down some time later.
Shagger's Start to Exit Groove by P Trower, I Wilson, April 1989.

1967 Feb. 4	**The Trap**	D E Alcock, G Rogan
1967 Feb. 4	**Ormuzd** (1 pt. aid)	J Brown, G Birtles, P Crew
1967 Feb. 5	**Belial**	P Crew, A Alvarez
1967 Feb. 11	**Britomartis**	D E Alcock, G Rogan

A gem of a find.

1967 Feb. 12	**Uhuru** (Wen Zawn)	D E Alcock, G Rogan (AL)
1967 Feb. 12	**Concrete Chimney**	P Crew, J Brown (AL)

Climbed direct by L J Wood, J Entwistle, September 1967.

1967 Feb. 18	**Genuflex**	P Crew, B Ingle
1967 Feb. 18	**Ipso Facto**	M Howells, B Whybrow
1967 Feb. 20	**Route 66**	J Brown, P Crew, B Ingle
1967 Feb. 26	**Nightride**	J Brown, G Rogan

*Named after an earlier attempt when the team got
benighted. As mountainous seas rose ever higher the
rescue team arrived. At first the team refused to be
'rescued', but as a huge wave broke over them three
climbers found themselves*
prusiking furiously up the same rope – or so the tale goes.

1967 Mar. 30	**Plimsole Line**	H Drasdo, N Drasdo, K Carr

Another traditional mis-spelling.

1967 Apr. 15	**Times Square**	F E R Cannings, D G Peers

Pitch 2 by F E R Cannings, T I M Lewis, 9 March 1969.

1967 Apr. 23	**North Face Route**	W Preece, P Duffield
1967 Apr. 30	**Phagocyte** and **Rotten Gut**	J Brown, P Crew (AL)
1967 May 6/7	**Mammoth** (6 pts. aid)	P Crew, E Drummond

*Climbed with two points aid by R Fawcett, J Hesleltine,
1973.
One point of aid by J M Redhead in 1980.
First free ascent: A Pollitt, S Andrews, 23 May 1984.
Direct Start by A Pollitt, M E Crook, 26 May 1984.*

1967 May 13	**Primate** and **Wrangler** (1 pt. aid)	J Brown, I G MacNaught-Davies
1967 May 14	**Hombre** (1 pt. aid) and **Praetor** (1 pt. aid)	J Brown, I MacNaught-Davies
1967 May 14	**Fluke** (2 pts. aid)	P Crew, A Alvarez
1967 May 19	**Doomsville** (2 pts. aid)	M Yates, A G Cram (AL), Judy Yates
1967 Jun. 4	**Serendipity**	C J S Bonington, M Thompson
1967 Jun. 11	**Left-Hand Red Wall** (2 pts. aid)	J Brown, P Crew (AL)

*First free ascent: H Barber, 1976.
'The cliff is such a pleasant spot that the day is not wasted
even if you don't climb. The bay is a suntrap, well
sheltered from the wind, yet light sea breezes keep the
temperature bearable. The demands of the female half of
the climbing community can easily be met by leaving
them to sunbathe on one of the large flat boulders next to
the sea. The bored second who could veto progress on
higher and colder cliffs is happy here with bronzed
females below to take his mind from his leader's tiresome
struggles. The weather is so mild that the climbing is
possible in the winter months. Previously only Tremadoc
could be counted on to avoid the miseries of frozen*

*fingers and toes, but now this new crag with vastly
superior climbing will enable climbers to stay at peak
fitness throughout the winter.*

Ken Wilson, Mountain Craft, Summer 1967

1967 Jul. 24	**Enchanter's Nightshade**	M Swain
1967 Jul. 27	**Nonentity**	D Durkan, D Williams
1967 Aug. 2	**Moonshine**	D Durkan, D Williams
1967 Aug. 26	**Brown Split**	M Swain, A Hughes
1967 Aug.	**Sea Level Girdle**, South Stack	J Brown, E Drummond (AL)
1967 Sep. 18	**Archway**	J Brown, B A Fuller

*'He took absolutely ages, and was three times
underwater: yet he must have been fifty or sixty feet
above sea level.'*

1967 Sep.	**Mulatto**	J Brown, G Rogan, A Wright
1967 Sep.	**Gringo** (1 pt. aid)	J Brown, J Cheesemond
1967 Sep.	**Point Blank**	J Brown, T Peck
1967 Sep.	**Auricle**	J Brown, B A Fuller

*The upper section had been climbed previously by J
Brown, M V Anthoine.
Variation Finish by D Durkan, 14 October 1970.*

1967 Oct. 1   **The Strand** (1 pt. aid)   E Drummond

*Unseconded due to fading light.
Another generation starts to make its mark, a brilliant
contribution, but a little over the top in the way
Drummond recorded it: XS 6b, and stated that it wouldn't
be repeated for twenty years. It actually only survived a
few weeks before the second ascent.*

1967 Oct. 1   **Yellow Scar**   L E Holliwell, L R Holliwell

*A portion of the route fell down and the route as
described was first climbed by L E Holliwell, M Howells,
23 March 1969.
The Cockney team get to grips with the crag.
'The Holliwells were extremely upset when Sceptic and
the top of Yellow Groove, two of their best (hardest)
efforts, fell down during the winter.'*

The McCallum Affair. *Late in 1967 four routes were
claimed on the Upper Tier of Gogarth by an unknown
climber: Hielan'man, HVS, was the steep wall right of The
Gauntlet; Tam Dubh, HVS, was the deep vertical crack
between Bezel and Fail Safe; A'Bhaisteir (The
Executioner), XS, was a groove, corner and chimney left
of Ceilidh; and lastly Gael's Wall, XS, was right of Fail
Safe. The descriptions of these routes appeared in New
Climbs 1968.
A whisper went round the climbing world that something
was amiss and eventually a statement appeared in the
August edition of Rocksport. 'Rumours that the very
existence of some of the routes in New Climbs 68 is not
above suspicion'. Worse still, there were other possible*

bogus routes in the Moelwyns. Leading climbers of the
day went 'to have a look' and were cynical, but who
should point the finger of suspicion? A drastic step was
needed as the integrity of the climbing world was at stake.
The story finally hit the national papers, and was reported
in the February 1969 edition of Rocksport.
'Gillman (1969) then spells out the suspicions and
evidence which mushroomed into controversy whose
seriousness was unprecedented in the history of British
rock-climbing:- the unavoidable loose rock encountered
by the Holliwell brothers on A'Bhasteir; the suspect dates
of the first ascents (mid-week); the abseil down Gael's
Wall which satisfied Crew that the route was ridiculous;
the discovery by Wilson that McCallum's seconds were
unknown to anyone in the Apollo Club and that the routes
were of a higher standard than they had ever known him
climb, etc.'
Holliwell and Mossman had needed three points of aid to
complete the line of Hielan'man – to give Sceptic.
Unfortunately, during February, whilst the controversy
raged, a colossal fall of rock wiped out the whole of the
route as well as the upper parts of Ceilidh and The
Gauntlet. The vultures searched the rock fall for any gear
or evidence of ascents, while Holliwell and Howells
attacked the remaining rock.
Nigel Rogers, without concrete evidence, remained
circumspect in the 1969 New Climbs: '... certain routes
published in the 1968 edition of the Bulletin are of
doubtful authenticity. I would like to emphasise the word
doubtful in the above statement; little if anything has
been proved.'
Ed Drummond must have been in no doubt about Gael's
Wall which needed several points of aid to complete
(nowadays it goes free at E3). The last of the bogus lines
had to wait until 1975 before it finally had an ascent by
Alec Sharp who recorded The Eternal Optimist. Honour
was finally restored.

1967 Oct. 7	**A Groove** and **Another Groove**	J Entwistle, L J Wood (AL)
1967 Oct. 7	**Gladiator**	L E Holliwell, L R Holliwell
1967 Oct. 15	**Black Spot**	L E Holliwell, L R Holliwell
1967 Oct. 22	**Park Lane**	L E Holliwell, L R Holliwell
1967 Oct. 22	**The Cracks**	J M Kosterlitz, R J Isherwood
1967 Nov. 4	**U.F.O.**	L E Holliwell, F Quigley, L R Holliwell

*The flying object was their car, which had left the road the
previous night via a patch of black ice!*

1967 Nov. 7	**Campion** (1 pt. aid)	R Edwards, J Edwards, F Hutchinson
1967 Nov.	**Transatlantic Crossing** (4 pts. aid)	E Drummond, S Brown

First free ascent: P Whillance, D Armstrong, 1977.

1967 Nov./Dec.	**The Big Overhang** (A3)	D K Scott, B Palmer (alternate stints)

'We reached the top after a total of 22 hours climbing spread over three weekends. The roof is climbed with some 40 pegs (a few were unfortunately left in place). The roof, in profile, is in the form of a saw blade with several hanging teeth of rock to be pegged down and up again. Long slings are essential to keep the ropes running free. RURPs were used at the lip.'

'Early in the winter Paul Denny soloed the Big Overhang at North Stack in a remarkably short time to complete the decline of a myth.'

February/March 1971 Rocksport

'An exercise was arranged for the purpose of comparing coast-guard and R.A.F. rescue techniques...Initially the area selected for the exercise was the main cliff of Gogarth, but whereas the R.A.F.'s 500- foot ropes could cope, the coast-guards' equipment was inadequate...The coast-guards had acquired some 200 feet of electron ladder to replace their heavy wooden and rope ladders and much fun was had allowing volunteers to go up and down, or rather down and up, The Big Overhang on the ladders, a feat which exhausted more than one person.'

Rocksport, October/November 1970

1968 Feb.	**Sunset Slab**	M S Shannon, M Evans
1968 Mar. 30	**Interrogator**	L E Holliwell, L R Holliwell
1968 Mar. 31	**Mordor** (1 pt. aid)	J Brown, D E Alcock
1968 Mar.	**Red Cracks** and **Triffid Groove**	R Conway, C T Jones (AL on latter)
1968 Apr. 7	**Prom**	J Brown, B A Fuller, D Alcock
1968 Apr. 14/15	**Suspender** (2 pts. aid)	A Willmott, M J Spring
1968 Apr. 21	**The Amphibian**	L E Holliwell, L R Holliwell
1968 Apr.	**Deygo** (5 pts. aid)	T Proctor, G Birtles.

Done on separate days, and involving some strange items, including a portion of plumbing, to be whacked into the cliff.

A difficult section near the top was eventually solved by abseiling and banging a specially made peg into a hole in the rock. The peg was then lassoed from below and used to pendulum into a continuation weakness...'

Mountain Craft, August 1968

First free ascent: R Fawcett, J Hesletine 1973.

1968 May	**Mousetrap Zawn Girdle**	M Howells, J M Kosterlitz.

Pitch I previously done by J Brown, B A Fuller, D E Alcock

1968 May	**The Whip**	D K Scott, B Palmer
1968 Jun. 5	**Nomad**	D Durkan, D Edwards
1968 Jul. 14	**Exit Chimney**	P Crew, B Ingle
1968 Jul. 20	**Hypodermic** (1 pt. aid)	L E Holliwell, L R Holliwell

'We did it on a paralysingly hot day, and after pitch one we both wanted to abseil off, we felt so horrible.'

1968 Jul. 27	**Rolla Costa**	D Durkan, D Williams
1968 Aug.	**Spider's Web** (some aid)	J Brown, P Crew

'And so it was with bated breath I awaited the "assault from the sea", prepared once more to be disappointed, but determined this time to discover why. At last the first transmission came and went. Likewise the second, and my disappointment was no less than I had feared. Joe and Mac calmly got on with the business (Mac didn't fall off – again!). Pete Crew and Don Whillans waltzed up Wen Slab with infrequent long-shots giving little away. The Holliwell brothers and Janet Rogers moved smoothly up Tyrannosaurus Rex with every promising sequence cut short just as it was getting interesting.
But then just as I was giving up, came the third transmission. Suddenly I was watching climbing, the real thing, actually on the screen! It looked like climbing, it felt like climbing. I was transfixed. Firstly for those few precious moments as Joe moved up the wall above the overhang of The Spider's Web; and then again as he seemingly battled with the final pitch. Both these sequences were pure gems. This was surely what live broadcasts should be like.'

Phil Watkin, Rocksport, October/November 1970

1968 Aug. 18/19	**A Dream of White Horses** E Drummond, D Pearce

Probably the most famous climb of its grade in Britain, Leo Dickinson's stunning photo providing the perfect illustration.

1968 Nov. 9   **The Quartz Icicle** E Drummond, B Campbell-Kelly
Pitch 2 by the same pair 31 August 1969.

1968 Nov. 19   **Citadel** (9 pts. aid) J Street, G Hibberd
Pitch 1 previously by J Street, G Birtles.
Aid reduced to 2 pts by A Sharp, then 1 pt by P R Littlejohn.
First free ascent: R Fawcett 1977.
If ever a climb was bludgeoned into submission, this certainly was. Hammered etrier rungs: the whole works.

1968 Dec. 1   **Gazebo** L E Holliwell, L R Holliwell, D Mossman

1968 Dec. 7   **Drag** (1 pt. aid) L E Holliwell. L R Holliwell.

1969 Jan. 19   **Sceptic** (3 pts aid) L E Holliwell, D Mossman
To the right of The Greatest an ascent of the bogus Hielanman. The route was completely destroyed by a huge rock fall four weeks later.

1969 Mar. 9   **Afreet Street** (4 pts. aid) E Drummond (unseconded)
An ascent of the bogus route Gael's Wall.
First free ascent: R Fawcett 1980.

1969 Mar. 16   **Broadway** (1 pt. aid) C J Phillips, D Cuthbertson, L Dickinso

1969 Mar. 23   **Valdini** L E Holliwell, M Howells (AL)

1969 Mar. 24   **The Horizon** (8 pts. aid) E Drummond, B Campbell-Kelly
The ascent took five days spread over several months.

1969 Apr. 7   **Perygl** (5 pts. aid) J Brown, P Crew (AL)
'Whilst writing the guidebook, Pete Crew has climbed a new route near Sind, with Brown, called Perygl, and

*because of its steepness and looseness the ascent took
five days.'*

Rocksport 1969

1969 Apr. 13   **Locarno** (1 pt. aid)   L E Holliwell, K Wilson
1969 Apr. 19   **Wonderwall** (2 pts. aid)   L E Holliwell, D S Potts
*'It looked preposterous to me: it wasn't as if he was
making for anything, just more overhanging rock.'
First free ascent: A Sharp, J Pasquil 1973 or 1974.*
The **I Wonder Why** finish by M E Crook, C Smith June
1986.

1969 May 3   **Left-Hand Red Wall Girdle** (5 pts. aid)   P Crew, J Brown (AL)
1969 May 17   **Swastika**   L E Holliwell, L R Holliwell (VL)
1969 May 18   **Igdrazil** (1 pt. aid)   L E Holliwell, L R Holliwell
1969 May 25   **If**   E Drummond, B Whybrow, J Rogers
1969 May 17/26 **Mantrap** (1 pt. aid)   Pitches 1 and 2 L E Holliwell, L R
Holliwell. Pitches 3 and 4 L E Holliwell, R J Isherwood.
*'Laurie Holliwell's Mantrap follows an extremely steep line
between Mousetrap and Bedlam; and Wonderwall, also
by Holliwell, is another line of withering steepness in the
Easter Island Gully. Holliwell's seconds on these routes,
Isherwood and Potts (hardly strangers to rock), were "very
impressed"!.'*

Mountain 4, July 1969

1969 Jun. 1   **The Savage**   L E Holliwell, L R Holliwell
1969 Jun. 7/8   **T Rex** (2 pts. aid)   E Drummond, L E Holliwell, D Pearce (AL)
Janet Rogers
First free ascent: P Littlejohn 1971.
Golden Bough Finish by E Drummond, C Dale July 1973.
Metal Guru Variation by S Long, C Parkin, 13 July 1989.
1969 Jun. 29   **Spider Wall**   L E Holliwell, D S Potts, L R Holliwell
*The guide appeared in June and bears witness to the
fantastic upsurge of Anglesey as a major climbing centre.
140 routes have been recorded – all climbed in the space
of five years. It seems fair to say that the development of
these sea cliffs will come to be regarded as one of the
great milestones of British climbing history.'*

Mountain 4, July 1969

*'Anglesey has provided one of the great sagas of post-war
Welsh climbing; this volume is a compensatory postscript
to the saga's end.'*

Paul Nunn, 1969, reviewing the 1969 guidebook

1969 Jul. 6   **Sulcus**   R Holliwell, J Fitzgerald
*'The trend towards the shattering of the old reputations
on Gogarth, with Minks and Molyneux, the Holliwells and
Eric Jones leading the shattering, has left few of the older
routes unscathed and affected many of the new ones.
Ormuzd, Pterodactyl, Citadel, Left-Hand Red Wall, Deygo,*

Uhuru and Spider's Web are among the unrepeated routes.'

Al Harris, Rocksport, June/July 1969

1969 Aug. 17 **Red Haze** (1 pt. aid)   J Brown, P Crew
'I...was just swinging from one big side-pull to another, when my last hold fell off. It wasn't a flake, it was the corner of an arête.'
First free ascent: probably J Moran, P Williams.

1969 Aug. 30 **The Bluebottle**   E Drummond. B Campbell-Kelly

1969 Aug. 30 **Obelisk** (A2)   D E Alcock, J V Anthoine (AL)
Aid reduced by D Pearce, P Trower in 1977.
First free ascent: S Haston, M E Crook 1981.

1969 Sep. 6 **Falls Road** (6 pts. aid)   J Gosling, E Thurrell, B Sullivan, B Cardus
'This finishes up the mind-boggling crack that all the Rat Race pioneers had prudently avoided.'

Mountain 6, November 1969

First free ascent: P Livesey.

1969 Sep. 13 **Bullitt**   L E Holliwell, D Mossman, L R Holliwell
1969 Sep. 14 **Black Light**   A C Wilmott, M J Spring, D Edwards
1969 Sep. 27 **Hash**   L E Holliwell, L R Holliwell
1969 Sep. 28 **Progeria**   J Gosling, T Brooder
1969 Oct. 4 **Gerontion**   G MacNair, J Gosling, E Thurrel, T Brooder (VL)
1969 Oct. 4 **Dementia**   J Gosling, T Brooder
Both Dementia and Progeria were thought to be very serious undertakings, owing to the lack of protection on the lower pitches, and the extremely poor rock on the upper wall.

1969 Oct. 12 **Direct Start to Diogenes**   J Kingston, D Mossman, L R Holliwell
'The development of Gogarth illustrated a basic difference between the southern sea cliff climber and the northern crag climber. The Anglesey cliffs were developed by crag climbers looking for the vertical way up. Even now the sea-level traverses are not complete, because the sea was seen as a threatening and alien-environment. Swimming to a route was rare, abseiling the norm; accident victims were hauled up the cliff and not taken off by boat; benighted climbers, of considerable repute were prepared to sit it out rather than take to the water which is common practice in the south'.

Peter Biven, Rocksport, October 1968

'In search of something new several large parties have been working along the Holyhead coastline lassoing spikes, penduling, swimming and performing Tyroleans with great enthusiasm. Although the climbing has turned out to be very hard and serious, it would seem that

these "cliffquanauts" are discovering a whole new world of experiences with their expeditions.'

Rocksport, November 1969.

1969 Dec. 14 **Icarus** P Buxton, D Durkan
A significant discovery that initiated the first wave of Rhoscolyn exploration
Variation by L Costello, D Durkan June 14 1970.

1969 Dec. 24 **December Days** D Durkan, D Birch

1969 **Atlantic Wall** D Barton, J Firth (AL)

1969 **Green Light** J Brown, C E Davies, J Smith
Smurf Zawn gets its first route some years before it became popular.

1970 Jan. 29 **Solo Slab** and **Solo Surprise** D Durkan (solo)

1970 Jan. 29 **Symphony Crack** D Durkan, J Baker

1970 Feb. 20/21 **A Brown Study** E Drummond, B Campbell-Kelly
'A bit of bad route finding gave Neil Robertson and Eric Roseberry a frightening experience and a new route to add to those on Red Wall. They set off on Red Wall, somehow got onto A Brown Study, and finally emerged at the top of the crag via the obvious line halfway between Red Wall and A Brown Study. They appropriately named their route Brown Trousers.'

Rocksport, August/September 1970

1970 Apr. 4 **Mustang** and **Maverick** T Taylor, D Garner

1970 May 2 **Wall of Horrors** (4 pts. aid) C J Phillips, N Horne
First free ascent: P Whillance, D Armstrong 27 August 1978.

1970 May 5 **Miura** T Taylor, M Barraclough

1970 May 9 **Poseidon** D McGonigal, J Doodson, W Sutherland
Direct finish by D Lyon, J Frost, K Robertson, C Lyon 1976.

1970 May 19 **Acid** D Durkan, T Armitage (AL)
Pitch 2 previously climbed by D Durkan.

1970 May 30/31 **The Maze** (1 pt. aid) E Drummond,
Jun. 20/21 B Campbell-Kelly
'The guru revived a long-standing love affair with the Red Wall.'

Mountain 12, November 1970

First free ascent: G Tinnings, L McGinley.

1970 Jun. 15 **S... Hawk Alley** D Durkan (solo)

1970 Jun. 15 **Truant** D Durkan, D Birch

1970 Jun. **Bagger's Crack** and **Crack and Corner** L Costello (solo)

1970 Jul. 8 **Trogg's Way** D Durkan, P Sandall

1970 Jul. 11/12 **Annie's Arch** (1 pt. aid) B Campbell-Kelly, A J D Ferguson

1970 Jul. 16 **E. P. Special** (3 pts. aid) L Costello, D Durkan
First free ascent: J Healey, P Williams May 23 1984.

1970 Jul. 19 **The Viper** (5 pts. aid) D Durkan, L Costello
The route was originally climbed in two pitches, traversing right into the top corner of what is now Centrefold. A prusik on the abseil rope was used for aid on this move. The obvious direct finish and first free

ascent were incorporated into the modern line, as described, by J Moran, P Williams May 27 1984.

1970 Jul. 22   **Tomorrow Has Been Cancelled (Due to Lack of Interest)**   L Costello, D Durkan

1970 Jul. 25   **El Dorado**   D Durkan, L Costello

1970 Aug. 1   **Cocaine**   L Costello, D Durkan

1970 Aug. 5   **The Wild Rover**   D Durkan (unseconded)

*The preceeding two routes lie on a slabby facet that was rediscovered in 1984 by P Williams and J Moran, who thought it unclimbed. They added three lines; **Waxwing, Little Queenie** and **Mainlining,** only to find that some of the climbing had been done before.*

1970 Aug. 5   **Sea Shanty**   D Durkan, D Earnshaw, J Barker

1970 Aug. 17   **The Nod** (aid)   D Durkan, P Sandall

Later freed in 1984 as The Cruise.

1970 Aug. 19/20   **Force 8**   D Durkan, P Sandall, P Brown

1970 Aug. 24   **Sunstroke**   D Durkan, M Tolley

1970 Aug. 25   **Minute Man**   L E Holliwell, L R Holliwell, J Rogers

'Done during their TV training.'

1970 May 7   **The Underground** (12 pts. aid)   D Durkan, M Brown, J Baker
Jul. 24/29
Aug. 30

1970 Sep. 5   **Zeus**   L R Holliwell, L E Holliwell

1970 Sep. 7   **Mestizo**   T Taylor, P Jones

1970 Sep. 21   **The Trip**   D Durkan, N Shea, P Williams

No, not that P Williams. Ed.

1970 Sep. 26/27   **Games Climbers Play** (aid)   D Pearce, E Drummond

'The climb involves 60 feet of sky-hook moves on the first pitch and a 50-foot pendulum on the second pitch.'

                                       Mountain 12, November 1970

By the Original Start which was freed by R Fawcett, Gill Kent Dec 1979.
Start as described (1 pt aid) by P R Littlejohn, R Harrison (AL) May 29 1977.

1970 Nov. 1   **Star of the Sea** (1 pt. aid)   D Durkan, A N Other

1970 Nov. 18   **Adrenalin**   D Durkan (solo)

Climbed with a raging hangover, this was the conclusion to the first onslaught at Rhoscolyn.

1970 Nov. 22   **Canned Laughter** (A2)   P L Seramur, D Durkan

Led by a visiting American.
Aid reduced to (1 pt. aid) by D Knighton, D Cronshaw Oct 2 1978.

1970   **Green Gilbert**   M Boater, S Johnson, R Perry

1970   **Toccata Crack**   D Durkin

1971 Mar.   **Positron** (5 pts. aid)   A P Rouse, P Minks

Rouse flew off the route whilst Minks was rather more interested in the songs on the accompanying transistor radio.
After a couple of previous attempts, whittling away at the aid points, A Sharp finally managed a free ascent.

'Positron saw its first and second free ascents on the same day from Fawcett and Gibb, and Livesey and Lawrence. It now ranks with the hardest half dozen routes in Wales.'

Crags 2

Soloed by S Haston around 1985.

1971 May	**Fifteen Men on a Dead Man's Chest** (3 pts. aid) M A Boysen, D E Alcock, D Jones

(2 pts. aid) P Whillance, D Armstrong.
First free ascent: around 1981 by an unknown team.

1971 Jun. 12	**Bubbly Situation Blues** (1 pt. aid) R Evans, C Rogers

A hard climb at the time, and it still has a mean reputation.

1971 Jul. 17	**The Moon** (4 pts. aid) E Drummond, A Barley

'Another crumbling horror.'

Mountain 17, September 1971

'On South Stack, Dave Ivory and Ed Hart made the second ascent of The Moon. Ivory, who took a fall from loose rock on the final pitch, later said that the climb was like an unrelenting, giant-sized Vector. The same pair were repulsed from the first pitch of Deygo, during an attempt to repeat The Pagan. Unjustified seriousness was cited as the reason for the withdrawal.'

Mountain 29, September 1973

First free ascent: J Allen, S Bancroft 1974, or, A Sharp, B Hall in 1973/4.
Yet another brilliant route.

1971 Jul.	**Mirage** L E Holliwell, B Whybrow
1971 Oct. 9	**Too Cold For Comfort** (5 pts. aid) R Conway, C Jackson
1971 Oct. 31	**Hysteresis** (3 pts. aid) L E Holliwell, B Whybrow

'Shortly before his death Lawrie repeated Hysteresis free and chopped the (drilled) peg. We had made a mistake, and Lawrie corrected it, or almost.'

1971 Oct.	**Ziggurat** (1 pt. aid) L E Holliwell, J Kingston

First free ascent: A Pollitt, N Clacher Oct 11 1981.

1971 Nov. 14	**Tsunami** (5 pts. aid) C Jackson, K Myhill
1971 Dec. 5	**New Girdle of Mousetrap Zawn** L E Holliwell, B Whybrow
1973 Apr. 30	**Steerpike** D Carr, D Lanceley
1973 May 12	**Peepshow** B Wyvill, R Evans (AL)
1973 May 19	**The Needle** R Evans, C Rogers

Direct Finish by A Evans, J Moran July 5 1978.

1973 May 26	**Puzzle Me Quick** B Wyvill, R Evans
1973	**Mistaken Identity** M C Royle (unseconded)
1973	**Pagan** P R Littlejohn, A Houghton.

'I carried on for a while, before realising that the difficulties weren't going to end so soon, and that I should have got better protection. I reversed until just above the wire, which seemed to be lifting out, then found I didn't have the strength to reverse any further.'

1974 Jul. 1	**The Camel** A Sharp, J J Zangwill

A difficult problem, that has given many teams the hump.

1974 Jul. 28	**The Mad Hatter** (1 pt. aid) R Mallinson, A Green
1974 Aug. 17	**Supercrack** (2 pts. aid) L E Holliwell
	The date of the first ascent is not known, as it was not recorded at the time.
	First free ascent: on this date by A Sharp, C Rogers.
1974 Oct.	**Creeping Lemma** A Sharp, S Humphries
	Loose and frightening on the initial ascent, it has cleaned up considerably to give a fine and popular route.
1975 Feb. 6	**The Eternal Optimist** A Sharp, S Humphries
	The last of the bogus routes to fall. This was Tam Dubh.
1975 Mar. 8	**Annihilator** (1 pt. aid) A Sharp, S Humphries
	First free ascent: S Haston, S Andrews 1986.
1975 Mar. 17/18	**Black Rod** (A3) M Barnicott, C Remy, Y Remy
	Previously attempted as some in-situ gear was found during the ascent. Three expansion bolts were used.
1975 Jul. 3	**Horse Above Water** A Sharp, C Dale
1975 Nov.	**Ordinary Route** A Sharp, C Dale
	Pitch 1 previously by A Sharp, J Whittle.
	Although using sections from other routes, this was a brilliant eliminate.
1976 Feb.	**Dream Seller** J Moran, G Milburn
	Climbed on-sight (rare at the time) as an escape route.
1976 May 8	**Redshift** P R Littlejohn, H Clarke
	Unfortunately climbed during the bird restrictions, although a fine effort.
1976 May	**Dogs of War** (1 pt. aid) M Howells, P Trower (AL)
	A fine on-sight effort.
	First free ascent: P Boardman, J Tasker some time later.
1976 Jun. 19	**Graduation Ceremony** A Sharp, R Toomer
	Pitch 1 previously by A P Rouse, M Geddes in June 1971.
1976 Jun. 26/ Jul. 10	**The Cow** (2 pts. aid) D Pearce, P Trower
	A very fine route; the first ascent was played down by Sharp probably because he had eyed the line himself.
	First free ascent: P Gomersall or J Healey 1980.
1976 Jul. 19	**Broken Mirror** R Fawcett, P Livesey (AL)
1976 Jul. 19	**High Pressure** P Livesey, R Fawcett (AL)
1976 Sep.	**Trunk Line** M Fowler, J Stevenson (AL)
	Fowler had previously attempted this line on several occasions.
1976	**Neutrino** A P Rouse, B Hall
1977 Jun. 1	**Blowout** (1 pt. aid) M Wragg, G Hardill
1977 Aug. 26	**Hyde Park** (2 pts. aid) B Wintringham, Marion Wintringham
	Names that were to become familiar over the next few years.
	First free ascent: Andy Sharp 1977.
1977 Aug. 28	**Heathen** B Wintringham, M Wintringham
1977 Sep. 9	**Atheist** (1 pt. aid) B Wintringham, M Wintringham
	First free ascent: L McGinley, S Haston 1981.
1977 Sep. 10	**Gobbler's Arête** B Wyvill, R Evans
1977 Sep. 17	**Puritan** B Wintringham, M Wintringham
1978 Mar. 16	**Bitter Days** B Wintringham, M Wintringham

The start of the blitz year.

1978 Mar. 27 **Freebird** A Evans, N Siddiqui (AL), G Milburn, J Moran
The start of excavations by 'The Rock Machine'.

1978 Mar. 27 **Street Survivor** D Knighton, J Tout
*Top-roped prior to being led. Accusations of pre-placed
chalk were not entirely serious.
Dave Knighton commented "Yes, it's a brilliant route. I'd
even go so far as to say it compares with some of the
better Lancashire routes".
C J Phillips had climbed the first part as a Direct Start to
Central Park in the early 70's.*

1978 Mar. 30 **Staying Alive** P Whillance, D Armstrong (AL)

1978 Apr. 7/8 **Ludwig** (3 pts. aid) M Fowler, M Morrison
*A typical Fowler horror that was graded as Extremely
Severe. No-one had even the remotest idea as to how
hard it might or might not be. Perhaps it said volumes
that no-one at the time was prepared to go for the second
ascent.
A nut was used to place a peg on the 2nd pitch, then
bypassed. Another peg was used to place the aid peg on
the top pitch. The route was then claimed with just the
one aid point.
The aid peg was by-passed free by L McGinley but the
pitch was not completed. Several other teams were
unable to complete the pitch free.
First free ascent: finally by A Pollitt, S Andrews 10 May
1984, the aid peg having since disappeared.*

1978 Apr. 16 **The Flytrap** (1 pt. aid) J Brown, P Jewell, D Cuthbertson
*Brown returns to Gogarth new routing after an absence of
nine years.*

1978 Apr. 22 **Blue Oyster Cult** D Knighton, A Hyslop (AL), M Tuerney

1978 Apr. 23 **Pequod** J Moran, A Evans
*On a previous inspection, 'Jim's first interpretation of a
wave of exploration was to abseil down into Easter Island
Gully, where huge seas were pounding onto the cliff.
Within a minute or two he was soaked to the skin, and
wild screams filtering up on the wind suggested that he
was too numb with cold to climb back up. The rope
which was thrown down to him promptly shot out to sea.
Through the spray I could make out two dark shapes: Jim
was the one with the rope, the other was a seal.'*

1978 Apr. 23 **Diatom** A Evans, J Moran

1978 Apr. 23 **Perpendicular** (pitch 2) A Evans, J Moran
Pitch 1 previously by G Milburn, S Horrox 20 May 1978.

1978 Apr. 29 **Microdot** and **Tumbling Dice** J Moran, G Milburn
*'No I didn't fall off...I jumped...to avoid skinning my knees
when I fell.'*

1978 May 1 **Energy Crisis** P Whillance, D Armstrong
A route for the turbo powered only.

1978 May 1 **True Moments** and **Caress of Steel** A Hyslop, D Knighton
(AL on former).

1978 May 1   **Paddington**   M Fowler, M Morrison
...blocks rained down in profusion...

1978 May 1   **North West Passage**   J Moran, A Evans (AL), G Milburn, N Siddiqui
On a foul festering day Al nobly gardened the big tower to the right of Atlantis. Huge blocks had to be prized off in succession but his hard work paid dividends the next day when the weather cleared up.

1978 May 2   **Belvedere** (1 pt. aid)   J Brown, F Corner, D Jones (AL)
First free ascent: M E Crook, N Craine June 1986.
'The Baron's keen nose had detected where the action was to be found. While on Swastika with Smiler Cuthbertson he had spotted Jim and me on Tumbling Dice, and seeing us close to an unclimbed line on which we had also got our eyes he nipped in two days later to polish it off'.

1978 May 6/7   **Merchant Man**   J Moran, G Milburn

1978 May 9   **Wandering Wall** (1 pt. aid)   J Brown, D Jones, P Jewell
A fishing rod, with a peg weighted line, was used to place a runner high up, so that the blank section could be missed out by climbing the rope!

1978 May 13   **Rock Island Line**   J Moran, A Evans (AL)

1978 May 14   **The Third Man**   J Moran, A Evans
A passing canoeist stopped for a chat.
'The Baron repeated it shortly after thinking it to be new but thorough cleaning of the top crack told its own story. Jim was tickled pink to think that he had grabbed one of Joe's lines, and it kept him amused for all of one afternoon.'

1978 May 27   **Tequila Sunrise**   A Evans, J Moran (AL), D Knighton

1978 May 27   **Manor Park**   J Moran, D Knighton, A Evans
'Named after our local Glossop climbing wall where a passing horse dislodged Jim from his holds!'

1978 May 28   **Where Puffins Daren't**   A Evans, G Milburn, N Siddiqui, S Horrox
'A fun route which was intended to relieve the tension which was caused by Moran's horror routes. Jim forgot his footwear and refused to take part in such a trivial jaunt. He was later gravely informed of the utter seriousness of the undertaking which he would regret at some future date. The original name of Where Eagles Dare somehow didn't fit!'

1978 May 30   **Barbarossa** (1 pt. aid)   J Moran, A Evans
At the start of cleaning operations, several big blocks disappeared safely into the depths of Bloody Chimney. A leader on the bottom pitch, hearing them rattling down above his head, was convinced that his time had come.
'Undoubtedly Al's optimism comes in very handy at times especially when he takes it into his head to brush off blank bits of rock such as the impending wall right of Bloody Chimney. Jim certainly did not believe that it would go at

*first but Al convinced him that it really was on, especially
if he pre-placed a peg on the first unprotected section.
This route was bouldering with a vengeance as Jim went
up and down each sequence of moves in turn. As the sun
came round onto the face things got even worse and on
the deck we were content to lounge about wherever there
was shade. Chalk cascaded down in handfuls and Jim got
really angry as the heat sapped his energy slowly but
surely...Next day he was back in the cool of the morning
and quickly powered up the wall with total physical and
mental comitment. Bouldering out a big pitch on Gogarth
was now the new cult and this ascent merely served to
point out a whole variety of big blank walls which were
just screaming out to be done.'*

G.M.

	First free ascent: J M Redhead July 6 1980. *A major achievement.*
1978 Jun. 8	**Hunger** P R Littlejohn, C King *Inspired by Livesey's training methods, Littlejohn weighed in with this impressive contribution. Climbed on-sight, it took some time to be repeated.* **Ramadan** *variation C Waddy, J Dawes 5 May 1988.*
1978 Jun. 11	**The Assassin** J Moran, G Milburn, A Evans *Later without knowing that Jim was actually inspecting the line by abseil at that very moment Ben Wintringham told us about the line as both he and Ray Evans had tried it without success. Jim, who had been down the wall, was strangely non-forthcoming about the pitch and would only say that, "It's really something. It's going to be a right tit-ender all the way up".*
1978 Jun. 13	**This Year's Model** J Moran, P Jewell (AL)
1978 Jul. 5	**Cartwheel** A Evans, J Moran
1978 Jul. 5	**Slow Dancer** J Moran, A Evans
1978 Jul. 8	**Minnesota Fats** A Evans, G Milburn *'Al and I felt that it was a pity that there were too many chossy finishes up steep vegetation above the Main Cliff. I pointed Al at the most obvious corner and left him to burrow for a few hours until he emerged black as the ace of spades and utterly exhausted.'*
1978 Jul. 8	**The Horrorshow** (1 pt. aid) J Moran, A Evans (AL), G Milburn *'Until this route Jim kept insisting that he couldn't lead 6a – whatever that means! In his personal philosophy he doesn't think that there are any 6a pitches on Cloggy yet as the rock has too many holds.'* *Graded E4 6a on the Moran scale (not as way out as the Bancroft scale, and not as suicidal as the Ray Evans scale).* *First free ascent: R Fawcett Jan 1980.*
1978 Jul. 10	**Stimulator** B Wintringham, P Jewell *Top roped first.*
1978 Jul. 23	**Aardvark** A Evans, G Milburn, B Wintringham, J Moran

'For most of the day we had smart non-conversations (you don't tell me your lines and I won't tell you mine) and with some of the barriers down, to round the day off I, as the non-match-fit member of the hit-team, was delegated to fraternise with the enemy and, accordingly joined Ben for an ascent of the poorly protected Dropout.'

1978 Jul. 23	**Dropout**	B Wintringham, G Milburn
1978 Jul. 24	**The Grim Reaper**	J Moran, G Milburn

'The highlight of the route was the monster trundle of a huge flake right at the top of the route. The noise as it struck the ground was deafening and as a great orange cloud mushroomed up the crag we could just make out the fragments bounding far out to sea. It gave the Baron a nasty moment as having finished their route he was standing above the descent gully and in that split second he got the distinct impression that the whole of the descent gully was collapsing under his feet.'

1978 Jul. 24   **Mayfair** (2 pts. aid)   B Wintringham, J Brown
Pitch 1 by above team two days earlier.
First free ascent: A Sharp, S Lewis, P Williams Aug 1978.

1978 Jul. 28   **The Wastelands**   J Moran, G Milburn
'While changing his trousers a large wave caught Jim fair and square and being sufficiently gripped up already his adrenalin took him easily up the first pitch while I sweated it out below as the extra-high tide drove me up from one belay to the next.'

1978 Jul. 29   **Smurf**   J Brown, B Wintringham
1978 Jul. 29   **Nice 'n Sleazy**   A Evans, G Milburn, J Moran
The beginning of serious forays onto this long overlooked wall.
'While Joe and Ben elected to explore for new rock at one end of the Gogarth complex I talked our team into going over to North Stack to have a look at the wall which jutted out into the sea. As soon as we stuck our heads over the top of the cliff we couldn't help but notice the soaring crack-line (South Sea Bubble). Al and I were really excited but the other two reserved judgement until later.'

G.M.

'Sitting on the old cannons in the zawn we just couldn't believe our luck. Why hadn't Joe been there long before?'

1978 Jul. 30	**Talking Heads**	J Moran, G Milburn, A Evans, S Horrox
1978 Jul. 30	**South Sea Bubble**	J Moran, S Horrox, A Evans, G Milburn
1978 Aug. 3	**Gnome**	B Wintringham, J Brown (AL)
1978 Aug. 6	**Alligator**	A Evans, P Williams, J Moran, B Wintringham
1978 Aug. 6	**Cannibal**	J Moran, A Evans, P Williams, B Wintringham.

Climbed direct by T Hodgson, P Pritchard 11 October 1986.

1978 Aug. 8   **Anarchist**   B Wintringham, J Moran
Variation by S Andrews 9 December 1987.

1978 Aug. 13   **Television Route**   J Moran, B Wintringham, P Williams
A free version of the old aid route.

*'I provoked Jim to rename it Land of the Blind to show
contempt for what seemed to me to be a major act of rock
rape by the original team. If ever a route deserved
renaming this was it for my money. Not only was it done
originally as an aid route but it was also done for
commercial reasons – perhaps not rape, more like
prostitution! Eventually Joe made me see reason on the
grounds that a route name is for identification and not to
cause confusion so I scrapped renaming just before the
Supplement went to press.'* (I didn't realise however that
Joe had led Television Route on the first ascent and had
accepted the pre-placed pegs and bolts.) G.M.

1978 Aug. 20   **Khmer Rouge**   J Moran, P Williams
*Accused of cheating, Moran, after a failure in the midday
sun, returned to lead the route in the cool of the evening.
A witness only saw the first effort before setting in motion
a series of acrimonious allegations.*

1978 Aug. 28   **Shell Shock** and **Reptile**   J Moran, G Milburn

1978 Sep. 2   **Infidel** (2 pts. aid)   B Wintringham, J Brown, M Wintringham
*First free ascent: G Tinnings 1978.
Climbed direct by J Moran, P Williams Nov 5 1978.*

1978 Sep. 2   **Blue Peter**   P Whillance, D Armstrong
               Sarah Green start by D Hersey, A Haynes 1983.

1978 Sep. 10   **Communication Breakdown**   D Cronshaw, D Knighton (AL)
*Possibly the same line as Roadrunner which was climbed
by R Perriment, D Carroll in 1976.*

1978 Sep. 13   **Rapture of the Deep**   J Brown, B Wintringham, M
Wintringham

1978 Sep. 17   **The Cad**   R Fawcett, C Gibb
*The line had previously been cleaned on 30 July 1978 by
Al Evans.*
*'Al decided to abseil down the compelling wall to the right
of South Sea Bubble and promptly started to brush a wide
swathe down the thick green lichen. It looked utterly blank
and improbable so the lads top-roped the line just for fun.
We all speculated as to whether such a line would ever go
free and if bolts might be used for protection and how
many would be needed. Laughing and joking on the way
back Al and I decided to start a rumour that this random
bit of wall was the most tremendous unclimbed pitch in
North Wales if not in Britain – and then we would wait to
see what happened. Looking back, the laugh was really on
us.'*

Geoff Milburn

*Eight weeks later, on the same day, two independent top
teams turned up to have a look.
The first ascent team barely beat Whillance to the first
ascent. Some holds had apparently been improved and
the culprit left undiscovered. Two bolts and a peg were
placed on the pitch. Whillance bypassed the first on the*

second ascent, and it was chopped by his anonymous second, who assumed a false name due to fear of being found out for cheating on the hut dues at Ynys Ettws. J M Redhead dispensed with, and then removed, the peg on the third ascent.
N Dixon led the route without the bolt in 1987, and the route was soloed by P Jewell in October 1987.
Direct Start by J M Redhead November 1988.

1978 Sep. 18	**Blackleg** R Fawcett, C Gibb	

Fawcett's second major addition in as many days.

1978 Sep. 22	**The Emotionary** D Knighton, D Cronshaw
1978 Sep. 23	**Elf** B Wintringham, M Wintringham, J Brown
1978 Sep. 30	**Shagorado** D Knighton, B Conlon
1978 Oct. 7	**The Missionary** M Fowler, P Thomas (AL)
1978 Oct. 16	**Heart of Gold** M Fowler, P Thomas

Pitch 1 previously by M Fowler, S Haston (AL) 20 August 1978.
An intimidating line that had interested teams for some time. The ascent involved attempts on five separate occasions, as the route was led on sight as a matter of principle. A very short section eventually had to be cleaned on abseil. Three points of aid were used to clean poor rock, but after each case a descent was made prior to making the moves free.
Climbed direct by P Pritchard, T Hodgson Oct 12 1986.

1978 Oct. 19	**Sprung** D Jones, J Brown
1978 Oct. 19	**The Tail** J Brown, D Jones
1978 Oct. 21	**Noddy** (1 or 2 pts. aid) D Cronshaw, D Knighton (AL)
1978 Oct. 22	**Balu** D Jones, J Brown, D Cuthbertson
1978 Oct. 23	**Smurf Zawn Girdle** B Wintringham, D Jones, J Brown, M Wintringham
1978 Oct. 27	**Run Fast, Run Free** (2 pts. aid) D Knighton, J Girdley

First free ascent: P O'Donovan 1980.

1978 Oct. 28	**Get the Stroll** D Knighton, J Girdley (AL)
1978 Oct. 28	**Fantasia** (1 pt. aid) B Wintringham, M Wintringham

First free ascent: J Moran, P Williams 1979.

1978 Oct. 28	**Not Fade Away** J Moran, G Milburn

*The direct start, **Penelope Undercling**, by M E Crook, D Kendal Aug 4 1987.*
'A rumour went round the Main Cliff that a body had been dragged up the wall at North Stack. The explanation was that above the cliff it was freezing cold but at sea-level it was quite hot. After abseiling down we tied several layers of clothing to the abseil rope; later when hauling this in the bundles looked like a lifeless body jerking about when seen from far away.'

1978 Nov. 5	**Dangerous Rhythm** D Knighton, D Cronshaw
1978 Nov. 5	**The Fast Buck** G Milburn, A Evans

'At a C.C. meeting I suggested that Al and I were going to produce a supplement to make 'a fast buck'. Ken Wilson took off and hit the roof. The storm eventually abated and

the supplement was written and published between two Guidebook Committee meetings.'

1978 Nov. 5   **Watership Down**   A Evans, G Milburn
'We needed a rabbit name to match The Fast Buck so after prolonged thought Al came up with a suggestion. I asked him why Watership Down. "Well", he said pausing, and with a sly little grin, "We've seen a ship, we went down to do the route...and there's a heck of a lot of water round here...".'

1978 Nov. 9   **King of the Swingers**   J Brown, B Wintringham (AL), M Wintringham
Climbed direct by G Tinnings, P Trower 1980.

1978 Nov. 11   **The Cree**   J Moran, G Milburn, P Williams
1978 Dec.   **Safer Start**   B Wintringham, M Wintringham
1979 May 5   **Morphine**   B Wintringham, M Wintringham
1979 May 19   **Hyena**   B Wintringham, M Wintringham
1979 May 20   **The Tet Offensive**   J Moran, P Williams.
P Williams led pitch 4.

1979 May 22   **Sebastopol**   J Moran, P Williams
1979 May 27   **Peasant in the Big City**   G Gibson, J Walker
1979 Jun. 9   **High Noon**   B Wintringham, M Wintringham
1979 Jun. 15   **Devotee**   B Wintringham, M Wintringham
1979 Jun. 23   **Revelation**   B Wintringham, M Wintringham
1979 Aug. 25   **Mein Kampf**   J Moran, D Cuthbertson, P Williams, P Aubrey
'It gets in your blood, does the Red Wall.'
Climbed direct by P Pritchard, G Hughes 1986.

1979 Sep. 30   **The Long Run**   P Whillance, R Parker, D Armstrong
A fine consolation prize after missing out on The Cad. The Long Run Direct was climbed by D Towse, J M Redhead in November 1988.

1979 Oct. 21   **The Three Musketeers**   R Fawcett (unseconded)
1979   **Mill Street Junction**   D Knighton, D Cronshaw
1980 Apr. 3   **Toiler on the Sea**   G Gibson, D Beetlestone (AL)
Only Pitch 2 was new, Pitch 1 probably by C Brookes.

1980 Apr. 4   **Vend T**   G Gibson (unseconded)
1980 May 16   **Alien**   P R Littlejohn, S Lewis
A much-eyed line that gave fellow stars a hard time when repeating the route.

1980 May 22   **The Big Sleep**   R Fawcett, P Williams, J Moran
1980 May 27   **Wall of Fossils**   J Moran, R Fawcett (AL), P Williams.
Two big lines fall in quick succession, the latter still awaiting a confirmed repeat.

1980 Jun. 30   **The Bells! The Bells!**   J M Redhead, C Shorter
Britain's first E7. A magnificent piece of cool climbing which left Redhead totally drained as he topped out. The route had to wait six years for a repeat. It remains an extremely serious proposition.
'Their respective girlfriends were sat at the top picnicking, and joking about the boys having a nice time climbing. Meanwhile on the cliff, John was climbing for his life!'

1980 Jul. 28   **Hurricane**   S Webster, P Trower

Climbed as **Hard Animals** *by M E Crook, N Craine some years later.*

1980 Aug. 1	**Blue Remembered Hills** G Tinnings, P Trower
	Pitch 1 by G Tinnings, D Parker August 1979.
1980 Aug. 3	**Another Roadside Attraction** (1 pt. aid) G Tinnings, P Trower.
	First free ascent: S Haston date uncertain.
	Two fine additions in intimidating situations.
1980 Summer	**Andover** J Donnelly
	Possibly done before.
1980 Summer	**Breaking the Barrier** J Donnelly
1980 Summer	**Grendel** K Robertson, M Gresham
1980	**Echo Beach** M Duff, T Dailey
1980	**Funky Gibbon** M Boysen, J Brown, B Wintringham
1981 Jan. 31	**Bran Flake** K Robertson, S Robertson
1981 Jul. 11	**Croissant** K Robertson, A Lewandowski
1981 Jul. 12	**Big Jim** K Robertson, A Lewandowski
	So named because it's hard to finish (see Pete's Eats menu).
1981 Jul. 26	**Seeyerlater** S Reid, W Parker
1981 Summer	**Teenage Kicks** S Jones, D Hazelaar
1981 Summer	**Apostrophe** D Hazelaar, S Jones
	Climbed direct by M Gresham, K Neal.
1981 Aug. 25	**Mr Seal** A D Newton, A J Howells, C M Parry
	The seconds were entertained by a watcher from the deep.
1981 Oct.	**Hydrophobia** C Jones, S Hoste, S Smith
1981 Nov. 21	**The Flakes of Wrath** P Williams, D Dent, J Hall, D Hall
1981	**The Dope** K Glass, D Martin
1982 Jan. 30	**New Boots and Panties** M Gresham, S Jones
1982 Mar. 20	**Tinseltown Rebellion** D Hazelaar, M Gresham
1982 Summer	**Mirrored in the Cleft** J M Redhead, P Perrin
1982 Summer	**Penny** J M Redhead, K Robertson
1982 Summer	**Blackfoot** M Gresham (Solo)
1982 Jun. 9	**Poo Dog, The Smog Monster,** and **Dog Poo** S Haston, P Williams (AL)
1982 Jun. 19	**Fantastic Day** A Hayes, D Hersey
1982 Aug. 7	**Death Trap** M Fowler, A Baker
	Direct Variation by C Waddy and partner 1988.
	Both appallingly serious additions.
1982 Sep. 3	**Colditz** A D Newton, J R Peart
	An escape route!
1982 Sep. 11	**Little Women** M Gresham, D Birch
1982 Sep.	**Limping Lisa** S Reid, C Jones
	Cleaning was carried out on a day when the crag was crawling with teams, and the name describes the resulting injury to a climber below the said cleaners.
1982 Oct. 10	**Sue** P. M Lyndon, D Towse (AL)
	'Quite possibly the worst route in the entire universe.'
1982 Nov. 14/15	**L'Affreuse** (A4) D Williams, J Williams
1982	**End Game** A D Newton, J R Peart

Evidence of previous exploration was found.

1983 Jan. 19	**C'est La Vie** M Gresham, D Hazelaar	
1983 Feb. 12	**Comfortably Numb** M Gresham, D Birch	
1983 Feb. 16	**Pleasant Surprise** D Hazelaar, A Lomas, D Birch, M Gresham.	

Supersedes an older route called **Birthday Passage**.

1983 Feb. 21 **Time to Reflect**   D Hazelaar, M Gresham
1983 Mar. 3 **Emmenthal**   S Haston, M Howerd
'There are not enough stars in heaven to give this route.'
1983 Apr. 3 **See Emily Play**   M Gresham, J Dalton
1983 Apr. 9 **The Echoes**   M Gresham, K Neal
1983 Jun. 17 **The Finisher**   S Reid, J Roberts
1983 Jul. 24 **The Unblue Crack**   M Gresham, K Neal, J Dalton
1983 Summer **Generation Gap**   J Dalton and party
1983 Autumn **Electric Blue**   S Haston, T Saunders
1983 **Laceration**   F Williams, D Williams
A previously top-roped problem.
1983 **Rhiannon**   D Durkan, D Birch
1983 **Derek and Clive**   A D Newton, P J Corbishley
1984 Feb. 5 **Wind**   M Gresham, K Neal
The top pitch had been climbed previously as a direct finish to Thread.
1984 Feb. 9 **Lost Hope**   M Gresham, I Williams
1984 Mar. 14 **Kissing the Pink**   D Towse, W Rees
Climbed soon after by L Clark, R Dean as **Insane, Insane Again**.
The start of exploration by UCNW Mountaineering Club members that was to lead, in turn, to the major development of this area.
1984 Mar. 14 **Triffids**   L Lovatt, D Liddy
1984 Mar. 16 **Flobalob** and **Eric**   R Wood, D Liddy (AL)
The latter was climbed as **Cape of Good Hope** *by C Waddy some years later.*
1984 Mar. 25 **The Human Camel**   R Wood, D Liddy
1984 Mar. **Blackbits**   D Liddy (Solo)
1984 Mar. **Twilight Passage**   R Wood (Solo)
1984 Apr. 25 **The Clown**   J M Redhead, D Towse, J Sylvester
Another big lead by Redhead - and more was to follow. This ascent, inspired by Stravinsky's Petrouchka, later became the subject of a film, using the route as a vertical ballet.
1984 May 2 **The Cruel Sea** and **The Sea Shall Not ...**   P Williams, T Jadwat
The former possibly done before. Jadwat, a local canoeist who had observed climbers at Rhoscolyn, said "Hey Paul, I know where there is a really good little crag which might be worth a visit." Thus was the development of the area triggered off.
1984 May 3 **White Water Wall**   P Willans, T Jadwat
1984 May 5 **Fear Test** and **Centrefold**   J Moran, P Williams

	The Full Frontal *Finish by P Williams, T Hodgson April 24, 1988.*	
1984 May 6	**The Sun** P Williams, J Moran	
	A line much fancied by previous explorers.	
1984 May 8	**Big Boys** and **The Cocktail Trip** J Moran, P Williams (AL)	
1984 May 10	**Magellan's Wall** and **Little Queenie** J Moran, P Williams (AL)	
1984 May 11	**Dreams and Screams** and **Mainlinin'** J Moran, P Williams	
	Wet Dreams *Start by C Smith June 29 1986.*	
	Wet Dreams/Dreams and Screams was previously an A3 peg route.	
1984 May 12	**Warpath** J Moran, P Williams	
1984 May 12	**Skinhead Moonstomp** A Pollitt, S Andrews	
	Pitch 1 climbed the day before - taken on-sight and carrying pegs, it was found to be too strenuous on pitch 2. The team returned the next day to make a complete ascent.	
	A very fine ascent of a major remaining line.	
1984 May 19	**The Mask of the Red Death** P Williams, T Jadwat	
1984 May 20	**The Savage Sunbird** P Williams, G Peters	
1984 May 23	**The Trail of Tears** J Healey, P Williams	
1984 May 26	**Godzilla** P Williams, J Healey, J Moran	
	The leader cleaned the section below the overhang while leading.	
1984 May 27	**Birth Trauma** and **Art Groupie** J M Redhead, A Pollitt (AL).	
	Both climbers plugging obvious gaps on the wall.	
1984 Jun. 2	**Medicine Man** J Moran, P Williams, J Sonczak	
1984 Jun. 4	**The Jub-Jub Bird** J Moran, P Williams, J Sonczak	
	The third man fell off the start of the overhang and swung so far out that he came back with an Irish accent!	
1984 Jun. 11	**The Demons of Bosch** J M Redhead, D Towse	
	A bolt was placed for protection, but the Demons unclipped the rope from the krab as the leader climbed past.	
	A Pollitt did without the bolt altogether in August 1988.	
1984 Jun. 17	**Tomorrow is Reinstated** E Jones, L Lovatt	
1984 Aug.	**Le Bon Sauveur** J M Redhead, K Robertson	
1984 Sep. 9	**Helmet Boiler** M Fowler, A Saunders (AL)	
	Another serious offering from the master of vertical rubble.	
1984	**The Cruise** J Moran, P Williams, J Sonczak	
	This free climbs The Nod, aided in August 1970 by D Durkan, P Sandell.	
1984	**Fan Fare** R Wood, D Liddy	
	*Climbed soon after as **Raging Bull Dyke** by P Williams, T Jadwat.*	
1984	**Old Boots** and **Cut-Offs, A State of Saturation** M Gresham, N Other	
1985 Apr. 9	**Charlie Don't Surf** M E Crook, A D Newton	

*Apocalypse Now had recently been reshown in Bangor.
This was another route climbed after failing to locate the
older, part aided lines.*

1985 Jun.	**Drying Out** J Donelly	
1985	**M. Wall** J Dalton, D Hazelaar	

Previously a 70's aid route.

1986 Feb. 15   **Relief** M Gresham, K Neal

1986 May 28   **Stroke of the Fiend** Pitch 1 - D Towse, M E Crook, J M Redhead. Pitch 2 - J M Redhead, D Towse
Another very serious creation.

1986 May 29   **Agrophobia** C Waddy, C Malem
Exploration in the Cryptic Rift begins. (Agoraphobia? Ed.)

1986 May   **Flower of Evil** J M Redhead, D Towse

1986 Jun. 26   **The Ancient Mariner** M E Crook, J Sylvester

1986 Jun.   **Boil All Irishmen** C Smith, M E Crook (AL)

1986 Jun.   **For Mad Men Only** C Smith (unseconded)

1986 Jun.   **Me** S Haston, R Kay, C Dale
*Pitch 1 by S Haston, L McGinley 1981.
The beginning of new interest in Yellow Wall - many big
plums were soon to fall.*

1986 Jun.   **Three Day Event** and **Captain Mark Phillips** M Campbell, E Stone (AL)
Finished in darkness and rain!

1986 Jul. 4   **Skinned Up** M Gresham
*Free climbs a 70's aid route called **The Peeler**, J Donnelly
had reduced the aid in 1980.*

1986 Jul. 15   **Sincerely El Cohen** M E Crook, F Lowe

1986 Jul. 18   **Headbutt** N Dixon, C Smith

1986 Jul. 18   **Tom's Shredded Slippers** J Redhead, B Drury, M Boater

1986 Jul. 26   **Dislocation Dance** C Waddy, D Holmes

1986 Jul.   **The Drunk** S Haston, J Tombs
*The leader was the aformentioned inebriate. "What's
green and gets you drunk?...A giro."*

1986 Jul.   **Isis is Angry** S Haston, R Kay
An audacious proposition.

1986 Jul.   **Sex Lobster** C Smith, M E Crook (AL)
'All very weird'

1986 Jul.   **Psychocandy** C Smith (unseconded)

1986 Summer   **Dreaming of Home** A Woodward, A Lawson

1986 Aug. 16   **Schittlergruber** P Pritchard, N Harms
Another big lead.

1986 Aug. 28   **The Enchanted Broccoli Garden** P Pritchard, M Thomas
A contender for the poorest belay on Gogarth.

1986 Aug. 30   **Twilight Zone** (1 pt. aid) K Neal, M Gresham

1986 Aug.   **Rosebud, The Electrification of the Soviet Union** and **Free Stone Henge** S Haston, R Kay
*'...good jams leading to a position of sickness and
dizziness, followed by some light-headed dynamics...'
An extremely impressive trio of routes.*

1986 Aug.   **Conan the Librarian** (1 pt. aid) J Dawes, C Smith (AL)
A magnificent piece of climbing, in a stunning position.

	Janitor Finish added later by the same pair.
	'Not so much Parmesan as a mature Cheddar which has been left after cracking to sweat and grow fungal.'
1986 Sep. 25	**Captain Nemo** A D Newton, M E Crook (AL)
1986 Sep.	**Come to Mother** J Dawes, P Pritchard
	Yet another horror show, the belay of which now resides at sea-level.
	'We are psychotic, we need help.'
1986 Oct. 2	**The Hollow Man** A Pollitt, J Dawes
	Originally given E8, it was thought to be of similar difficulty to The Bells! The Bells! on the second ascent.
1986 Oct. 10	**Snakebite Wall** K Neal, M Gresham
	'Shunt' practised beforehand.
1986 Oct. 10	**The Electric Spanking of War Babies** M Gresham, K Neal.
	'Shunt' practised beforehand.
1986 Oct.	**Ceefax** P Barbier, P Pritchard
1986 Oct.	**Katana** E Roseberry, J Peake, P Hawkins
1986 Dec. 23	**Winnie The Pooh** A Moore, T Brindle, C Reilly
1986	**Ancient Mariner** M E Crook, J Sylvester
1986	**Mordor Newydd** T Hodgson, S Haston
1986	**Ain't Goin' Down, Goin' Down Slow** J Dalton, D Birch
1986	**Into The Deep** C Parkin, P Blackburn
1987 Jan. 23	**Tigger** T Brindle, A Moore, C Reilly
1987 Jan. 24	**Kanga** A Moore, T Brindle
1987 Jan. 29	**The Super Calabrese** P Pritchard, R Drury
	A totally terminal proposition, the hardest lead in this guide.
1987 Apr. 28	**The Red Sofa** J Dawes, N Craine
1987 Apr.	**A Sea Change** R Brookes, M Murray
1987 Apr.	**Free Bourn** M Murray, B Wisheart
1987 May	**FEU 123 ELF** S Haston, P Norton, R Kay
	A well known form of local transport.
1987 Jul. 12	**The Unridable Donkey** P Pritchard, N Dixon (AL)
	Flurries of falling rocks marked the leader's progress up the groove, as the second cowered under the arête. The second pitch suffered a serious rockfall twelve months later.
1987 Jul. 26	**Evidently Chickentown** C Waddy, D Holmes
	The hardest addition to this enigmatical area.
1987 Jul. 28	**Arnold Seafood** J Dawes, S Haston
1987 Jul. 29	**The Escapegoat** C Waddy, J Dawes
1987 Jul. 29	**20,000 Leagues Under The Sea** M E Crook, D Kendal
	A good find on a painfully obvious feature.
1987 Jul.	**Zed** D H Jones, J Brown
1987 Aug. 1	**The Pipes, The Pipes** M E Crook, D Kendal, N Craine
	'Strictly Fowler territory.'
1987 Aug. 15	**Into The Light** M E Crook, A Popp
1987 Aug. 15	**This is The Sea** M E Crook (J Toombs hit by rockfall and unable to second).
1987 Sep. 15	**Thunderbird** D Jones, R Kay (AL)
	A venture into new territory

1987 Sep. 29	**Mondo Hard**	M E Crook, D Kendal, J Toombs
1987	**Cracked Slab, Crackers, Cracked Up, The Crack, The Groove, The Chimney**	J Brown, C E Davis
1987	**Chimney Climb, Overlapped Groove**	J Brown, M V Anthoine.
1987	**Crackers, Sirplumb**	J Brown, D H Jones

Some climbers just cannot retire gracefully!

1988 Jan. 21	**Outside The Asylum**	P Pritchard, P Johnson

The inmates stage a break-out!

1988 Jan. 31	**Salem**	P Pritchard, P Johnson

Pitch 1 by P Pritchard, C Waddy Aug 1988.

1988 Feb. 9	**The Crimson Crimp**	P Pritchard

Mr. Bold turns his hand to another game.

1988 Mar.	**The Terrible Thing**	G Smith

Eight belayers had completed cold stints at the base of the wall.

1988 Mar.	**The Compass**	R Kay, L McGinley (AL)
1988 Mar.	**Oijee Wall**	C Waddy, G X Percival
1988 Apr. 24	**The Motombo**	P Williams, T Hodgson
1988 Apr. 25	**Daddy On Sight**	M Edwards and party.
1988 Apr. 25	**Hi, Jack**	M Edwards, C Johns
1988 Apl. 25	**Cape of Good Hope**	C Waddy (solo)
1988 Apr. 25	**Round The Horn**	C Waddy, T Hodgson
1988 Apr. 27	**Tetrion, Aquaseal** and **Ciment Fondue**	M Barnicott, P Williams
1988 Apr. 27	**Wellectic**	T Hodgson, M Barnicott, P Williams
1988 Apr.	**The Hitcher**	C Waddy (Solo)
1988 Apr.	**Holyhead Revisited**	C Waddy, B Pritchard
1988 May 5	**Arachnid**	G Smith, G Hughes.

The 'Route Machine' turns up another goody.
Variation finish J Dawes (solo).

1988 May 5	**Seal's Song**	S Haston, C Bull

'Turbo glide is the only way to describe it.'

1988 May 6	**The Real Keel**	P Pritchard, C Waddy
1988 May 6	**Vicious Fish**	C Waddy, P Pritchard
1988 May 6	**A Limpet Trip**	G Smith, G Hughes, M E Crook
1988 May 15	**Hardback Thesaurus**	J Dawes, B Drury

Wales' first totally on sight E7, a very fine effort.

1988 May 20	**A Wreath of Deadly Nightshade**	A Pollitt, A Hughes

'No wonder Andy doesn't smile very often.'

1988 May 22	**An Unimportant Wave**	J Dawes (solo)
1988 May	**The Dark Side of Growth, Fatty on Sight**	G Smith I Sherrington (AL)
1988 May	**Babes In Consumer Land**	M E Crook
1988 May	**Gumshoe**	M E Crook
1988 May	**Aliens Ate My Bewick**	M E Crook (Solo)
1988 Jun. 3	**Hang Ten (In The Green Room)**	P Pritchard, C Waddy

A serious and difficult addition.

1988 Jun. 5	**Drunk on Arrival**	R Kay, L McGinley

Another alcohol assisted ascent, the result of a particularly fine birthday party.

1988 Jun. 8	**Hieroglyphics**	C Waddy, P Williams, T Hodgson

1988 Jun. 8	**Gorgonzola Slab, Midsummer Madness** P Williams (solo)	
	Direct Variation to former by C Waddy, the same day	
1988 Jun. 8	**Waddy's Edge** C Waddy (solo)	
1988 Jun. 9	**Icameosaurus** C Waddy, J Dawes	
1988 Jun. 9	**Flake Out, Nempnett Thrubwell** P Williams, T Hodgson (AL)	
1988 Jun. 10	**Grimper** C Parkin, P Williams (both solo)	
1988 Jun. 13	**Lord Snooty** P Jiggins, G Stamp	
1988 Jun. 18	**Sai Dancing** M Gresham	
1988 Jun. 22	**Bye Bye Sunday Blues** B Kemball, A White, G Jordan	
1988 Jun.	**(Will Mawr gets the) Vulcan Lip Lock** S Haston, C Bull	
1988 Jun.	**Elephant Talk** N Biven, I Sherrington	
1988 Jun.	**Free Nelson Mandela Now** S Haston, P Trower	
	'Hard Extremely Marvellous'	
1988 Jun.	**Camel Crack, Big Wednesday** M Murray, R Austin (AL)	
1988 Jul.	**The Angle Man** D Towse, J M Redhead (AL)	
	These boys just never give up, yet another line on this criss-crossed wall.	
1988 Aug. 1	**Natalie** S Haston, G Everett, C Bull	
	'Original belay despatched, without effort, into the sea.'	
1988 Aug. 2	**The Cruel Seam** G Smith, S Howe	
1988 Aug. 8	**Boogie Woogie** C J Phillips, M Wallis	
1988 Aug. 9	**The Twilight Zone** P Jiggins	
1988 Aug.	**Sting Ray** S Haston, C Bull	
	'Find Thunderbird, a secretive thing, down and left roosts another species, where perhaps it would be advantageous to grow wings.'	
1988 Sep. 28	**Snatch in the Storm** P Jenkinson, C Waddy	
1988 Sep. 28	**The Featherstone** C Waddy	
1988 Sep. 30	**The Walls of Jericho** C Waddy (solo)	
	'Remember what happened to those walls?'	
1988 Sep.	**Eraserhead** G Farquhar, C Waddy (AL)	
	A good find on this crowded section of the Main Cliff.	
1988 Sep.	**Live at the Witch Trials** C Waddy (unseconded)	
	'Not as serious when the tide's in...'	
1988 Nov.	**The Light That Didn't Shine** S Haston, C Bull	
	'...length-measureless, quality – unsurpassable, grade – sporting.'	
1989 Feb. 8	**Kira His** M E Crook, D Kendall	
1989 Feb. 11	**Helios** P R Littlejohn, T Jepson	
1989 Mar. 7	**Hanging Hippies** J Kiernan, J Simpson	
1989 Mar. 7	**Indiana Fudge and the Tuck Shop of Doom** J Simpson, J Kiernan	
1989 Aug. 28	**Angel Dust** S Haston, R Kay	
1989 Aug. 29	**Sea Witch** S Haston, C Bull	
1989 Oct.	**Dichotomous** C Parkin, A George	
1990	*Watch this space there's more to come!*	

Index of Climbs

Mountain Rescue

In the event of a serious accident where assistance is required, a message giving all the factual information about the patient(s) location (crag, climb, pitch etc.) should be passed on to the North Wales Police at the nearest Police Station, or at the Headquarters (Telephone – Colwyn Bay 57171), or by dialling 999.

The Police will contact the respective Rescue Team, and as co-ordinators, will obtain further assistance (e.g. helicopter) as directed by those affecting the rescue.

After an accident, please report in writing directly to the Hon. Secretary, Mountain Rescue Committee, 9 Milldale Avenue, Temple Meads, Buxton, Derbyshire, giving particulars of the date of the accident, extent of injuries, name, age and address of the casualty, details of the MRC equipment used and the amount of morphia used (so that it can be replaced). Normally this will be done by the local Police and/or the Rescue Team involved, who will also require the names and addresses of the persons climbing with the injured party.

Avoid making rash or unconsidered statements to the press; refer any journalists to the mountaineer who has overall charge of the rescue.

HELICOPTER NOTES

In the event of a helicopter evacuation ALL climbers ON or OFF the cliff should take heed. A helicopter flying close to a cliff will make verbal communications between climbers difficult and small stones etc. will be dislodged by the rotor downdraft. All loose equipment must be secured and climbers in precarious positions should try to make themselves safe. A smoke grenade may be dropped from the helicopter to give wind direction.

The persons with the injured party should try to identify their location. NO attempt should be made to throw a rope to the helicopter, but assistance should be given to the helicopter crew/personnel if required.

A helicopter will always be flown into the wind to effect a rescue and on landing there are three danger points; the main rotor, the tail rotor, and the engine exhaust. The helicopter should not be approached until directed to do so by the air crew.

Smurf Zawn (for exploration)

Geoff slightly off route on Gogarth in 1986.
Photo: Alan Milburn